OLD SOLDIERS
NEVER DIE

BY

PRIVATE
FRANK RICHARDS
D.C.M., M.M.

*Late of the Second Battalion
Royal Welch Fusiliers*

Printed and bound by Antony Rowe Ltd, Eastbourne

CONTENTS

CONTENTS

CHAPTER I

THE START

I was a reservist belonging to the Royal Welch Fusiliers whom I had first joined in the year that Queen Victoria died. I had served eight years with the Colours, very nearly seven of them in India and Burmah, and had been back in civil life for another five years and a half, when all this commenced. My job now was coal-mining; I was a timberman's assistant.

On the fourth of August, 1914, I was at Blaina, Mon., having a drink in the Castle Hotel with a few of my cronies, all old soldiers and the majority of them reservists. One had took us around South Africa; there wasn't a Boer left in South Africa by the time he had finished his yarn. Next I had took them around India and Burmah, and there wasn't a Pathan or Dacoit left in the world by the time I had finished mine. Now another was taking us through North China in the Boxer Rising of 1900; and he had already got hundreds of Chinks hanging on the gas brackets when someone happened to come in with a piece of news. He said that war had broken out with Germany and that the Sergeant of Police was hanging up a notice by the post office, calling all reservists to the Colours. This caused a bit of excitement and language, but it was too late in the evening for any of us to proceed to our depots so we kept on drinking and yarning until stop-tap. By that time we were getting a little top-heavy, and an old artilleryman wound up the evening by dropping howitzer shells over the mountain and destroying a mining village in the valley beyond.

The next day I proceeded to the Regimental Depot at Wrexham, arriving there about 9 p.m. On my way to barracks I called at a pub which I used to frequent very often when I was a recruit, and found it full of Royal Welch reservists. We hadn't seen one another for years, and the landlord had a tough job to get rid of us at stop-tap. We arrived at barracks in a jovial state and found that the barrack rooms were full, so about thirty of us had to sleep on the square that night. I was medically examined next morning, and afterwards got my equipment and kit out of stores. On the evening of the 5th a draft of reservists who had arrived early in the day had left the Depot to join the Second Battalion which was stationed at Portland. The Second was the battalion I had served with abroad and had arrived back in England about March 1914, after eighteen years absence. The First Battalion was stationed at Malta, just beginning its tour overseas. On the evening of August 7th the Depot Sergeant-Major called for ten volunteers to join the Second Battalion. Every man volunteered and I was one of the selected ten. We went by train to Dorchester, where the Battalion, which had left Portland, was now billeted in the Town Hall. Two old chums of mine, Stevens and Billy, who were Section D reservists like myself, were posted to the same platoon in

A Company. When I went on reserve there were eight companies in a battalion, and four sections in each company; now there were four companies in the battalion, four platoons in each company, and four sections in each platoon. We reservists were a little muddled at first by all this. A battalion at full strength consisted of twelve hundred, officers and men, which roughly meant about a thousand bayonets. All bandsmen became stretcher-bearers. We sailed from Southampton about 2 a.m. on August 10th, and arrived about 3 p.m. in the afternoon at Rouen, where we were billeted in a convent. I had never visited France before.

I believe we were the first infantry battalion to enter Rouen, and the inhabitants gave us a wonderful reception, and cheered us loudly all the way from the docks to our billets in a convent. On arrival at a new station we pre-War soldiers always made enquiries as to what sort of a place it was for booze and fillies. If both were in abundance it was a glorious place from our point of view. We soon found out that we had nothing to grumble about as regards Rouen. Each man had been issued with a pamphlet signed by Lord Kitchener warning him about the dangers of French wine and women; they may as well have not been issued for all the notice we took of them. Billy and I went out the following evening and called in a café. The landlord was very busy, the place being full of our chaps. Billy used to boast that no matter what new country he went to he could always make the natives understand what he required. He ordered a bottle of red wine, speaking in English, Hindustani and Chinese, with one French word to help him out. The landlord did not understand him and Billy cursed him in good Hindustani and told him he did not understand his own language, threatening to knock hell out of him if he did not hurry up with the wine. One of our chaps who spoke a little French told the landlord what Billy required. The wine was brought but we did not care for it very much, so we left for another café. I remonstrated with Billy and told him we could not treat the French who were our allies the same as we treated the Eastern races. He said: "Look here, Dick, there is only one way to treat foreigners from Hong Kong to France, and that is to knock hell out of them." Billy and I spent a very enjoyable evening and the two young ladies who we picked up with proved true daughters of France. Billy said that Rouen was a damned fine place and he hoped that we would be stationed there until the War finished. I went out by myself the following evening, Billy being on guard. Going by the cathedral I struck up an acquaintance with a young English lady who informed me that she was an English governess to a well-to-do French family in Rouen. She took me around Rouen, showing me the places of interest and informed me that the opinion of the upper and middle classes of Rouen was that Great Britain had only come into the War for what she could make out of it, and that if she could see there was nothing to be gained she would soon withdraw her army that she was now sending over.

On the evening of the 13th my company was ordered to Amiens, the other three companies remaining at Rouen. At every railway station on the way the villagers turned up with bottles of wine and flowers. Duffy, a time-serving soldier with six years service, said it was a glorious country. In those early days British soldiers could get anything they wanted and were welcomed everywhere, but as the War progressed they were only welcomed if they had plenty of money to spend, and even then they were made to pay through the nose for everything they bought. We billeted in a school outside Amiens and were allowed out in the afternoon when not on duty. It was no uncommon sight for the first few evenings we were there to see about fifty young ladies lined up outside the school. A man simply had to hitch his arm around one of them and everything was plain sailing. Amiens proved an excellent place and we were sorry to leave it. General French had his Headquarters at the Hotel Moderne and we found a guard for him there. About the 16th August we attended a funeral of two of our airmen who had crashed; all the notabilities of the town were present. We also brought General Grierson's body from the railway station to the Town Hall. He was Chief-of-Staff to General French. All sorts of stories were going around regarding his death. One was that he had been poisoned when eating his lunch on the train, but I believe now it was just heart failure from the strain and excitement. We took his body back to the railway station where a detachment of Cameron Highlanders took it down-country. Stevens and I visited the cathedral and we were very much taken up with the beautiful oil paintings and other objects of art inside. One old soldier who paid it a visit said it would be a fine place to loot. Nothing had been removed from the cathedral at this time. On the evening of the 22nd August we entrained with the remainder of the Battalion who had came up from Rouen that day, and early next morning detrained at Valenciennes and marched to a little village named Vicq. We, with the 1st Middlesex, 1st Cameronians, and the 2nd Argyle and Sutherland Highlanders formed the 19th Brigade. We did not belong to any division: we were a spare brigade. The majority of men in my battalion had given their cap and collar badges to the French ladies they had been walking out with, as souvenirs, and I expect in some cases had also left other souvenirs which would either be a blessing or curse to the ladies concerned.

CHAPTER II

LE CATEAU: THE RETIREMENT

It was at Vicq that we first realized that there was a war in progress. We advanced out of the village across open country. High shrapnel was exploding in the air some miles in front of us, and an officer and twelve of us were sent out about half a mile in front of the company and took up an outpost position at some crossroads. About midnight orders came for us to rejoin our company which was now lined up on a railway. Rations for the next day were issued out. The bread ration was a two-pound loaf between four men. It was the last bread ration we were to get for many a day, for our service had now begun in earnest. We marched all that night and the greater part of the next day and dug trenches on the evening of the 24th August, outside a little village, the name of which I never heard, or else I have forgotten it. Old men and women from the village gave a hand in the digging. Whilst visiting outposts that evening Major Walwyn was shot through the foot with a spent bullet—the Battalion's first casualty in the War.

We were only in those trenches a few hours before we were on the march again; we didn't know where to, or why. We were issued out with an extra fifty rounds of ammunition, making in all two hundred rounds to carry. We marched all night again and all next day, halting a few times to fire at German scouting aeroplanes but not hitting one. At one halt of about twenty minutes we realized that the Germans were still not far away, some field-artillery shells bursting a few yards from my platoon, but nobody was damaged. We reservists fetched straight out of civil life were suffering the worst on this non-stop march, which would have been exhausting enough if we had not been carrying fifty pounds weight or so of stuff on our backs. And yet these two days and nights were only the start of our troubles.

We arrived in Le Cateau about midnight, dead-beat to the world. I don't believe any one of us at this time realized that we were retiring, though it was clear that we were not going in the direction of Germany. Of course the officers knew, but they were telling us that we were drawing the enemy into a trap. Le Cateau that night presented a strange sight. Everyone was in a panic, packing up their stuff on carts and barrows to get away south in time. The Royal Welch camped on the square in the centre of the town. We were told to get as much rest as we could. The majority sank down where they were and fell straight asleep. Although dead-beat, Billy, Stevens and I went on the scrounge for food and drink. We entered a café, where there were a lot of officers of other battalions, besides a couple of staff-officers, mixed up with ordinary troops, all buying food and drink. For three days officers and men had been on short rations. This was the only time during the whole of the War that I saw officers and men buying food and drink in the same café. I slept the sleep of the just that night, for about three hours. I could have done with forty-three, but we were roused up at 4 a.m. and ordered to leave our packs and greatcoats on the square.

Everyone was glad when that order was issued; the only things we had to carry now, besides rifle and ammunition, were an extra pair of socks and our iron rations which consisted of four army biscuits, a pound tin of bully beef, and a small quantity of tea and sugar. Iron rations were carried in case of emergency but were never supposed to be used unless orders came from our superior officers. Haversacks were now strapped on our shoulders and each man was issued with another fifty rounds of ammunition, which made two hundred and fifty rounds to carry. At dawn we marched out of Le Cateau with fixed bayonets. Duffy said: "We'll have a bang at the bastards to-day." We all hoped the same. We were all fed up with the marching and would have welcomed a scrap to relieve the monotony. But we were more fed up before the day was over. The Second Argyles who went to the assistance of the East Yorks lost half of their battalion during the day, but we simply marched and countermarched during the whole time that this was going on.

We kept on meeting people who had left their homes and were making their way south with the few belongings they could carry. One little lad about twelve years of age was wheeling his old grandmother in a wheelbarrow. They all seemed to be terror-stricken. In every village we marched through the church had been converted into a field-hospital and was generally full of our wounded. At about twilight we lined up in a sunken road. I was the extreme left-hand man of the Battalion, Billy and Stevens being on my right. Our Colonel was speaking to our Company Commander just behind us when up the road came a man wheeling a pram with a baby in it and two women walking alongside. They stopped close by me and the man, speaking in English, told me that the two women were his wife and mother-in-law, and that his only child was in the pram. He was an Englishman, the manager of some works in a small town nearby, but his wife was French. They had been travelling all day. If they had delayed their departure another hour they would have been in the enemy's hands.

Just at this moment a staff-officer came along and informed our Colonel that all our cavalry patrols were in and that any cavalry or troops who now appeared on our front would be the enemy. He had hardly finished speaking when over a ridge in front of us appeared a body of horsemen galloping towards us. We immediately got out of the sunken road, and standing up opened out with rapid fire at six hundred yards. I had only fired two rounds when a bugle blew the cease-fire. This, I may say, was the only time during the whole of the War with the exception of the German bugle at Bois Grenier, that I heard a bugle in action. The light was very bad, and the majority of the bullets had been falling short because we couldn't clearly see the sights of our rifles, but several horses fell. The horsemen stopped and waved their arms. We had been firing on our own cavalry who, I was told later, belonged to the 19th Hussars: I never heard whether any of them had been killed.

When we got back down in the sunken road the women were crying and the child was bawling, but the man seemed to have vanished. Stevens said: "Where has he got to?" I asked the women but couldn't get a word out of them, only crying, when out from under the cover of the pram crawled the man. He commenced to storm and rave and wanted to know what we meant by all that firing which had terrified his wife and child. (He didn't say a word about his mother-in-law.) He said that he would report us. Billy got hold of him and said: "Call yourself an Englishman! What the hell do you reckon you were going to do under that pram? For two pins I'd bayonet you, you bloody swine!"

"Fall in!" came the order, and we were on the march again. It was now dusk and I expect that family fell into the hands of the enemy during the night.

We retired all night with fixed bayonets, many sleeping as they were marching along. If any angels were seen on the Retirement, as the newspaper accounts said they were, they were seen that night. March, march, for hour after hour, without no halt: we were now breaking into the fifth day of continuous marching with practically no sleep in between. We were carrying our rifles all shapes and it was only by luck that many a man didn't receive a severe bayonet wound during the night. Stevens said: "There's a fine castle there, see?" pointing to one side of the road. But there was nothing there. Very nearly everyone were seeing things, we were all so dead-beat.

At last we were halted and told that we would rest for a couple of hours. Outposts and sentries were posted and we sank down just off the road and were soon fast asleep. Fifteen minutes later we were woke up, and on the march again. We had great difficulty in waking some of the men. About ten yards from the side of the road was a straw rick, and about half a dozen men had got down the other side of it. I slipped over and woke them up. One man we had a job with but we got him going at last. By this time the Company had moved off, so we were stragglers. We came to some crossroads and didn't know which way to go. Somehow we decided to take the road to the right.

Dawn was now breaking. Along the road we took were broken-down motor lorries, motor cycles, dead horses and broken wagons. In a field were dumped a lot of rations. We had a feed, crammed some biscuits into our haversacks and moved along again. After a few minutes, by picking up more stragglers, we were twenty strong, men of several different battalions. I inquired if anyone had seen the 2nd Royal Welch Fusiliers, but nobody had. By the time that it was full daylight there were thirty-five of us marching along, including two sergeants. We got into a small village—I had long since lost interest in the names of the places we came to, so I don't know where it was—where we met a staff-officer who took charge of us. He marched us out of the village and up a hill and told us to extend ourselves in skirmishing order at two paces interval and lie down and be prepared to stop an attack at any moment. About five hundred yards in front of us was a wood, and the attack would come from that direction. The enemy commenced shelling our position, but the shells were falling about fifteen yards short. The man on my left was sleeping: he was so dead-beat that the shelling didn't worry him in the least and the majority of us were not much better. We lay there for about half an hour but saw no signs of the enemy. The staff-officer then lined us up and told us to attach ourselves to the first battalion we came across. I had to shake and thump the man on my left before I could wake him up. We marched off again and came across lots of people who had left their homes. Four ladies in an open carriage insisted on getting out to let some of our crippled and dead-beat men have a ride. We packed as many as we could into the carriage and moved along, the ladies marching with us. Late in the afternoon we took leave of the ladies. The men who had been riding had a good day's rest and sleep. If the ladies had all our wishes they would be riding in a Rolls-Royce for the rest of their lives.

During the evening when passing through a village I got news that the Battalion had passed through it an hour before. I and a man named Rhodes decided to leave the band and try and catch them up. During the next few days we attached ourselves to three different battalions, but immediately left them when we got news of our own. We wandered on for days, living on anything we could scrounge. It seemed to us that trying to find the Battalion was like trying to chase a will-o'-the wisp. But we were going the right way. All roads seemed to lead to Paris. One day, when we were on our own, not attached to any unit, Rhodes and I came across a band of gypsies in a wood and made them understand that we were very hungry. They invited us to the meal they were about to have, and I think we surprised them by our eating abilities. We thanked them heartily, and with bellies like poisoned pups staggered along again. It was the first square meal we had had since we left Amiens. The following day we came to a railhead. A train was in and an officer inquired if we had lost our unit. We said that we had, so he ordered us to get into the train which was full of troops who were in the same fix as ourselves.

No one knew where we were going to, but we all believed that we were going to Paris. One battalion that we had been with had been told by their officers that they were going to Paris for a rest. Everybody seemed to have Paris on the brain. We had a long train journey and I slept the greater part of the way. We detrained at a place called Le Mans. The only thing I can remember about this place was a large French barracks where we stayed and a street named after one of the Wright brothers of aeroplane fame. I expect I was too dulled with marching to notice anything more. We were there about a week and then got sent up country again. We picked the Battalion up just after they had passed through Coulommiers. I could not find Billy or Stevens; when I asked what had become of them I was told that Stevens had been missing after the Battalion left St. Quentin. Then a man named Slavin said that Billy and himself had left the Battalion about fifteen miles from Paris. Billy had a touch of fever. They had got a lift in a motor lorry into Paris where Billy was admitted into hospital. Slavin said that he had stayed in Paris for four days and the last day he was there he saw Billy riding in a grand motor car with two French ladies; the way Billy waved his hand to him, anyone would have thought he was a bloody lord. Billy was lucky enough to be sent home, and I never saw him again.

CHAPTER III

THE MARNE TO THE AISNE

We had finished with our retirement and were facing in the right direction. We marched up some rising ground. Down in the valley in front of us ran the River Marne. On each side of the river was a village. A fine bridge had spanned the river but it was now in a half, the enemy having blown it up. We advanced down the hill in extended order. The enemy were supposed to be holding the two villages, and we had to take them. We were met by a hail of bullets. The men on the right and left of me fell with bullet wounds in the legs, and a sergeant just behind me fell with one through the belly. We were having heavy casualties, but couldn't see one of the enemy. We lined the edge of a little copse and opened fire on the villages, aiming at the windows of the houses. But the hidden enemy were still keeping up an intense rifle-fire, so we doubled back up the hill and under cover. Some of the men had remarkable escapes, several having their water-bottles pierced. A man named Berry happened to ask me to undo his haversack from his shoulders, saying that he had a spare tin of bully and some biscuits in it. When I did so he found that whilst lying on the slope of the hill his haversack must have flopped up and a bullet must have just missed his head, gone through his haversack, right through the tin of bully, and through one of his folded socks; because here it was now, reposing in the other sock. No, Berry didn't know what a narrow squeak he had had until I pulled his haversack off.

When it was dusk we carried on with the attack. We advanced and got into the grounds of a big château. Everything was now quiet, and from the château my platoon advanced quietly into the village. The first house we came to was locked. We heard some groans in the yard of the house and found an officer of the King's Own Lancaster Regiment who was badly wounded. He told the Second-in-Command of the Battalion, who was with us, that the enemy was strongly entrenched the other side of the river. He said it was quite possible there were still a lot of them left in the village we were now in. We also came across the dead bodies of three other officers of the same regiment; I expect they had been reconnoitring the village earlier in the day.

Six of us and a young lance-corporal were told to occupy the nearest large house, and if we found any of the enemy inside not to fire but use the bayonet. The doors and the wooden shutters of the windows were securely fastened and we tried to burst a door open, but failed. We then knocked a panel out of the bottom of it, which left a space just big enough for one man to crawl through. The seven of us looked at one another: no doubt each one of us had thought it out that if any of the enemy were still inside the house the first man that crawled in didn't have a ghost of a chance. We were all old soldiers except the lance-corporal, who had about twelve months service. One old soldier had very nearly persuaded him that it was his duty as a lance-corporal to lead the way, when our officers came on the scene and ordered us to get in the house at once, also warning me to take the lead. It took me a couple of seconds to crawl through, but it seemed like a couple of years. I had every prospect of being shot, bayoneted, stabbed, or clubbed whilst crawling through; but nothing happened and the remainder soon followed. We searched the house. There was not a soul inside, but we found a small back door wide open which a few minutes before had been securely fastened.

I went out to report and going down the street came across one of our majors and half a dozen men knocking at the door of a house which had a Red Cross lamp hanging outside. The major had just given orders to burst the door in when it was opened and a German Red Cross nurse appeared in the doorway. We went in and found twenty-seven wounded Germans, including two officers, inside. Our major, who was an excitable man, was cursing and raving and informing the German officers that if one weapon was found in the house he would order his men to bayonet the bloody lot of them. We searched the house but did not find a weapon of any description. One of the German officers who spoke English told me that we were the first British troops he had seen in action since the War commenced. He had a slight wound in the leg.

I went back to the house I had left, with orders that the seven of us had to stay the night there. We were lucky in that house. In one room we found the remains of a big dinner—roast chickens, ducks, vegetables all nicely cooked, and bottles of wine. By the look of it half a dozen men had just sat down to dine when they were disturbed and had to leave in a hurry. One man said he was going to have a feed and chance whether it was poisoned or not, and that he didn't believe pukka soldiers would ever poison good food and drink. We all agreed with him. Stories had been going around that the Germans had been poisoning the water in the wells and we had been warned to be very careful not to eat or drink anything where they had been. We never took much notice of the stories or warnings. So now we got down to that feed and eat until we very nearly busted, and washed it down with good wine. We retired upstairs and got into some nice beds just as we were and were soon fast asleep.

We were woke up next morning by one of our own eighteen-pounder shells, which had dropped short, hitting a house a few yards away. The street below was full of our men. Some were drumming up—that is, making tea—others wandering about on the scrounge, when suddenly a machine-gun opened fire from across the river, sweeping the street. Second-Lieutenant Thompson of my battalion was badly wounded; most of the men had taken cover as soon as the gun opened out. Two men named Jackson and Edwards rushed forward, in spite of the machine-gun, and carried him to safety, Jackson getting shot through the wrist. The young lieutenant, who had been shot low down, lived about half an hour. Jackson was awarded the Distinguished Conduct Medal, also the French Medaille Militaire on the recommendation of some French staff-officers who were in the village and happened to be witnesses. Edwards only got the French Medaille Militaire, because his wrists escaped injury. Jackson went home with his wound but came back to France to the First Battalion, and I was told he got killed at Festubert; Edwards was killed at Loos.

The enemy were fighting a rearguard action and the seven of us were told to get up in the tollet of the house and make loopholes in the walls with our entrenching tools. We found a couple of picks in a toolhouse and we soon made the loopholes. We could now see right across the river and the rising ground behind the village the other side. There were a few more bursts of machine-gun fire from the other side of the river and then silence. We spotted some of the enemy making their way up the rising ground and opened out with rapid fire which we kept up until we could see no one to fire at. We had some excellent shooting practice for about five minutes and saw a lot of men fall.

A few hours later the Engineers had constructed a pontoon bridge across the river which we crossed without having a shot fired at us. There were a lot of dead Germans in the village the other side of the river and they were soon relieved of any valuables they had on them. As fast as we retired on our retirement, the Germans were equally as fast on theirs from the Marne to the Aisne. Our rations were very scarce at this time. Bread we never saw; a man's daily rations were four army biscuits, a pound tin of bully beef and a small portion of tea and sugar. Each man was his own cook and we helped our rations out with anything we could scrounge. We never knew what it was to have our equip-

ment off and even at night when we sometimes got
down in a field for an all-night's rest we were not allowed
to take it off. One night just after we had got down to
it a man lying beside me was spotted by a sergeant to
have slipped his equipment off. He was brought up the
next morning before we moved off and was sentenced
to twenty-eight days Number One Field Punishment.
After many days of hard marching, which we did not
mind so much now because we were advancing, not
running away, we crossed the Aisne and arrived at
Venizel Wood. We were there a few days and on the
day we left we were shelled with large shells which we
called Jack Johnsons, because they burst with a black
smoke.

We moved to a little village not far from Soissons
where my company was billeted in a linseed-cake factory. Whilst there a General Army Order from the
Commander-in-Chief, General Sir John French, was
read out, in which he thanked the officers and men for
the magnificent spirit they had shown since the twenty-
third of August and also said that it was only a question
of hours or days before they would be in pursuit of a
beaten enemy. Twenty-four hours later another General Army Order from Sir John French was read out, in
which he stated that it had been brought to his notice
that men did not salute their superior officers, and that
the men were probably of the opinion that they did not
have to salute their superior officers whilst on active
service. But officers must be saluted on active service
the same as in peace time, and officers commanding
units must see that this is carried out. Ever since we had
landed in France we had been under the impression

that we did not have to salute officers now; our officers were under the same impression and never pulled us up for not saluting them: we simply stood to attention and answered "Sir" when they were speaking to us. The following day we were on saluting drill, and each one of us tried to outdo the other in our flow of language. There were two parades. The old pre-War soldier heartily disliked saluting parade and church parade. Duffy said we didn't have a ghost of a chance under this sort of conditions and that we were bound to lose the War. I have often thought since then that our time would have far better been employed if we had been learned something about a machine-gun.

During the time we were on the Aisne our brigade were in reserve and during our leisure hours we played Kitty Nap, Pontoon, Brag, and Crown and Anchor. A pukka old soldier's Bible was his pack of cards. Corporal Pardoe of my section and I won quite a lot of money. Mine came in handy afterwards for having a good time, but Corporal Pardoe was thrifty with his winnings, and didn't spend hardly a penny. Duffy told me I was in God's pocket but that he had no doubt in his own mind that I would get killed during the next action I was in, and that all men who were lucky at gambling very soon had their lights put out. Duffy was a pessimist in his way but a first-class soldier and good all-round chap.

About sixty men who had got separated from the Battalion on the Retirement and had been serving with other units, rejoined us on the Aisne. One man had taken part in a bayonet charge forty-eight hours before. There was an order by Sir John French instructing commanding officers not to punish any men who had left their battalions on the Retirement and had since rejoined. Our Commanding Officer, Colonel Delmé-Radcliffe, took no more notice of that order than a crow. We all had to parade in front of him and he wouldn't listen to no explanations. He said that no man should have left the Battalion for five minutes, and punished us by giving us extra route marching in the afternoon to improve our marching. Three or four young officers were in the same boat with us and they had to do the same punishment as we did. In the Royal Welch at this time no good soldier would ever dream of falling out on the line of march unless he was ill with fever. I have seen men hobbling along with blistered feet and skinned heels, chafed between the thighs and backside, cursing and grousing but still with the Battalion after weeks of marching. We thought it very unfair of our Colonel in punishing us, as there were exceptional circumstances in the majority of cases. The man who had taken part in the bayonet charge offered up some beautiful prayers for the Colonel's soul: they would have been a revelation to any bishop who could have overheard them.

CHAPTER IV

FROMELLES: THE FIRST BATTLE
OF YPRES

The first week in October we left the Aisne to march north, and were issued with topcoats but no packs. We folded our topcoats and tied them on our shoulder-straps with string. We marched by night and rested by day. My gambling money came in very handy: we could buy food in the villages where we rested. There were three of us mucking in and we lived like fighting cocks. Our clothes were beginning to show signs of wear, though, and some of the men were wearing civilian trousers which they had scrounged. A lot of us had no caps: I was wearing a handkerchief knotted at the four corners—the only headgear I was to wear for some time. We looked a ragtime lot, but in good spirits and ready for anything that turned up. About eighty per cent of us were Birmingham men: I never saw better soldiers or wished for better pals. Our Colonel was very strict but a good soldier: the Adjutant likewise. We all admired the Adjutant very much: he could give us all chalks on at swearing and beat the lot of us easily.

Our Company Commander had left us on the Retirement, and during the last day's march from the Aisne a new one took over the company: he was a First Battalion officer and the majority of us had never seen him before. We were loading a train when he first appeared on the scene and he commenced to rave and storm, saying that everything was being loaded up wrong and that we were a lot of ruddy idiots. Company-Sergeant-Major Stanway and Sergeant Fox, who was my platoon sergeant, were directing the loading of the train, and what they didn't know about loading trains was not worth knowing. Stanway had about fifteen years service and Fox about twelve, the greater part of which they had spent abroad. They were the two best non-commissioned officers I ever soldiered under. In any battalion of men there were always a number of bullies, and it's natural to expect one or two among the officers: our new Company Commander was agreed to be a first-class bully. Bullies as a rule are bad soldiers, but he was an exception to the rule.

We entrained that evening and arrived at St. Omer. We were on the move next morning, and a couple of days later we had a brush-up with some German Uhlans who were fine cavalrymen and excellent raiders; there were bands of them operating around the Bailleul area. One lot had done a good deal of damage to Steenwerk railway station, between Armentières and Bailleul, blowing up the points. We were advancing by platoons in extended order over open country when rifle-fire opened out from somewhere in front. We judged it to come from a fair sized wood about six hundred yards away, and laying down opened out with rapid fire at it. A few more shots were fired at us and then the firing ceased. We advanced again and through the wood but saw no one. No doubt the Uhlans had seen us advancing and opened fire with their carbines from inside the wood, then mounting their horses and using the wood as a screen had galloped safely out of sight. My platoon had no casualties, but Number 2 and Number 3 platoons had about half a dozen during the day. The men of Number 3 told us later in the day that they had killed four Uhlans and their horses as they had galloped out of a small wood on their right front about five hundred yards away.

One of our badly wounded men was taken to a lone farmhouse; McGregor, a stretcher-bearer, volunteered to stay the night with him. The next morning he told us that he had been through a bit of torture: the wounded man had been carried upstairs and during the night six Uhlans had rode up to the farm, tied their horses up outside and entered. They had made the old lady of the farm put them out food and drink. McGregor was wondering whether they would have a scrounge through the house after they had finished their meal. The wounded man was delirious too and might easily have given the show away. The Uhlans left as soon as they had finished their meal but McGregor reckoned that he had lost a stone in weight during that short time they were in the house.

We entered Bailleul in the afternoon and the people there were very glad to see us. The place had been in possession of the enemy for a few days and the Uhlans had intended to billet there that night. At this place Stevens rejoined the Battalion. His wanderings on the retirement had been similar to my own: he had also been to Le Mans and had been in hospital a week with fever and ague, after which he had been sent up country and had been serving with another unit for a fortnight. The next morning as we left Bailleul on our way to Vlamertinghe we saw about a dozen Uhlans galloping for all they were worth back from the outskirts. We fired a few shots but they were too far away for us to do any damage. The sight of one Uhlan would frighten the French people more than if half a dozen large shells were exploding in their villages. They told us that the Uhlans were brigands of the first water and would pinch anything they could carry with them. Although the French were our allies we used to do much the same. But we had to be careful: at this early date in the War the penalty for looting was death. We were at Vlamertinghe a few days and then marched for thirteen hours, arriving at a place named Laventie the following morning; we must have come a roundabout way to have taken that time. We moved off again at daybreak and relieved some French troops the further side of Fromelles on the Belgian frontier: two days later we retired back through Fromelles and dug our trenches about four hundred yards this side of that village.

Little did we think when we were digging those trenches that we were digging our future homes; but they were the beginnings of the long stretch that soon went all the way from the North Sea to Switzerland and they were our homes for the next four years. Each platoon dug in on its own, with gaps of about forty yards between each platoon. B Company were in support, but one platoon of B were on the extreme right of the Battalion's front line. On our left were the 1st Middlesex, and on our right was a battalion of Indian native

34

infantry. Our Company Commander used to visit the other three platoons at night; he, the Second-in-Command of the Company and the platoon officer stayed on the extreme right of our trench. We dug those trenches simply for fighting; they were breast-high with the front parapet on ground level and in each bay we stood shoulder to shoulder. We were so squeezed for room that whenever an officer passed along the trench one man would get behind the traverse if the officer wanted to stay awhile in that bay. No man was allowed to fire from behind the traverse: because the least deflection of his rifle would put a bullet through someone in the bay in front of him. Traverses were made to counteract enfilade rifle-fire. Sandbags were unknown at this time.

A part of our trench crossed a willow ditch and about forty yards in front of us we blocked this ditch with a little bank which was to be our listening post at night. The ditch was dry at present. Every order was passed up the trench by word of mouth, and we found in many instances that by the time an order reached the last man it was entirely different from what the first man had passed along. When our Company Commander passed along the trench we had to squeeze our bodies into the front parapet to allow him to pass. If a man did not move smart enough, out would come his revolver and he would threaten to blow the man's ruddy brains out. During this time he had a perfect mania for pulling his gun and threatening us one and all for the least trifling thing we done. Our platoon officer followed his example, but he used to pull his gun in a half ashamed manner. The platoon nicknamed them Buffalo Bill and Deadwood Dick. I got on very well with Deadwood

Dick and he was a decent platoon officer. We always numbered off at night: one, two, one, two—odd numbers up, even numbers down, and change every hour. It made no difference whether we were down or up: we could only lay over the parapet by our rifles and with our heads resting on the wet ground try and snatch an hour's sleep.

About the third day we were there Buffalo Bill came up to our part of the trench: I got behind the traverse to allow him to get in the bay. He ordered us to keep a sharp look-out, as the enemy were attacking on our extreme right, and said that it was quite possible the attack would develop all along the front. About four hundred yards in front of us was a road leading into Fromelles. Just behind the road were some trees. I spotted a few of the enemy advancing among the trees and, forgetting for a moment that I was behind a traverse, I rose my rifle to fire, but recollected in time and put it down again. At the same time a man in the next bay below me opened fire. Buffalo Bill turned around. He was red in the face, the veins in his neck had swelled, and he looked for all the world like a cobra ready to strike. "You dog!" he shouted. "You fired!" I replied that I hadn't. He did not go for his gun but picked up a big clod of earth and threw it at me, hitting me on the chest. All my discipline vanished at that moment. "You dirty swine!" I said. By a bit of luck he didn't hear me, for at that moment the enemy's artillery happened to open out and shells began bursting all along our front; but I could hear *him* all right. "Get in that next bay," he roared. I squeezed myself in the next bay. Some of the enemy had now come out of the trees and no doubt intended to advance a little way under cover of their barrage. But the shelling was not severe enough to prevent us opening out rapid fire at them. I don't think any one of them ran twenty yards before he was dropped. To good, trained, pre-War soldiers who kept their nerve, ten men holding a trench could easily stop fifty who were trying to take it, advancing from a distance of four hundred yards. The enemy now put up a tremendous barrage on our trench, but fortunately for us the shells were dropping short. Some more of the enemy had advanced at the run under cover of this barrage and had dropped down behind some little tumps of ground about two hundred and fifty yards away. I was watching the ground in front but it was very difficult to make anything out through the smoke and showers of dirt being blown up by the exploding shells. Buffalo Bill came into the bay I was in: he had his glasses out and was peering through them but seemed unable to see more than we had done. Most of us now had our heads well below the parapet, waiting for the barrage to lift. The enemy opened out with rifle-fire, and although they could not see us their bullets were kicking up the dirt all around. Buffalo Bill was as cool as a cucumber: he had plenty of guts, I'll say that for him. He passed down the trench warning us as soon as the barrage lifted to be prepared to stop an attack.

At last the barrage lifted: the shells were now exploding about a hundred yards behind us. We were all on the alert and stood to. The enemy rose up and started to advance. They were stopped at once: with the parapet as a rest for our rifles it was impossible to miss. The attack was over before it had hardly commenced. From somewhere under cover by the trees the enemy then opened out with rifle-fire on our trench and a couple of men in the next bay to me were shot through the head. We directed our fire in that direction. Stevens shouted to me to look at one of the men in our bay: he had his head well below the parapet and was firing in the air. We made him put his head well up and fire properly. The whole of the men in the bay threatened to shoot him dead if he done it again. If Buffalo Bill had seen him he wouldn't have given him that chance, but soon put daylight through him.

The left platoon of Indian native infantry on the extreme right of the Battalion had lost their white officer and the enemy's shelling had put the wind up them properly. While the enemy was advancing toward them our men on their left noticed that none of the Germans were falling; so they got a cross fire on them which soon held the attack up. The Indians were firing all the time as if they were mad, but they must have had their heads well below the parapet, like the man in our bay, and been firing up in the air. Every evening after, until the native infantry were relieved by a British battalion, twelve of our men were sent over to their trench with orders to stay the night there; they went over at dusk and returned at dawn. Every man of the twelve had served in India. One of the men told me later that the first night they went over they found the natives wailing and weeping; no one was on sentry and they hadn't attempted to remove their dead out of the trench. Our fellows cursed the natives in Hindustani and finding that of no avail commenced to kick and hit them about and also threatened to shoot or bayonet the lot of them if they did not put their heads over the parapet: in fact, they put the wind up them more thoroughly than what the German shells had. It was quite possible that the natives might have hopped it in the dark, but if they had attempted to in the day they would have been mowed down by our own men as well as by the enemy. Native infantry were no good in France. Some writers in the papers wrote at the time that they couldn't stand the cold weather; but the truth was that they suffered from cold feet, and a few enemy shells exploding round their trenches were enough to demoralize the majority of them. But there was one thing about them: over three years later the Battalion passed through a village they had been billeted in, and I saw several half-caste mites playing in the street. One old Expeditionary Force man remarked to me that if the bloody niggers were no good at fighting they were good at something else that sounded much the same.

That night we heard the enemy working on our front, but we didn't know whether they were entrenching themselves or not. The next morning a heavy mist hung over everywhere and it was impossible to see ten yards ahead. Buffalo Bill decided to send a patrol out, consisting of a corporal and two men; in my battalion throughout the whole of the War no privates were ever warned to go out on patrol—volunteers were always called for. Corporal Pardoe, Private Miles and I went out on that patrol; our orders were simply to proceed as far as we could up the willow ditch and to discover what we could. We had gone a considerable way past our listening-post when we halted. Pardoe said: "How far do you think we have come?" "Over two hundred yards," said Miles, and I agreed with him. The mist was still heavy and we were listening intently. Presently we heard voices not far off and the sounds of men working. We were wondering whether to work up closer or to go back and report, when all of a sudden the mist blew away, and there, a little over a hundred yards in front of us, were new enemy trenches. The enemy were taking advantage of the mist and working on the parapet: some were a good thirty yards from their trench—they had been levelling some corn-stacks so as to have a clear line of fire. Pardoe got one side of the ditch, and Miles and I on the other, and opened out with rapid fire. We had our rifles resting on the bank. The three of us had been marksmen all through our soldiering: each of us could get off twenty-five aimed rounds a minute and it was impossible to miss at that distance. We had downed half a dozen men before they realized what was happening; then they commenced to jump back in the trench. Those that were out in front started to run, but we bowled them over like rabbits. It put me in mind of firing at the "running man" on a peace-time course of musketry. Against we had expended our magazines which held ten rounds there wasn't a live enemy to be seen, and the whole affair had not lasted half a minute. We quickly reloaded our magazines, which took us a couple of seconds, turned around, and ran towards our trench, each of us in turn halting to fire five rounds covering fire at the enemy's trench.

The mist had now lifted everywhere: we could see our own trench quite plainly and bullets were zipping around us. Our men on the extreme left of the platoon had opened fire on the enemy's trench, but the men in line with the ditch were not allowed to fire for fear of hitting us (we learned this when we got back). We arrived at our listening-post, jumped the little bank and laid down, properly winded. We were not out of the soup yet: we still had forty yards to travel before we got back in our trench. We were safe from rifle-fire as long as we crawled on our bellies to the parapet but when we got to the end of the ditch we would have to jump out in the open before getting into the trench, and we knew full well that the enemy would be waiting for that move. We arrived at the end of the ditch and there we heard Buffalo Bill shouting over for us to remain where we were for a couple of minutes, and then to get back in the trench one by one. He passed word up the trench for the whole platoon to open out with rapid fire which would make the enemy keep their heads down and give us a decent chance to get home without being hit. We got back safely; I never knew how well I could jump until that morning. I was out of the ditch and into the trench in the twinkling of an eye: Duffy said that I cleared the parapet like a Grand National winner. The corporal made his report to Buffalo Bill who was delighted at our brush-up. Miles and I did not know what narrow squeaks we had had until someone noticed a bullet-hole through Miles's trousers and two more through the right sleeve of my tunic.

About an hour later Miles was busy sniping. In those early days of trench-warfare both sides were pretty reckless, and it was no uncommon sight on our front, and especially on our right front, to see a German pop up out of his trench and make a dart for the village. He did not always get there, and as time went on both sides respected the marksmanship of each other so much that no one dared to show a finger. Miles had just claimed to have popped a German over when he got a bullet through the head himself. That same evening Corporal Pardoe also got killed in the same way, after getting away with that stunt in the morning it was tough luck on the both of them.

Our dead we used to put on the back of the parapet and we carried them at night to a place just behind the line and buried them there. All companies carried their dead to the same place. If a dead man's clothes or boots were in good condition we never hesitated to take them off him, especially when they would fit a man. My own puttees were in ribbons, so I took the Corporal's, which were in good condition. In a belt that Corporal Pardoe wore next to his skin they found about sixty English sovereigns, besides French money. None of it went back to his next-of-kin. I could have had some but I didn't want to touch it: I was satisfied with his puttees. We began to sap out to our left and right platoons and dug a trench from the officers' bay back to a dip in the ground about twenty yards from a farmhouse. We used to fill our water-bottles at the farm at night, and each man's water-bottle had to last him twenty-four hours.

There was no such thing as cooked food or hot tea at this stage of the War, and rations were very scarce: we were lucky if we got our four biscuits a man daily, a pound tin of bully between two, a tin of jam between six, and the rum ration which was about a tablespoonful and a half. Even at this early period the jam was rotten and one firm that supplied it must have made hundreds of thousands of pounds profit out of it—the stuff they put in instead of fruit and sugar! One man swore that if ever he got back to England he would make it his first duty to shoot up the managing director and all the other heads of that particular firm. Tobacco, cigarettes and matches were also very scarce. We had plenty of small-arm ammunition but no rifle-oil or rifle-rag to clean our rifles with. We used to cut pieces off our shirts for use as rifle-rags, and some of us who had bought small tins of vaseline (in villages we passed through during our Aisne advance) for use on sore heels or chafed legs, used to grease our rifles with that. A rifle soon got done up without oil in these conditions. Our sanitary arrangements were very bad: we used empty bully-beef tins for urinating in, throwing it over the back of the parapet. If a man was taken short during the day he had to use the trench he was in and then throw it over the back of the trench and throw earth after it.

One night there was an enemy attack which we beat off and the next morning some corpses were to be seen lying just out in front of us: they were wearing spiked helmets. We crawled out the next night and went through their packs, taking anything they had of value from them. The spiked helmets we intended to keep as souvenirs, but we soon came to the conclusion that it was no good keeping souvenirs of that sort when any moment we may be dancing a two-step in another world. So we used them as latrine buckets, throwing them over the parapet at the back when we had used them. A few days later we had completed a trench back to a dip in the ground where we dug a square pit which we used as a latrine: we could go back in the day to it and be quite safe from rifle-fire.

The only artillery covering our front were two eighteen-pounders who had a limited number of shells to fire each day. They were so hard up for shells that they couldn't spare a shell to fire at a large straw rick on our right from which some enemy snipers were causing us casualties. The young artillery officer with the guns often used to come up to our trench during the night, and sometimes bring us tobacco and cigarettes: he was a very cheery soul. Two companies of Argyle and Sutherland Highlanders were in reserve to the whole of the Brigade front.

The 29th October, 1914, was a miserable rainy day. One young soldier remarked that he did not believe anyone was in support or reserve to us. But Duffy said "What the hell does it matter about supports or reserves? We have plenty of small-arm ammunition, and as long as our rifles hold out we can stop any attack, especially if they make it during the day." The night before a party of Engineers had come up to our trench and had driven some posts in the ground about fifteen yards in front with one strand of barbed wire stretching across them. It looked like a clothes line during the day. We had put a covering party about thirty yards in front of them while they were doing the work. The Old Soldier of the platoon remarked that the British Government must be terribly hard up, what with short rations, no rifle-oil, no shells, and now sending Engineers up to the front line to stretch one single bloody strand of barbed wire out, which he had no doubt was the only single bloody strand in the whole of France, and which a bloody giraffe could rise up and walk under. It was enough to make good soldiers weep tears of blood, he said, the way things were going on. This was the first and last time Engineers put out wire in front of the Battalion: after this we always put out our own, no matter where we were.

Well, it was still raining on the night of the 29th when heavy rifle-fire broke out on the extreme right of our front. At the same time our listening-post sent back to say that the enemy were getting out of their trenches, so the post was called in at once, and presently we could see dim forms in front of us. Then our right platoon opened out with rapid fire. We opened out with rapid fire too. We were firing as fast as we could pull the trigger: no man can take a sight in the dark so we were firing direct in front of us. One of our eighteen-pounders had fired a star shell which enabled us to see the enemy dropping down on their stomachs. Five or six ordinary shells were fired too, and one of them set fire to the straw-rick on our right front which was soon burning merrily. The enemy in front of us were held up for the time being, so we opened fire on our right front where we could see some more of them quite clearly by the light of the burning rick. On the left of our left platoon the enemy had captured one platoon-frontage of trench from the Middlesex, but a company of the Argyles had been rushed up and soon recaptured it. The platoon of Middlesex holding that trench had lost a lot of men a few days before, and the trench was thinly manned.

One of our chaps in turning to get another bandolier

of ammunition out of the box, noticed three men coming towards our trench from the back. "Halt! Hands up! Who are you?" he challenged. We turned around. We knew it was quite possible for some of the enemy to have got through the gap between us and our left platoon and come around the back of us. Instead of answering the challenge two of the men dropped on their stomachs and the other mumbled something which we did not understand. Two men opened fire at him and he dropped; then one of the men on the ground shouted: "You bloody fools! We're artillery signallers and you've shot our officer." We asked them why they did not answer when challenged. They said that they had left it to the officer to answer, and that they were running a telephone line out to our trench. He was the young officer who used to visit us: one bullet had gone through his jaw and the other through his right side. The two men carried him back and we all hoped that he would recover from his wounds; but we never heard any more news of him.

The attack was still going on: we kept up a continuous fire on our front, but one by one our rifles began to jam. Word was passed up the trench for Richards and Smith to go down to the officers' bay. When we two arrived there we were warned to stay in that bay for the night. In a short time mine and Smith's rifles were about the only two that were firing in the whole of the platoon. Then ours were done up too: the fact was that continual rain had made the parapet very muddy and the mud had got into the rifle mechanism, which needed oiling in any case, and continual firing had heated the metal so that between the one thing and the other it was impossible to open and close the bolts. The same thing had happened all along the Battalion front.

About a couple of hours before dawn, word was passed along the trench for every man to get out and lay down five paces in front of the parapet and be prepared to meet the enemy with the bayonet. When everyone was out Buffalo Bill walked up and down the platoon and told us all that we would have to fight to the last man. He had his sword in one hand and his revolver in the other; officers carried their swords in action at this time. We were all dead-beat, and if any man had slept two hours during the last seven days without being disturbed he had been a very lucky man. Smith said to me: "I expect this is our last time around, Dick, but I hope we take a few of them on the long journey with us." I replied that I was going to do my level best in that way. The straw-rick had practically burned itself out, but it had now stopped raining and we could see more clearly in front of us. The enemy were about thirty yards away. They had halted and begun talking together. One of them fired a rocket; it was a very poor one, it spluttered into sparks and fell only a few paces in front of them.

There was no firing all along our front. The enemy were not firing either; perhaps their rifles were done up the same as our own. In spite of the danger I had great difficulty in keeping my eyes open, and the man on the left of Smith had commenced to snore. Smith drove his elbow into his ribs. The Second-in-Command of the company had dozed off too. Buffalo Bill spoke to him sharply a few times before he answered; even the knowledge that it might be their last minute on earth did not prevent some of the men from dozing off. Sleep will beat any man and under any conditions. It was passed along for us to get up on our feet to receive the charge. But no charge came. It was getting a little lighter, and just before dawn broke the enemy turned around and hurried back to their trench; and we didn't have a single good rifle to fire a round at them. We had two machine-guns in the Battalion at this time, one in the centre and the other on the extreme right, and both had done good work during the night; but they were done up too, the same as our rifles.

We got back in our trench wet through to the skin (but we were getting used to that) and commenced to clean our rifles. This proved a difficult job; but the metal had cooled now and some of us who still had some vaseline left handed it around and we got them all in working order again. A sentry was posted in each bay and we snatched a few hours sleep, the best way we could. Our rations that day, October 30th, were three biscuits, a tin of bully between four, a spoonful of jam and our rum ration. To hungry, half-starved men it was a flea-bite. The Old Soldier remarked that the Government was trying to make us as fierce as Bengal tigers so that all the Germans we killed in future we would also devour as well. We could now see the effects of our night's work: a lot of the enemy dead lay out in front. One of the men in our left platoon threw his equipment off, jumped on the parapet with his hands above his head and then pointed to a wounded German who was trying to crawl to our lines. He then went forward, got hold of the wounded man and carried him in, the enemy

48

clapping their hands and cheering until he had dis-appeared into our trench.

We were constantly sapping out to our left and right platoons whenever we had the chance and now had plenty of room in the trench. There was a decent orchard in the farm at the back of our trench, and Stevens and I used to slip over in the night and fill his pack full of apples—Stevens was the only man in the whole platoon with a pack. We had to fill our bellies with *something*. There was one cow and one pig left in the farm. Buffalo Bill had the pig killed and sent back to the company cooks with instructions to melt a lot of the fat down and cook the remainder; the pork came up the following night and we enjoyed it greatly although we had no bread to eat with it. The fat that was melted down we used for greasing our rifles with. With the exception of one dicksee of tea, which was stone-cold against it reached us, this was the only occasion that the cooks had to do anything for us the whole of the time we were there.

One morning the officers were about to have break-fast at the end of the trench leading to their bay, from where it was possible by stooping low in a ditch to get into the farm by daylight. One of the officers' servants, whose duty it was to milk the cow so that the officers could have milk in their tea, reported that the cow had broken loose and that they would have to do without milk that morning. Buffalo Bill jumped to his feet, re-volver out, and roared at the man: "My God, you'll catch that cow and milk her or I'll blow your ruddy brains out!" The cow was grazing about twenty yards away where there was a dip in the ground. The man ran after her, the cow ran up the slope in the rear, the man following; if they kept on they would soon be in full view of the enemy. Buffalo Bill saw the danger the man would soon be in. He shouted: "Come back, you ruddy fool, and never mind the cow!" The man evidently did not hear him, but kept on. One or two bullets hit up the dirt around him. The enemy had been sending over a few light shells that morning, and now they sent over one or two more. One burst quite close to the cow. The cow got killed and the man received a nice wound in the leg which took him back to Blighty. I expect when he got home he blessed Buffalo Bill, also the cow and the German who shot him: even at this time we used to reckon that anyone who got a clean wound through the leg or arm was an extremely fortunate man.

One night some of the men in the company on our right were pinching chickens out of the farm when Buffalo Bill appeared on the scene. He roared like a lion and threatened to blow their ruddy brains out if he caught them again and told them that everything on the farm belonged to *him*. Not many hours later there wasn't a feathered fowl left on that farm: the men had pinched the lot. His favourite punishment from now on was forty-eight hours continual digging in a support trench. Yet he never troubled himself to see whether the punishment was being done or not, and in some instances that punishment was a blessing in disguise because we took things far easier behind than in the front trench. I never remembered him having any favourites: he treated all men in the same way—like dirt.

The enemy made a half-hearted attack on us a few

nights after the 29th, but we stopped them before they had come far. After this we settled down to ordinary trench-warfare, and were finally relieved on the night of the 15th November. By this time we were as lousy as rooks. No man had washed or shaved for nearly a month, and with our beards and mud we looked a proper ragtime band of brigands.

CHAPTER V

TRENCHES AT HOUPLINES

Twenty-four hours later, after a wash, shave and sleep we were different men, and in another twenty-four hours we had marched through Armentières and relieved some troops in trenches on the right of Houplines. We were relieved eight days later and billeted in a cotton factory in that place. We thought we were going to have a rest, but we were wrong: every night we had to go up the line digging communication trenches leading back from the front line. During this time we were issued with caps and packs. It was the first cap I had worn since August.

About one hundred of us were sent to a village outside Armentières, where the King inspected some of his Army. I hadn't seen the King since he was Prince of Wales, when early in 1905 he held a garden party in the grounds of Sikundra Taj, about six miles from Agra in India. I was present as a signaller at that party, and although over nine years had elapsed he did not look a day older. No king in the history of England ever reviewed more loyal or lousier troops than what His Majesty did that day. To look at us we were as clean as new pins, but in our shirts, pants and trousers were whole platoons of crawlers. His Majesty decorated one of our sergeants with the Distinguished Conduct Medal, who had won it at Fromelles.

There were fifty-eight Number One Field Punishment prisoners in the Battalion at this time. When out of action they were locked up and had to do all the dirty jobs that wanted doing, and were tied up two hours a day (by the ankles and wrists, generally) to the carts and wagons in the transport lines. Outside the factory on the one side of the street was a wall with some iron railings sunk in. One afternoon the fifty-eight prisoners were tied up to the railings and I should think three parts of the female population of Houplines and Armentières paraded that street in the afternoon. Some were sympathetic and some were laughing. The prisoners resented this very much, and one remarked that he didn't mind being tied up but he didn't want a bloody lot of frog-eating bastards gaping at him. There were some hard cases among the Number One's and the majority were continually in trouble, but these on the whole were the finest soldiers, in action, that I ever saw. During the first four months of the War, if a man was sentenced to imprisonment he left the Battalion to serve his sentence, but afterwards it was only an isolated case that was sent away. I have known men who were sentenced to five or ten years imprisonment stay with the Battalion, and in less than a month's time have their sentences washed out for gallant conduct in the field.

One man in my company whom we called Broncho was the hardest case of the lot. Whenever we were out of action he was always up in front of the Colonel for some crime or other. He was a grand front-line soldier, and most of his crimes were caused by overbearing non-commissioned officers. There was an old saying that in the Army they tamed lions; but Broncho was never tamed. I was one of the escort to him one morning when he was in front of the Colonel. His crime was too serious for the Company Commander to deal with. It was insubordination to an N.C.O.—he had told a corporal that he was no bloody good. The Colonel gave Broncho the usual twenty-eight days Number One and warned him that he would be put up against the wall and shot if he did not alter. Broncho then reminded the Colonel that it was the third time he had given him that warning and that he didn't care a damn whether he was shot or not. "March him out!" shouted the Colonel. He was brought up again next morning and sentenced to another twenty-eight days Number One for insubordination to his Commanding Officer.

But he got the whole lot washed out a fortnight later in the following manner. The enemy had been shelling so badly in the rear of us that all communication had broken down, and Buffalo Bill called for a volunteer to take a message back to Battalion Headquarters. Anyone who took the message back would have to make his way through the barrage and the communication trench had not yet been dug. Broncho shouted out: "I'll take the bloody message," and it was handed to him. It was a hundred to one he would be blown to bits before he had gone sixty yards—he not only arrived at Battalion Headquarters with the message but also came back with an answer. He was recommended for a decoration for this. A week previous when returning from a night-patrol one of the patrol had got badly wounded by unaimed fire; and it was Broncho who carried him back safely to the trench. For these two acts he had a term of imprisonment washed out and about six months accumulated Number Ones; but he got no decoration.

About the 2nd of December we took over some trenches in front of Houplines. Our trench ran into the River Lys and we were exactly eighty yards from the enemy's trench, which was dug in front of a brewery. Duffy said that there was some sense in digging a trench in front of a place like that and that only good soldiers could have chosen such a spot. Ten yards behind our trench was a house which had been badly knocked about, but which had a good cellar. A small trench led from the front line to the house. Buffalo Bill and Deadwood Dick, who was now Second-in-Command of the company, stayed in the cellar. In a château five hundred yards behind the front line were Battalion Headquarters. Colonel Delmé-Radcliffe had gone home with a nervous breakdown and our senior major, Major Williams, had taken his place. Just below the château on the other side of the road was a block of houses, and a corporal and four of us who were sent out to do police duty for a week were billeted in one of them. The people living in the block were given twenty-four hours in which to clear out, but if they failed to do so we had to turn them out and drive them back into Houplines. At the end of twenty-four hours not one of them had budged, so we had a very unpleasant duty to perform, especially as it was snowing heavily at the time. We entered every house and in two cases had to pull the ladies out of their beds, but we finally turned them all out with the exception of one very old lady who was over eighty years of age, and she absolutely refused to budge an inch, and we didn't want to use force on an old lady that age, so we gave her best. The end house of the block was the Battalion's Aid Post and three young French ladies were allowed to stay in that house. They were always up during the night and doing what they could for our wounded men who were brought there before they were evacuated down the line. The communication trench leading to the front line had not yet been completed and our wounded had to stay in the trench until dusk before they could be brought back.

No civilians were allowed up this road during the day and they were only allowed to visit one of the houses in the block if they had permits signed by the Assistant Provost-Marshal of the police. At night a password was used and anyone coming up that road was challenged and asked for the password. Our orders were that if anyone came up the road at night and didn't have the password we were to march them to Battalion Headquarters, and if they attempted to run away to either shoot or bayonet them.

That week we lived like lords. There were plenty of ducks and chickens about, pigeons in the toilet of the house we were staying in, and vegetables in the gardens. We also scrounged a lot of bottles of champagne and other wines and made up for the starvation diet we had been on for some time. Our usual rations were also more plentiful now and we were getting a bread ration. One morning a man came up with a permit. He had formerly occupied the house we were staying in and he told us he wanted to take two pigeons away. We had killed some pigeons the day before and only that morning I had killed another four which were boiling merrily away with a couple of chickens in a dicksee. He went up to the toilet and came down crying. He made us understand by pointing to the photographs of two pigeons hanging up on the wall that they were the two finest pigeons in the whole of Northern France and that they had pedigrees as long as ships' cables. But we also made him understand by pointing to our bellies that they were as empty as drums. The finish was that we told him to take as many pigeons as he liked and clear off. I expect we had had a very expensive feed during one of the days we were in that house, because the man could not find those two pigeons anywhere.

Early in October the Germans had occupied Houplines, Armentières and other villages for a day or two before they were driven out. One old lady had had twelve billeted in her house, and one night after they had retired upstairs for the night one of them came down and commenced pulling her grand-daughter about. Her screams awoke the other Germans who came downstairs, seized hold of the dirty dog and gave him a good hiding. They then tied him to a post outside the house, where he spent the night (the old lady said), and it was raining heavily at the time. Another woman keeping a café in Houplines told me that a lot of German soldiers had looted her place, but a German officer came in while the looting was going on; there was hardly anything left by this time and he paid her in gold marks for the damage that had been done. A café near the cotton factory in Houplines was the scene of a remarkable fight, with only the lady of the café and her daughter as witnesses. When our troops drove the enemy out of Armentières one man who, I expect, was on the scrounge, wandered into Houplines, which was joining Armentières, and entered this café. He came on six Germans drinking: they had their rifles leaning against the wall by them. He recovered from his surprise first and attacked them before they knew where they were. Finally he killed the six but received a very bad wound himself. The old lady and her daughter carried him upstairs and laid him on the bed, dressing his wound the best way they could, but he died within an hour, she told me. They buried the seven in the garden behind the café, the six Germans side by side and the British soldier a few paces from them. The old lady had the man's identity disc and pay-book, which she was keeping as souvenirs. He belonged to the Buffs (the East Kents) who were in the Sixth Division. The old lady wouldn't allow anyone to sleep in that bed. She used to say that a grand soldier had died in it; and she was right: the man of the Buffs must have had the heart of a lion, and if ever a man won the Victoria Cross, he did. In the early days of open warfare, where a man fell so he was buried.

We were back in the trenches again and the five of us had gained about a stone each during the week. Our trenches were flooded. We were knee-deep in some places, and it was continually raining; but we had handpumps which we had scrounged from Houplines and worked them day and night. At night, we numbered off, one, two, three, one, two, three—ones up on sentry, twos and threes working. Every evening at twilight the order would come "Stand to!" and every man in the trench would get up on the fire-step and gaze across no-man's-land at the enemy's trench. The same thing would happen at dawn in the morning. After standing to about five minutes the order would come "Stand down!" A sentry would be on from stand to in the evening until stand to the next morning, which during the long winter nights meant fourteen or fifteen hours continual standing on the fire-step and staring out at no-man's-land. At night all sentries stood head and shoulders above the parapet: they could see better and were less liable to be surprised. Also when enemy machine-guns were traversing or enemy sentries firing it was better to be hit through the chest and shoulders than through the head; although that was all according to a man's luck. Twos and threes were working all night, some carrying R.E. material from Houplines—this consisted of duckboards for laying on the bottom of the trench when the water was cleared out, barbed wire, sandbags and other material for building trenches. Some were carrying rations, others filling sandbags. There was a great dump of sand just behind our trench on the river bank which came in very useful. Some were putting out barbed wire in front, and others strengthening the parapet. A good standing trench was about six foot six deep, so that a man could walk upright during the day in safety from rifle-fire. In each bay of the trench we constructed fire-steps about two feet higher than the bottom of the trench, which enabled us to stand head and shoulders above the parapet. During the day we were working in reliefs, and we would snatch an hour's sleep, when we could, on a wet and muddy fire-step, wet through to the skin ourselves.

If anyone had to go to the company on our right in the daytime he had to walk through thirty yards of waterlogged trench which was chest-deep in water in some places. We took turns in one part of the trench bailing out water with a bucket; we had to lift the bucket and empty it in a little ditch, on the back of the parapet, which led into the river. Of course we kept our heads well down during the operation. One morning a man named Davies had his thumb shot off whilst bailing. Every one of us volunteered to take his place, but one man got the bucket first. He deliberately invited a bullet through one of his hands by exposing them a little longer than was necessary; but the bucket got riddled instead and he spent the remainder of the day grousing and cursing over his bad luck. Everyone was praying for a wound through the arm or leg, and some were doing their level best to get one.

Behind the back wall of the house behind the trench was a pump and we could safely get to it by day and draw drinking water. The pump was about a foot from the edge of the wall, and if a man rose the handle to the full extent of his arm, his arm would be seen by the enemy. Two men got shot through the forearm within five minutes of one another, and then Buffalo Bill wisely gave orders that no more water was to be drawn from the pump in the daytime. He would have lost some more men in a short space of time if he hadn't given that order. During the whole of the 1914-15 winter we endured enough of physical hardships, one would have supposed, to break men that were made of iron; but we suffered more in our morale than in our health, for casualties from sickness were comparatively few.

About this time the 5th Scottish Rifles, a Territorial battalion, joined our brigade. They were in billets at Houplines. I was ordered one night to proceed to Houplines and guide a platoon of them into our trench; they were coming to us for instructional purposes; I was also warned to bring them along the communication trench which had just been completed. I had never been through this trench and the only way I knew back and forth to our trench was along the river bank. I met the platoon not far from the mouth of the communication trench, reported myself to their officer, and we started on our way. I came to a part of the trench which branched off in two or three directions, and made a wrong guess. Soon I found myself in C Company's part of the front line. I worked my way to B which was the company on our right, and then had to decide whether I would take the platoon through that water-logged trench or over the top. An enemy machine-gun was traversing every now and then and the enemy sentries were busy with their rifles too. As soon as the machine-gun packed up for the moment I decided to make my way over the top and we arrived at our trench without a casualty. It took us an hour and a half to do that journey. If I could have brought them the way I knew along the river bank it would have taken us ten minutes. Old regular soldiers never held a very high opinion of the Territorials, but as time went on we got to like the 5th Scottish Rifles very much. They were the best Territorial battalion that I ever saw, and after they had been a few months with us we never worried if they were on the left or right of us in the line or in attacks.

The enemy in front of us had about half a dozen

stoves in their trench, and the stove pipes were sticking up like periscopes above the parapet. Some of us used to do snap-shooting at them until the smoke would be coming out of dozens of holes. We used to fix iron plates in the parapet of our trench, concealing them as cleverly as we could, but in a day or two the enemy generally discovered them and would rattle bullets all around. Later they had a bullet which would penetrate them; a man was never safe even when firing from behind them. The hole in the iron plate was just large enough to put the muzzle of the rifle through, and one morning I saw the greatest shooting feat that I ever saw during the whole of the War. A man named Blacktin was firing behind one of the plates. He had fired two rounds and was just about to pull the trigger to fire the third when he seemed to be hurled against the back of the trench, his rifle falling from his hands. A German sniper had fired and his bullet had entered the barrel of Blacktin's rifle, where it was now lodged fast, splitting the top end of the barrel the same way as a man would peel a banana. Blacktin's shoulder was badly bruised.

About halfway between our trench and the enemy's were two large mounds about ten yards from the bank of the river: we didn't know whether the enemy were using them for some purpose or not. So one night Deadwood Dick asked me to go out on patrol with him, and we were going to endeavour to find out for sure. We got out of the trench and started to crawl on our stomachs towards the enemy's trench: it was very misty and we were about five yards from the bank of the river. We approached the mounds very warily and had a good hunt round, but discovered nothing. We went on another ten yards when Deadwood Dick whispered to me to stay where I was and he would go on a little further on his own: he would signal when he was returning by a low whistle. I didn't like the idea and told him so, but he insisted on it. We were now only about thirty yards from the enemy's trench, but it was so misty that we could hardly see five yards in front of us. It takes a man a long time to crawl a little distance on his stomach and the minutes seemed hours whilst I was waiting for his return. I was straining my eyes trying to pierce the mist; but this was now clearing a little. Presently I spotted what I thought were two men approaching me; one was crawling and the other seemed to be walking in a crouching attitude behind and now and again dropping down. In a couple of seconds many thoughts rushed through my head. Had Deadwood Dick been captured and was this a German patrol coming towards me? I rose my rifle to fire, but put it down as the thought struck me that he might be still safe and that I would be putting him in danger by firing. I now made up my mind to lay still and when they were very nearly on top of me to spring up and, trusting to the element of surprise, bayonet the one and capture the other. I could now see the man that was crawling quite plainly but the other had disappeared. The crawling man gave a low whistle, which I did not answer. I couldn't make it out; he whistled again and stood up on his feet. I answered the whistle this time and recognized Deadwood Dick. When he had been crawling over the tumps in the ground his legs would go up in the air, and I now think that that's what I took for the man walking and dropping down. He informed me when we arrived back in the trench that he had crawled until he could dimly see them working on the barbed wire and that he had come across no listening-post of theirs. He had plenty of guts. When I told him what a fright he had given me by the way he was crawling, he said that I had had an optical illusion caused through the mist.

CHAPTER VI

CHRISTMAS, 1914

On Christmas morning we stuck up a board with "A Merry Christmas" on it. The enemy had stuck up a similar one. Platoons would sometimes go out for twenty-four hours rest—it was a day at least out of the trench and relieved the monotony a bit—and my platoon had gone out in this way the night before, but a few of us stayed behind to see what would happen. Two of our men then threw their equipment off and jumped on the parapet with their hands above their heads. Two of the Germans done the same and commenced to walk up the river bank, our two men going to meet them. They met and shook hands and then we all got out of the trench. Buffalo Bill rushed into the trench and endeavoured to prevent it, but he was too late: the whole of the Company were now out, and so were the Germans. He had to accept the situation, so soon he and the other company officers climbed out too. We and the Germans met in the middle of no-man's-land. Their officers was also now out. Our officers exchanged greetings with them. One of the German officers said that he wished he had a camera to take a snapshot, but they were not allowed to carry cameras. Neither were our officers.

65

We mucked in all day with one another. They were Saxons and some of them could speak English. By the look of them their trenches were in as bad a state as our own. One of their men, speaking in English, mentioned that he had worked in Brighton for some years and that he was fed up to the neck with this damned war and would be glad when it was all over. We told him that he wasn't the only one that was fed up with it. We did not allow them in our trench and they did not allow us in theirs. The German Company-Commander asked Buffalo Bill if he would accept a couple of barrels of beer and assured him that they would not make his men drunk. They had plenty of it in the brewery. He accepted the offer with thanks and a couple of their men rolled the barrels over and we took them into our trench. The German officer sent one of his men back to the trench, who appeared shortly after carrying a tray with bottles and glasses on it. Officers of both sides clinked glasses and drunk one another's health. Buffalo Bill had presented them with a plum pudding just before. The officers came to an understanding that the unofficial truce would end at midnight. At dusk we went back to our respective trenches.

We had a decent Christmas dinner. Each man had a tin of Maconochie's and a decent portion of plum pudding. (A tin of Maconochie's consisted of meat, potatoes, beans and other vegetables and could be eaten cold, but we generally used to fry them up in the tin on a fire. I don't remember any man ever suffering from tin cr lead poisoning through doing them in this way. The best firms that supplied them were Maconochie's and Moir Wilson's, and we could always depend on having a tasty dinner when we opened one of their tins. But another firm that supplied them at this time must have made enormous profits out of the British Government. Before ever we opened the first tins that were supplied by them we smelt a rat. The name of the firm made us suspicious. When we opened them our suspicions were well founded. There was nothing inside but a rotten piece of meat and some boiled rice. The head of that firm should have been put against the wall and shot for the way they sharked us troops.) The two barrels of beer were drunk, and the German officer was right: if it was possible for a man to have drunk the two barrels himself he would have bursted before he had got drunk. French beer was rotten stuff.

Just before midnight we all made it up not to commence firing before they did. At night there was always plenty of firing by both sides if there were no working parties or patrols out. Mr. Richardson, a young officer who had just joined the Battalion and was now a platoon officer in my company wrote a poem during the night about the Briton and the Bosche meeting in no-man's-land on Christmas day, which he read out to us. A few days later it was published in *The Times* or *Morning Post*, I believe. During the whole of Boxing Day we never fired a shot, and they the same, each side seemed to be waiting for the other to set the ball a-rolling. One of their men shouted across in English and inquired how we had enjoyed the beer. We shouted back and told him it was very weak but that we were very grateful for it. We were conversing off and on during the whole of the day. We were relieved that evening at dusk by a battalion of another brigade. We were mighty surprised as we had heard no whisper of any relief during the day. We told the men who relieved us how we had spent the last couple of days with the enemy, and they told us that by what they had been told the whole of the British troops in the line, with one or two exceptions, had mucked in with the enemy. They had only been out of action themselves forty-eight hours after being twenty-eight days in the front-line trenches. They also told us that the French people had heard how we had spent Christmas day and were saying all manner of nasty things about the British Army.

Going through Armentières that night some of the French women were standing in the doors spitting and shouting at us: "You no bon, you English soldiers, you boko kamerade Allemenge." We cursed them back until we were blue in the nose, and the Old Soldier, who had a wonderful command of bad language in many tongues, excelled himself. We went back to Erquinghem on the outskirts of Armentières and billeted in some sheds. Not far from the sheds was a large building which had been converted into a bath-house for the troops. We had our first bath one day in the latter end of November, and on the twenty-seventh of December we had our second. Women were employed in the bath-house to iron the seams of our trousers, and each man handed in his shirt, under-pants and socks and received what were supposed to be clean ones in exchange; but in the seams of the shirts were the eggs, and after a man had his clean shirt on for a few hours the heat of his body would hatch them and he would be just as lousy as ever he had been. I was very glad when I had that second bath, because I needed a pair of pants. A week before whilst out in the village one night I had had a scrounge through a house and found a magnificent pair of ladies' bloomers. I thought it would be a good idea to discard my pants, which were skin-tight, and wear these instead, but I soon discovered that I had made a grave mistake. The crawlers, having more room to manœuvre in, swarmed into those bloomers by platoons, and in a few days time I expect I was the lousiest man in the company. When I was stripping for the bath Duffy and the Old Soldier noticed the bloomers, and they both said that I looked sweet enough to be kissed.

Some drafts of reinforcements had joined us since the retirement and one of the lieutenants, a Third Battalion officer, who had joined us at Fromelles, had lately been with my company. He was a very brave man and popular with us all and was always quoting Kipling. Amongst ourselves we always called him Jimmie. He lasted in France, off and on, longer than any officer but Lieutenant Yates, the Quartermaster, of those who were with us in 1914. More than once he was in temporary command of the Battalion and I am glad to hear from a friend that he survived the War. The last time I saw him was in June 1918, on the Somme: he was then Second-in-Command of one of our Service battalions which we passed on the road. He stopped me and shook hands and said: "Well, well, Richards; it takes a hell of a lot to kill us old 'uns!"

CHAPTER VII

TRENCHES AT BOIS GRENIER

The first week in January 1915 we took over some trenches at Bois Grenier; they were about six or seven hundred yards in front of the village. There were only three houses occupied in the village; the remainder of the population had vanished. Early in October the Germans had been in possession of Bois Grenier for twenty-four hours before they were driven out. In a farm where we had our Battalion Headquarters a Frenchman was still living and tilling the land. A few yards from the farm was a tall new red-brick house in which lived an old lady and her daughter, and a very old lady was living next door to them. Three of us and a lance-corporal were left behind in the village for ten days to do police duty. The village used to get shelled every day, but we noticed that no shells ever fell near the farm or the red-brick house. So we billeted in a house opposite them.

French people could come up to the village at their own risk and take their furniture away, but they had to have a permit signed by the Assistant Provost-Marshal of police before they were allowed to come. Bois Grenier consisted of one main street and a side street, with farms dotted here and there. We stayed in the side street. Our chaps would come from the front line at night and take anything that might be useful to them in the trench. Also rations and R.E. stores were brought up to the village at night. Very few French people took the risk of fetching their furniture, but one hunchbacked Frenchman came into the village four days running with a deep French cart and took loads of furniture away. He took his own and he pinched other people's as well. One old man came up with a cart one day, and when he arrived at his house there was hardly a rag left in it: the hunchback had been there the day before. The old man commenced to cry and blamed the British troops, but I made him understand that one of his own countrymen had taken the furniture. So he commenced to shout "Brigand!" I then took him to another house which was full of grand furniture and told him to help his self: there was not much left in that house by the time that deep cart was full, and I assisted him to load some of the heavy pieces. I thought it queer that he did not hesitate to steal another man's furniture but had cried when he had found his own was stolen. Of course it was only a question of time before everything would be blown to bits, and not one of us four cared a damn whether a man who had the guts to come up to the village took away his own furniture or someone else's, or both. The hunchback was coming up to the village the following morning when a shell exploded just off the road near him. His horse was killed and his cart was smashed but he himself was not hurt in any way. He picked himself up and ran back down the road like an hare. It was the last I ever saw of him; I expect he became a prosperous furniture dealer somewhere in France. He was eminently gifted that way. He must have told a good tale, because I never saw anyone come up to the village for furniture after that morning.

The old lady's daughter living in the red-brick house was about twenty-eight years of age and could speak English. In a conversation I had with her she told me that the German officers had better manners than the English officers and that some of them had stayed in her house when they had occupied the village. Both she and her mother did not seem to like British soldiers and we always suspected them of being spies. Every morning about 11 a.m. a priest used to come up to the village and visit them. He would stay about two hours and then depart, and we noticed that during the time he was in the village it was very rare that an enemy's shell came over. It might have been a pure coincidence, or it might have been that the German artillery always packed up about this time for their dinners, but we thought it very queer. We had never asked him to produce his permit but decided one day that whoever was on duty the following morning would ask him to produce it, and if he did not have one to rush him to Battalion Headquarters, where the Assistant Provost-Marshal would be phoned for to send up some police to take him away.

I happened to be on duty next morning; the enemy had been shelling the village for a couple of hours and some houses about twenty yards to the right of us had been practically demolished. About 10.30 a.m. the shelling ceased, and at 11 a.m. the priest appeared on the scene. I halted him a few yards from the red-brick house and asked him to produce his permit. He didn't have one. I ordered him to put his hands up. He pretended that he didn't understand that order, so I put the muzzle of my rifle into his belly. His hands shot up like lightning: he understood that all right. I turned him around and marched him to Battalion Headquarters. The Adjutant was standing outside and he called the Colonel out. They both burst out laughing. I expect it was enough to make anyone laugh, the priest with his hands above his head and I with the muzzle of my rifle in his back, marching along. I explained to the Adjutant why I had arrested him, and later in the day some police came up and took him away. That evening the four of us were ordered to rejoin our companies in the trenches and four nights later, when I was back in the village drawing rations, one of the Battalion Headquarters' signallers told me that the priest had put in an appearance at the village that morning again, for the first time since I had arrested him. He evidently had explained himself, but I honestly believe to this day that he and the young lady were spies.

Our trenches at Bois Grenier were as bad as the Houplines ones and we were working day and night to put them in shipshape order. There was no communication trench and we used to travel back and forth to the village at night over a corduroy track which looked like a long black winding snake stretching over the top of the ground. Some of the men would be carrying up the rations during the night and then would be carrying up R.E. stores until stand-to in the morning. We were now getting plenty of sandbags, barbed wire, duckboards and other trench materials. We were also getting a ration of coke and charcoal. We scrounged buckets from the village and by stabbing holes in them converted them into fire-buckets. Half the duckboards that were brought up at this time we chopped up for firewood. Rations were also more plentiful and we were getting more bully beef and jam than we could eat, also plenty of biscuits; but the bread ration was still small—we were always short of that. Each man still drew his own rations and was his own cook: the regimental cooks were back with the transport and only cooked for us when we were out of action. It was not until the following September that hot tea and cooked food were sent up to the trenches for the Battalion. A man who had plenty of tea and sugar, a tin of milk, bread and some candles was looked upon as a millionare; but there were ways and means to get those things, especially if a man had a pal on the transport who was working in the Quartermaster's stores.

A willow-ditch with about two feet of water in it ran from the enemy's trench through no-man's-land and through our trench; we drew water from it for drinking and cooking purposes. One night a patrol who had gone forward along it about one hundred and fifty yards discovered some dead bodies lying in it, who I expect had been killed early in October; the ditch may have been dry at that time. Orders were then issued that we were not to drink any more of the ditch water. But we still continued to drink it; our insides were now as tough as the outsides of our bodies.

Our trenches were about three hundred yards from the enemy's and we frequently sent out night patrols, generally an officer and two men, sometimes a sergeant

74

and two men. The main object of patrols was to try and discover where the enemy had their listening-posts and also what regiment was holding the trenches in front of us. Sometimes the Germans would send out a strong patrol of between twenty and thirty men, which would spread out like a fan over the ground they were travelling, and it was quite possible, when they had a large patrol out like that, for one of our patrols to get right in the centre of theirs before spotting them, and if the German patrol spotted them first their flank men would simply have to close in and our patrol would be surrounded. When a patrol went out, word was passed up and down the line and no shots were fired until they returned, unless it was to fire a flare telling them to return. One night three of us went out on patrol: we had gone out about one hundred yards walking and then began to crawl. We had crawled a considerable way towards their trench when we spotted forms moving to right and left of us: we knew at once that we were inside the ring of a large German patrol. They were walking and there was a possibility that they hadn't seen us, so we did what another patrol had done a fortnight before—we separated and lay very still, pretending we were dead men. I crawled into a shell hole which was half full of water, and laid down with half my body in the water. We had blackened our faces and bayonets before going out. I unfixed my bayonet and put it underneath my leg. Shortly after I could hear whispering voices and knew that the enemy patrol was returning, and two of them passed by me on each side of the shell hole. I lay there a little longer and then had a quick look to my front and could see their forms disappearing in the distance. The trick had worked all right with the three of us, and we got back to our trench quite safe. But we *were* in a state, and I believe I never felt so cold during the whole of the War as what I did when I was laying in that water in the shell hole. I don't know whether the patrol spotted us or not, but their flank men had closed up when they were returning.

One very dark night, with not a star in sight, a sergeant and two men from B Company were out on patrol. Some hours later the two men returned without the sergeant. The two men reported that after wandering about no-man's-land and falling in shell holes here and there the sergeant decided to return. They started to argue the point as to which direction their trenches lay, the sergeant saying they lay one way, and the men the other. The enemy had not sent up any flares or fired any shots—they must have had a working party out or a patrol. The sergeant then commenced to walk to what he thought was his own lines, but was really the Germans, informing the men that he would report them when he got back. The men decided to wait where they were for a bit until either a German flare or one of their own went up. Suddenly machine-gun and rifle-fire rung out and up went a German flare, which told them that they had been right and the sergeant wrong. The sergeant no doubt had walked up to the edge of the German barbed wire, shouted in English that it was one of the patrol returning and had been absolutely riddled. Next day a body could be seen lying over the enemy's wire which had not been there the day before.

About February periscopes were introduced in the trenches: they were little mirrors stuck up on the back parapet, and day-sentries could sit on the fire-step of the trench and view no-man's-land in front. Before they were introduced day-sentries would have to get up on the fire-step and take a sharp look ahead every now and then. Many a day-sentry had been drilled through the head before periscopes had been introduced. One morning Stevens and I were watching a man fixing a hand-pump; the trench at this point took a sharp turn to our right front and we were on the corner. It was Berry, the man who had that bullet in his haversack on the Marne. He had his boots, socks and puttees off, with his trousers rolled up above his knees, and his language was delightful to listen to. Soon he slipped on his back in the water and we burst out laughing. Then suddenly Stevens too dropped down in a sitting position with his back against the back of the trench; but this was no laughing matter. A sniper on our right front had got him right through the head. No man ever spoke who was shot clean through the brain: some lived a few seconds and others longer. Stevens lived about fifteen minutes. We buried him that night in Bois Grenier cemetery. He was a married man with children and one of the cleanest white men I ever met. He was different to the majority of us, and during the time he was in France never looked at another woman and he could have had plenty of them in some of the places we were in, especially during our first fortnight in France. We now discovered that there was a slight dip in the ground on our right front, and anyone who stood at the corner of the trench would expose his head to the enemy.

There was a ruined farm at the back of our trench where we had a cunningly concealed sniping-post.

There were no hard and fast rules as regards sniping, and although we had one recognized company sniper any man could go sniping if he wished to. I felt very sore after Stevens and for a number of days I spent many hours in that sniping-post. A man needed plenty of patience when sniping and might wait hours before he could see a man to fire at. I was very fortunate on two days and felt that I had amply revenged Stevens. We could always tell when a man had been hit by an expanding bullet, which caused a frightful wound. Whenever one of our men got shot by one of those bullets, some of us would cut off the tips of our own bullets which made them expanding and then go on sniping with them. It would be very difficult to decide which side used those bullets first, but one man of ours whom I knew very well never went sniping unless he had cut the tips of his bullets off.

We liked the hard and frosty weather: we could move about better. We could also keep ourselves much warmer than when it was raining, which caused us a lot of misery, generally being up to our eyebrows in mud. At night when it was freezing hard we sometimes used to hang our shirts on the barbed wire in front and fetch them in before dawn. The idea was to freeze the crawlers. We would brush as many dead ones off as we could find, then rub the stiffening out of the shirts and put them back on. In a few minutes time those that we had not found would be coming back to life and were soon hale and hearty. Being very hungry after their night out they would commence to bite us as if they had had no food for weeks. We tried many experiments to get rid of them, but they always beat us. The Old Soldier used to say that if a man had the craftiness of a woman and the staying abilities of a louse he could easily conquer the world.

We had one man in the Company who suddenly started a queer habit. In the day he would curl himself up for an hour or two's sleep, and as soon as he woke up he would seize hold of his rifle and a bandolier of ammunition, get up on the fire-step and with head and shoulders fully exposed fire fifty rounds rapid at the enemy's trench. He would then get down, clean his rifle and curl up for another sleep; but as soon as he woke up again he would repeat the performance. How he didn't have his head drilled through we could never make out. He didn't believe in iron plates. Any other man who exposed his head for a few seconds would have had a hole drilled through it. After a week of this he was ordered not to fire any more during the day. But when he was on sentry during the night, if there were no working parties or patrols out, he would be blazing away all the time and wouldn't cease until his rifle became too hot to hold. There were always boxes of spare ammunition in the trench, and I daresay this man fired more rounds in a week than what the majority of men fired in a year.

It was very rare that Buffalo Bill pulled his gun now, but he used a different threat, which was to tie us on the ruddy wires at night for an hour. It was impossible to make a dug-out in the earth in this sector owing to striking water at a couple of feet down, so we built an upright timber shack for him in the back parapet, with some sandbags on the top. When it was completed he had a stove carried up to it which he had picked out in the village. A few nights later he went back to the village and picked the best feather bed he could find and ordered it to be taken up to his shack. We didn't mind his shack or stove, but the bed was the limit; at this time although we were working little shacks under the front parapet of our trench the majority of us still had only a wet and muddy fire-step to rest on, and we rather resented that bed being a feather one. Duffy and I carried it up, and when about ten yards from his shack dumped it in a shell hole which was full of water. Then we pulled it out, rolled it in the mud, and handed it over in that condition to Buffalo Bill's servant.

We made our way back to the village and met the remainder of the carrying-party with the N.C.O. in charge, who inquired if we had landed with the bed all right. We replied that we had, but that we had fell down on a few occasions through ducking from shells and that perhaps the bed had got a little wet. We also told him that Buffalo Bill was somewhere along the trench and that we had handed the bed over to his servant. He told us to remain in the village until he came back: we generally used to make four or five journeys during the night. The N.C.O. and the party arrived back and they were cursing flashes, for just as they had got to the trench with their loads Buffalo Bill had rushed out of his shack bellowing like a bull and shouting for the ruddy N.C.O. in charge of the carrying-party. The N.C.O. went up to him wondering what was the matter, but as soon as he saw the bed he knew at once what all the commotion was about. He informed Buffalo Bill that the two men carrying the bed had fell down a few times when ducking from shells, and that's how the bed got wet and muddy. "Wet and muddy," roared Buffalo Bill. "By the look of the bed it has been drawn through every shell hole in France; but by God, you'll find me another bed to-night if you have to pull it from underneath the President of the French Republic. And I'll hold you responsible that it is brought here bone dry, and if it isn't you'll not be wearing those ruddy stripes of yours by this time to-morrow." Another bed was found, and Duffy and I volunteered to carry it, but the N.C.O. wouldn't let us touch it at any price: he knew perfectly well what had happened to the other. So all our good intentions for our worthy captain's comfort had come to nothing, and we had caused extra work for the carrying-party. The N.C.O. saw that the second bed arrived all right: he accompanied the two men that were carrying it the whole of the way.

The most powerful searchlight that I ever saw during the whole of the War was operated by the enemy on this part of the Front. Whenever we came in the full rays of it when carrying up to the trench, we stopped dead in our tracks, sinking our heads on our chests so that we would resemble stumps of trees, or posts. One man used to say that when the war was over the ghosts of dead soldiers would be marching over these fields every night, cursing and grousing as they were moving along, and that no farmer would be ever able to live around these parts again. As time went on we worked quite a lot of shacks in the front parapet of our trench which we could crawl into head first. The only time we were ever dry was when it was freezing, but nobody ever had a cold during the whole of this winter. My company never had a case of trench fever or frostbitten feet either.

When we had a few hours sleep we wrapped sandbags around our boots and legs.

The conditions in the enemy trenches must have been equally as bad as our own and several Germans had been deliberately inviting a bullet through their hands or arms, which would take them back out of it. One morning the sentry in my bay called my attention to a German opposite us who was rising a trench mallet and leaving his hands and arms hanging for a few seconds before bringing it down. We watched him for a minute through the periscope and saw what his game was. To oblige him we started to take pot-shots at his hands or arms, but were afraid to take too careful an aim as we might have had our own heads drilled through. We had another man looking through the periscope who gave a shout whenever the mallet rose, and we on the fire-step crouching down behind the parapet would spring up and take a pot-shot. The German evidently got fed up with our bad shooting as he jumped right out of the trench and exposed his whole body, chancing his luck whether he got hit through a vital part or not. We both fired. By the way he fell back in his trench we knew he had been unlucky. Two men in the Company when they were using a trench mallet were always trying the same experiment, but they never got hit. Hands and arms holding a mallet was not an easy target for a quick snap-shot.

We commenced to work five days in the line and five days out, being billeted in huts and farms about two thousand yards behind the front line and on the outskirts of Armentières. But the five days we were out we had to go up the line every night digging communication trenches. After these were completed we could walk from the front line into the village of Bois Grenier in safety from rifle-fire. Very nearly opposite the entrance of the communication trench was a solitary house which an elderly Frenchman from Armentières had taken possession of, and he was soon selling beer and ving blong and doing a roaring trade; many a day if we had any money we would slip down the communication trench with rum jars, pretending we were going for water. We would get them full of beer and with a couple of ving blong bottles which we carried in a sandbag would arrive back in the trench and have a drink amongst ourselves. Ving blong was very cheap at this time and a man could get a decent pint and a half bottle for a franc; but as the War went on it got very dear and was also not so good as the stuff we were buying at this time. This was a grand drink; a drink to make a man talk about his relations.

One day, early in March 1915, we paraded to go back to the front line after five days behind. A man called "Fizzer" Green who was the outside man of his section of fours and who was very drunk and staggering, fell into the ditch by the side of the road, which had about two feet of water in it. It was freezing at the time. Green was fished out spitting and cursing and the platoon officer seeing that it was impossible for him to keep up with the Company, detailed two men off to conduct him to the trench. The next time we were out of the line Green was tried for the crime of being Drunk whilst Proceeding to the Front-Line Trench. I was one of the escort to him when he appeared in front of the Commanding Officer. After the platoon officer and the platoon sergeant had given their evidence of the drunken state of Private Green, the C.O. asked Green if he had anything to say in answer to the charge. Green replied that the charge was a terrible mistake and that he was as sober as a judge on that particular evening. In fact for the last six weeks he had been a strict teetotaller; during that period he had given his daily rum ration to his comrade Private Elliot, who could bear him out in this statement. He could quite understand the platoon officer and sergeant thinking he was drunk when he staggered and fell into the ditch, but ever since he was a lad he had been subject to sharp lightning attacks of rheumatic paralysis in the legs which caused him to stagger and fall, no matter where he was. His father, grandfather and many generations back in his line had suffered in the same way, and one of his uncles had collapsed in this way in front of a horse-tram and got killed. He would like very much if the C.O. could see his way clear to adjourn the case so that he could get medical evidence from home to support his statement. By the time Fizzer had finished everybody in the Orderly Room had a difficult job to refrain from laughing and the C.O. instead of awarding him a court-martial awarded him twenty-eight days Number Ones. I think it was the horse-tram that saved him. When we were outside the Orderly Room and dismissed, Fizzer said he was very lucky; but he considered the yarn he had spun was good enough to get a man dismissed on a charge of murder.

If we happened to be out of the line on a Sunday we were compelled to attend Church Parade which ninety-five per cent of the Battalion thoroughly detested. Any pukka old soldier would have much preferred a dose of opening medicine, and we were on many Church Parades when heavy guns on the right and left of us had been firing and also our eighteen-pounders in front of us, so that enemy shells would be coming over in answer. One Sunday they were bursting so close to the parade we were holding in the open air that we had to be dismissed before half the service was over and scatter in all directions; that was the only time that we offered up a genuine prayer for the welfare of German gunners. I expect J.C. and his angels were doing a quiet grin as they were looking down on some of the Church Parades held around that area. After that incident Church Parades were held in a barn. We had a mouth-organ band who used to play the hymns: we liked the tunes of some of the hymns, but not the words. We much preferred our own words which we set to the tune and sung with great gusto when we were having a jollification. These words set to the tune of the well-known hymn "O God, our Help in Ages Past" was a great favourite amongst us:

> John Wesley had a little dog,
> He was so very thin,
> He took him to the Gates of Hell
> And threw the bastard in.

There were six verses to this hymn, and each one a little more racy than the first.

We had some grand parsons with us during the War. One who was with us a considerable time had a wonderful reputation: he could drink our Quartermaster-Sergeant blind, and he had to be a great man to do that. Parsons always stayed with the transport when we were in the line, but on two occasions when we were in a quiet part of the front line this one paid us visits. The first time he called on each company commander at company headquarters and did not shift until they had each in turn run out of whiskey. Yes, he drunk them out of house and home and walked down the communication trench as sober as a judge. The second time he visited the front line he didn't get a drink anywhere: each company commander said how sorry they were when they told him that they had completely run out of whiskey. So he didn't stay long that time and never visited the front line again. The old hands of the Battalion admired him very much, and often used to say that when he went west he would be put in charge of the largest and finest drinking bar in Hell. We had another parson just before him who never came up at all. One of our grooms who had a very good billet with an old lady and her daughter was asked if he would mind giving up his billet for the parson, who was supposed to have a poor one. Of course if he had refused he would have been ordered from there just the same, so he moved out and the parson moved in. A few days later the groom called at his old billet for a few things he had left there. The parson met him and said: "Look here, my man, I don't want you coming around here after my little bit of meat." The groom, who was a bit of an hard case and didn't care a damn for any man, called him a dirty old pig, not to mention a few other good names as well. The best parson we ever had was one who came to us a few months before the War finished; we also had a young Wesleyan minister with us during that time and he was very good, but if he had listened to me one morning he might have still been preaching sermons in this world instead of preaching them in the other.

When we were out of the line the trimmings to our walking-out dress was a rifle and a bandolier of ammunition which held fifty rounds; and it was no uncommon sight when we were drinking in a café to see us leave our drinks and start firing at a German aeroplane which was flying overhead, and then resume our drinks when he had passed out of sight. One day two of our chaps with a drop on shot up all the bottles and glasses in a café. Another man absolutely riddled everything that was hanging up in a butcher's shop. Perhaps he mistook the carcases for Germans. The butcher was dancing a two-step around the corner of the house and yelling for the military police. They quickly appeared on the scene as soon as the man had expended his bandolier of ammunition. Shortly after that, walking-out dress was abolished.

Buffalo Bill bought a large and powerful dog with harness and got the Pioneer Sergeant to make a little cart. All over Flanders it was a common sight to see dogs in harness working and pulling little carts about, which in England is against the law. Buffalo Bill calculated that the dog would be able to pull as much trench stores to the front-line trench in one journey as six men could carry, thereby saving six men who could work repairing the trenches. He appointed a man to take charge of the dog, whom we afterwards called the Dog-Major on the lines of the Goat-Major, the lance-corporal who has charge of the Regimental Goat. He told this man he would hold him responsible for the dog's safety. The idea was all right but the dog had other ideas. On the first night that the dog made the trip it was deemed advisable to send another man with the Dog-Major. I was detailed off to accompany him. We loaded the cart up with reels of barbed wire and other small trench materials and set off for the trench. The dog strode out resolutely along the road and the Dog-Major remarked that we would put a little heavier load on for the next journey. I replied that we had not completed this one yet, and that it was time to talk when we had safely landed in the trench with the load we had got.

As soon as we left the main road and got on the corduroy track our troubles began. We had not proceeded very far when the dog left the track, the cart upset and everything was in the mud. We cursed, got the dog and cart back on the track, loaded up and got going again. We had not proceeded very far when a small shell exploded some distance from us. The dog gave a leap off the track, pulling cart and stores into a shell hole which was knee-deep in mud and water. It took us about an hour to get the dog and cart back on the track and load up again. This happened a couple more times, and then I carried as much as I could of the load whilst the Dog-Major tried to guide him. But it made no difference. He would have left the track even if the cart had been quite empty. I tried to persuade the Dog-Major to let me shoot the dog or bayonet it, and he could report to Buffalo Bill that a piece of shrapnel had did the trick. But he wouldn't agree to it. Just before dawn we landed in the trench thoroughly exhausted. We reported to Buffalo Bill the trouble we had had, but he said that the dog was strange to the work, and after a few nights would be making six or eight trips a night.

A sandbagged kennel was made adjoining the officers' shack where the dog rested during the day. The following night another man accompanied the Dog-Major. Only one journey was made, and when he arrived in the trench he was too exhausted to curse. This man believed in the transmigration of souls, and later in the day he told us that the souls of ten old soldiers and ten Indian crows had entered the dog when he was born, and no human being on this Ball of Clay would ever succeed in making him work. He was right. The dog was too artful to work, and was as wronk as a wagonload of old soldiers and Indian crows put together. One night the dog had a rest, and when the Dog-Major went to his kennel the next morning he found six bayonet thrusts in the sandbags inside the kennel, which he reported to Buffalo Bill. No doubt as some of the men had moved along the trench they made a quick jab at the dog in passing by. The Dog-Major was now struck off all trench duties and ordered to take up his abode in the kennel with the dog. Buffalo Bill warned him, pulling out his revolver, that if anything happened to the dog something just as serious would happen to him. Then the cart which used to be left some yards from the kennel was blown to pieces. I don't know whether the dog knew that his troubles were over for the time being but for the rest of the day he was yelping and barking with delight.

When Buffalo Bill left us, the dog stayed with the Company, but never did no more work. He got used to shells and rifle grenades when they were coming over, and it was very funny to see him flatten his body against the wall of a trench when he heard the whine of a shell which he knew would be falling somewhere near him. He used to wander around the trench, but he would never attempt to jump on top during the daytime. He seemed to sense that it was not safe. We all got to like the dog which used to go in and out of the line with us. I may as well tell his whole story now and get it over. About a month before we left the Bois Grenier Sector and during one of our little spells out of the line, he got lost. I expect a Frenchman pinched him. Nine months later when we were in Bethune two old soldiers of A Company were having a stroll around the town when a large dog came running up to them barking and wagging his tail with delight. They recognized him at once and took him back with them. He was given a permanent home with the transport. In the autumn of 1917, when we were around the Ypres Sector, he was killed by a shell splinter when the transport lines were shelled. He had survived four or five months in a front-line trench but was killed miles behind one.

Sometimes the rations would come up to a farm outside the village and more near the front line, and carrying-parties would take their loads down a road which ran behind the trenches. One night in February a man named Bolton and I were each carrying a sandbag of bread down this road. Bolton's puttees became undone and I stayed with him until he had put them right, the remainder of the party going on in front. We were just about to start off again when the enemy opened out a terrific bombardment, the majority of the shells bursting on the road in front of us. We ran for the nearest trench, which happened to be B Company's, and jumped into a hole just behind their front line. It turned out to be their latrine pit, and we sank knee-deep in it. We were in a grand mess but we still had our bags of bread safe. We scrambled out and made our way into the front line where everyone was standing to. The shells were now falling just behind our front line and all the way back to the road. We heard a bugle blow in the enemy's trench, followed by a lot of shouting and yelling, and then the whole of the enemy opened out with rifle-fire. Bolton and I had got on the fire-step and the whole of our front returned the fire. After a bit the enemy ceased firing, and we the same: they had simply been trying to put the wind up us, pretending they were going to make an attack.

Every man on our fire-step now commenced to sniff. "What the hell stinks?" exclaimed one. I explained what had happened. We passed along the trench to our own company lines and the men were holding their noses and pretending that they had never smelt anything so bad in all their lives, and against we had reached our own platoon we had been called all the stinking hounds and dirty names imaginable. We met Mr. Richardson, who was pleased to see us safe: the majority of our ration party had been killed by the barrage on the road. Bolton's puttees had undoubtedly saved us. Mr. Richardson was holding his nose and inquiring what was the matter with us, as we smelt like polecats. We explained to him what had happened, but that anyway we had saved the bread. We scraped ourselves with our knives and then plastered ourselves with clean mud. Later in the night it commenced to freeze and we were a decent weight by morning. That day we started scraping ourselves again and got not as clean as new pins but decently clean. We had to undergo a bit of chaffing for the next few days.

It was as hard to get a new suit of khaki as it was to get a Divisional general to come up the front line and see for himself how we were existing. During the whole of the War I never saw a general above the rank of brigadier-general in a front-line trench. The Brigadier that we had at this time used to pay us a lightning visit now and again on fine days, but he had no conception of what we were going through: he didn't have to live in the trenches.

Six weeks later Bolton met his death in a very peculiar way. At this time there was a great demand for the nosecaps of enemy shells which we used to sell to men in Back Areas who were not coming in the line. Just behind our trench was a shack which had a small table in it. One afternoon Bolton and some friends were in there with an enemy's shell which had failed to explode. They had unscrewed the nosecap and were trying to detach the detonator from it. Three men were around the table and a fourth was standing behind Bolton and looking over his shoulder. They all had a try to detach the detonator but couldn't do it, so one of them threw the thing down on the table in disgust, saying: "Oh, bust it!" The detonator exploded and killed the three of them; but the man that was looking over Bolton's shoulder did not receive a scratch. Bolton's body was absolutely perforated, but we noticed that there was not a mark on his face.

We had bombs made out of jam tins with a fuse attached. Later stick-bombs arrived and later we had another kind of bomb called the cricket ball, but these had to be lighted with a match. They were very crude compared to the Mills bombs which were introduced the latter end of 1915 or the beginning of 1916. Some bombing raids were made with the stick-bombs in April: they were the first raids I can remember in the Battalion.

Mr. Richardson left us to go to the First Battalion. We were very sorry to lose him: he was popular with all of us. We heard he was killed at Fricourt on the Somme in the following spring. Shortly after, Buffalo Bill left us, also for the First Battalion which had been having a great many casualties since their arrival in early October. At the time of our Fromelles fighting they were reduced to about fifty men under command of a recruit officer and made into a 5th Company to the Queen's. Buffalo Bill was a great soldier and a great bully. The man who believed in the transmigration of souls used to say that Buffalo Bill had only had two existences on this earth before the present one. In one he had been a great general and in the other a great slave-driver, and that now he had the combined qualities of both, and that he had no doubt that Buffalo Bill in his next existence would be a bloody roaring Bengal tiger. Buffalo Bill got some fine decorations and a brigade in the end, and survived the War. Our next Company Commander was Captain G. O. Thomas, who was a very efficient soldier and was soon very popular with all the Company: it was a pleasure to serve under him. Company-Sergeant-Major Stanway had been granted a commission in Fromelles, and was now with C Company, Sergeant Fox now being our Company-Sergeant-Major.

The French people were devils for jam and when we were out for five days we used to sell them a lot of it at four tins for a franc, which was twopence halfpenny a tin. Three of us went out one afternoon with fifty tins of jam to sell. The Company was parading that evening at 5 p.m. to return to the trenches. We got rid of our stock, entered a café and decided to leave at 4 p.m., which would give us ample time to get back before the Company paraded. We were drinking ving blong and stout mixed, and before we could look around it was 4.30 p.m. We hurried back and would have still been in time if the other two hadn't been so busy arguing the point about something that had happened years before when the Battalion was in Burmah. The argument had cropped up just before we left the café. When we were stationed at Shwebo in North Burmah, at one race meeting that was held there was a race called the Shwebo Grand National. One man argued that a certain officer in the Battalion at the time had won it; and the other man argued that he hadn't won it when we were stationed there but in another year. I knew which of them was right, but I thought, to save further argument, it was better to tell them they were both wrong. I only made it worse. They wouldn't accept my decision and pulled their coats off. They appointed me as referee and had exchanged a good few blows when the enemy commenced to shell one of our heavy batteries about fifty yards away. Some shells burst only a few yards from us, but we had flattened ourselves in a ditch by the side of the road just in time: we could hear them coming. Those shells finished the fight but delayed us for some minutes; we ran back to billets to find that the Company had moved off, and that we were absent from parading to go in front-line trenches.

This was a crime punishable by death, and at the very least meant ten years imprisonment. We reported ourselves in the front-line trench, of course, as soon as ever we could, but we were prisoners and would be tried when we got back out of the line again. When we went back out of the line for the usual five days we were brought up in front of Captain Thomas and our crime was read out to us. We were charged with being absent from parading with the Company when about to proceed to the front line, until reporting ourselves in the front line an hour later. We knew perfectly well that our crime was too serious for the Captain to punish and that he would have to pass us on to the Colonel, who no doubt would have given us a court-martial. But we also knew that a company commander could use his own discretion and squash any crime of that description if he chose to do so. Not one of us had been in any trouble before, we had been very lucky in that way, and we were on excellent terms with Deadwood Dick, who was still Second-in-Command of the Company. "What have you got to say?" asked Captain Thomas.

All old soldiers believed that any excuse was better than none and I replied, speaking for the three of us, that we had gone for a little stroll and when returning about 4 p.m. the other two had been taken suddenly ill with colic from something they had eaten and were doubled up with pain for about an hour: it was impossible for them to move so I had to stay with them. We had arrived in the trench only fifteen minutes after the

Company. The other two supported me in my statement and one said that it was the most severe attack of colic he had experienced since he had left India. We had been rehearsing this yarn for the last five days. Captain Thomas did a good grin and then gave us a severe talking to and warned us that if we ever appeared in front of him again he would pass us on for the Commanding Officer to deal with. He then tore the crime up and dismissed us. Duffy and the Old Soldier were delighted at me getting away with it, but they both said that if they had been up for the same crime they would have been shot at dawn. The argument about the Shwebo Grand National was finally settled by me suggesting to them to accept the Old Soldier's decision on the matter, to which they both agreed. The Old Soldier was an authority on races, particularly where regimental officers were concerned, and soon put them right.

One night Smith and I were on sentry in adjoining bays in the trench. An enemy sentry had been persistently firing for a couple of hours and we decided to fire in his direction when our wiring party came in. At night the flash of a rifle could be seen a fraction of a second before hearing the report. About an hour before dawn our wiring party came in; they had just arrived in the trench when the sentry fired again. "See——" but that was the only word Smith uttered, and then he crashed off the fire-step. Another man took my place on sentry, and I rushed around the traverse to warn the stretcher-bearers. I found a stretcher-bearer already attending to Smith by the time I got back, and he informed me that it was a bloody bake as Smith had stopped it through the pound. The bullet had entered by the side of the nose and had come out by the back of the neck. In about fifteen minutes time Smith came around and with great difficulty called me by name. I knew then that the bullet, which was a clean one, had not touched the brain. We carried him down to the Aid Post in the village. The doctor examined him and said that he was the luckiest man in France. Smith managed to ask the Doctor if he had a chance. "Why?" said the Doctor. "Have you got the wind up?" "No," replied Smith, "but I want to know the bloody truth." The Doctor then explained to us how by an hair's breadth the bullet had missed so and so many vital parts after entering by the nose, and that it had come out lengthways at the back of the neck. Smith was sent home and recovered from his wound but I was told that he was sent back out to France and was wounded again in the head whilst serving with the First Battalion on the Somme.

One day a few of us were warming ourselves by a fire and debating whether the spirits of the soldiers that were killed early in the War could wander through space and could look down upon us and see how we were existing. "Of course they can," exclaimed one, "and I wouldn't mind betting that at this very moment they are looking down on us and dancing a two-step and clicking their heels together in holy glee to think that they have scrounged out of this blasted misery, whilst the most of us here after enduring all kinds of hardships are bound to be popped over in the course of time, the same as them. They were the lucky ones and we are the unlucky ones." Our idea of Paradise during the 1914-1915 winter was a shelter over our heads and dozens of buckets of fire around us and buckets of fire suspended by chains hanging over our bodies.

When we were out of the line we got on fairly well with the French people. A lot of them could speak a little English and were very proud of it, but it was proper old-soldier's English they spoke. Some of them could curse better than some of us, and not know it. We got on a lot better with the people living near the line than what we did, as we found out later, with the people that were living a long way from it. We had a few young officers join the Battalion, most of whom had been in the Artists' Rifles. Two were posted to my company. We always judged a new officer by the way he conducted himself in a trench, and if he had guts we always respected him. The two new officers soon won our respect. One of them had been Brigade dispatch-rider on the Retirement and had been granted a temporary commission in the Regiment when we were on the Aisne. Since then he had been with B Company. His name was Mr. Fletcher, and all the men in B swore that he was not only the bravest man in France, but had more brains than all the Battalion officers put together. He had done some brave and brainy deeds at Fromelles where he was always out on night patrols, along with a man of his company. He could talk German like a native and once or twice mixed with their patrols, for the fun of it and to pick up what information he could. When we were in the Houplines trenches he had planted a British flag right on the enemy's parapet. We soon agreed with B about Mr. Fletcher; but he was not long with us. One morning when we were in the line he was informed that he had been awarded the Distinguished Service Order, and it happened that only a few minutes after he took a sharp quick look over the parapet and got sniped through the head. During the whole of the War I never saw men so cut up over an officer's death as in this case. The following December when we were out on rest, his father, who was an Oxford professor and wrote history books, came out from home and paid a visit to the Battalion.

We had one officer attached to us during this time who I always considered had the worst job in France. He had no trench duties to perform but generally went out in no-man's-land three nights out of five. He was an expert in the German language and his job was to get as near as he could to the enemy's lines and listen to their conversation which he used to memorize and then write down after he had come back. He had every prospect of being shot by unaimed fire and spotted by a German patrol or working party, who would have soon made short work of him. Private Lloyd, a young time-serving soldier with about two years service, but one of the old Expeditionary Force, generally accompanied him. For over a month they went out on their job, but one night young Lloyd returned carrying the officer. He reported that they had got quite close to the enemy, who were putting barbed wire out, and could distinctly hear them speaking; they had returned when the enemy were going back to their trench. They had crawled a considerable way and then began to walk. Shots were now ringing out from the enemy's lines and he knew that all their parties and patrols were in. They hadn't walked very far before the officer fell: he had been shot through the head and only lived about a minute. Lloyd then slung his rifle and managed to get the officer across his shoulder to carry him back. Lloyd was a small man and the officer was a good two stone heavier than him, and it must have taxed his strength to the utmost to have carried him back over that uneven ground. I don't believe he even got recommended for all that he had done; in our estimation he should have had at least a D.C.M.

I have read in some paper about troops in the War being doped with rum before going into action. In my battalion we never got enough of rum to make a louse drunk. Of course some of us had certain ways and means to get a drop extra, but our proper ration was about a tablespoonful and a half and we were lucky if we got as much as a tablespoonful. The rum came up with the rations and was handed over to the Company-Sergeant-Major. If he liked his little drop he took his little drop; then the platoon sergeants would draw the allowance for each platoon, and they would take their little drops; sometimes the section corporals would draw their allowance from the platoon sergeants and by the time they had had a few little sips there was damned little left for us. Sometimes platoon officers would issue it out and the majority I knew were very honest, but we had one in the Company who was a proper shark. His platoon sent up many prayers for his soul, which were not answered, as he went away sick and never rejoined the Battalion again. I have seen non-commissioned officers and men drunk in action, but it wasn't on their rum ration: it was rum they had scrounged from somewhere else. Our ordinary ration was very beneficial to us and helped to keep the cold out of our bodies, but any man who had had an extra drop before he went out on patrols, night raids or attacks was looking for trouble; a man needed all his wits and craft when he was taking part in any of those, and an extra drop made one reckless.

We had a man in our platoon who was one of the most windy men I ever saw in France, and when working on the parapet at night the report of a rifle was enough to make him jump back in the trench shivering with fright: it was pitiable to see him when the enemy were shelling our line. We decided one evening to see what effect an extra drop of rum would have on him. When the rations came up to the village the Old Soldier exchanged two nosecaps for about a pint of rum (this deal had been arranged the night before) with one of the transport men. We were issued out with our rum ration in the trench, and later in the night we gave the windy one who was working on the parapet a few swigs out of the pint. His own ration never had any effect on him, but those swigs did. For the next half hour he was the bravest man in France. He danced and yelled like a Red Indian on the warpath, shouting across to the Germans to come over and meet him halfway so that he could bayonet the bloody lot of them. We had a job to prevent him from going across and attacking the German Army single-handed.

We had a sergeant called Billy Townshend who was middle-weight boxing champion of the Battalion in India, and one year had reached the final of the All-India Boxing Championships held at Simla. On being transferred to the Reserves he joined the Metropolitan Police Force; he did not look tall enough for a London policeman and must have scraped in by raising on his toes when they were not looking. He was very proud of the fact that he did not swear like the rest of us, but always used words that was something like the swear words we used but didn't mean so much, which I often told him was a damned sight worse than swearing properly. About April, Billy and two other men were out in front erecting barbed wire. It was very quiet, hardly a shot coming from the trenches opposite. After they had been working a couple of hours the enemy sentries suddenly began firing as if they had gone mad, and a machine-gun opened out too. The three men rushed back in the trench, one holding his face in his hands. A bullet had gone neatly through his two cheeks. Billy came into a little upright shack where Duffy and I were, to recover his breath. By the light of a candle we noticed that Billy's trousers was ripped and his backside was bleeding. No doubt in his rush back to the trench he had caught his trousers on the wire and a prong had pierced his flesh but in the excitement he had not felt it. Duffy gave me the wink and suddenly exclaimed: "By Christ, Billy! You've been shot through the bloody arse! You'd better let one of us bandage you." Billy put his hand to his backside and seeing blood on his hand was out of that dug-out like a madman and making his way back to the Aid Post in the village as fast as his legs would carry him.

He did not come back to the trench that night, and we began wondering whether he had been hit out with a shell when making his way down the communication trench. The following evening he returned to the trench with a ration party and explained to some of the men what a marvellous escape he had had from that bullet, which had just penetrated the cheek of his backside sideways and came out about an inch from where it had entered. He swore that the Doctor wanted to evacuate him to hospital, but he told the Doctor bravely that he would much prefer to be back with the boys in the trench. For a long time after that Duffy and I were constantly asking him if he felt any ill effects from his bullet wound; but he simply used to grin and turn the conversation into other channels. It took a lot to ruffle Billy. He got wounded early in 1917 when we were around the Clery sector.

During this time we often carried on conversations with the enemy, and one night one of them shouted across in excellent English: "Hello, Second Royal Welch Fusiliers, how are you?" We shouted back and enquired who they were. "The same regiment that you spent your Christmas day with in Houplines," came the reply. The enemy always seemed to know who was opposite them in the line. We were never opposite a German regiment during this time but what didn't have a few men who could speak English. In one German regiment they had a wonderful violin player who often played selections from operas, and in the summer evenings when a slight breeze was blowing towards us we could distinguish every note. We always gave him a clap and shouted for an encore.

The Old Soldier had been reading in a paper that our bishops and ministers had been praying for a speedy victory and also that the German clergy had been praying for the same. "God's truth!" he exclaimed. "That poor old Chap above must be very nearly bald-headed through scratching His poll, trying to answer the prayers of both sides. If I had my way I would collect all the parsons and ministers of the both countries and stick the whole bloody crowd of them in a waterlogged trench. After they had been in it a week it's a hundred to one they would be offering up the same kind of prayers that we do now."

I might mention here that about April or May latrine pits were abolished in standing trenches, and latrine buckets introduced which the sanitary men emptied every night.

CHAPTER VIII

LAVENTIE, GIVENCHY, CUINCHY

About June we commenced to go on leave. At this
time men were only granted five days' leave—one
day to go, three at home, and one day to return—and
they had to take their one hundred and fifty rounds of
ammunition with them. At 4 p.m. one afternoon I left
the front-line trench and at 6 p.m. the following evening
I was in Newport, Mon., which was about nineteen
miles from my home. There were no rest camps at
Boulogne or other ports at this time: they came into
being a little later. Just before I went on leave the Battalion had their trousers cut short and every man had to
have his hair closely cropped, which was a good idea
especially when a man received a shrapnel wound in
the head. My friends were delighted to see me but were
disappointed because I hadn't brought a few German
helmets. When I told them what use I had made of a
couple of them they laughed and put it down to an old
soldier's yarn. Those three days I did nothing but
booze; if I called in a pub everybody wanted me to have
one. There was no restrictions on public houses.

Returning from leave, Victoria Station was open to
the public: they were all old regular soldiers returning

to France and there were little groups here and there dancing and singing with their relatives and friends, the majority a little top-heavy and to the onlookers as happy as birds. I wonder how many of them saw Victoria Station again. On my remaining leaves the public were not allowed on the platforms where the leave trains were coming in or returning back: they had to stay outside a barrier erected on the platform. There were always the ladies soliciting outside and I expect many young soldiers who went with them wished afterwards that they had been blown to pieces in France. I was never foolish enough to go with one of those birds, not because I was different to some but because I was afraid of the consequences. When a man is between twenty and thirty nature rules his brain, but between thirty-five and forty-five brains should rule nature. I wasn't a young soldier any longer, so I was a bit careful. I left my home at 9 a.m. in the morning and was back with the Battalion at 8 a.m. the following morning. Some time later leave was increased to seven or eight days and men might be detained for days in the rest camps at the ports, both going and returning. Also the carrying of ammunition was abolished and any man caught with a round on him was sent back to his battalion and was supposed to forfeit his leave.

About July we left the Bois Grenier sector and relieved a Territorial battalion in the trenches in front of Laventie. They informed us that they had arrived in France in March and had been on this part of the Front for the last few months. We noticed that the trenches were in a very bad state, in some places being only breast-high and the parapet and traverses were crumbling to pieces, and very little barbed wire had been erected in front; there were stacks of barbed wire and sandbags on the back of the trench which had not been used. We asked them why they hadn't made their parapet higher so that in the day they could walk upright instead of having to crawl about in their two doubles. They replied that it wasn't safe to work out on the parapet or out in front during the night, as the enemy were continually firing and sometimes a machine-gun would open out. If Buffalo Bill had been with us he would have shot the lot of them at sight. I never saw a more windy crowd, and before they had filed out of the trench the majority of us were up on the parapet working and cursing flashes. One of their officers ordered us to keep quiet until they had left the trench: we replied by making more noise and the Old Soldier told him to put a sock in it and clear out with his men as they only made good soldiers weep. If the Germans had made a raid on them they would have had a beanfeast.

Our Brigade was sent to that sector simply to rebuild the trenches: it was a quiet place and we had very few casualties during the time we were there. In one part of the line the ground dipped in the rear of us and we could walk through a little trench and out into the open. One afternoon we were filling sandbags on this spot and some of the men who were digging discovered a large chest and some smaller ones. The smaller ones contained glass and crockery and household stuff, and one was full of ladies' clothes, but no jewellery. The large chest was the most useful to us: it was full of bottles of wine including some champagne well packed with straw. They had been probably buried by the owner of a ruined café which was close by. At stand-to that evening most of the men who had been filling sandbags were three sheets in the wind and one man had drunk so much that he fell insensible off the fire-step and had to be carried down to the Aid Post on a stretcher. The Old Soldier remarked that every man in a front-line trench should be carried out in the same condition. The man was sentenced to five years' imprisonment, but had the sentence washed out a few months later.

During the time we were there I was warned to go back on the signallers. I had been a signaller during my pre-War soldiering and had been asked to go back on the job several times by the signalling sergeant, but had refused. Now I was warned and had no option in the matter. There were at this time eighteen signallers to a battalion, with a sergeant in charge; in the front line there were generally three signallers in each company and the remainder in Battalion Headquarters, but sometimes four were posted to a company. Signallers were also runners; in the Royal Welch there were no Battalion runners except signallers until July 1916. Signallers had to do no trench work or patrols and were the only men in the trench that were exempt from stand-to. When going in the line we were not always posted to our own companies, and although I belonged to A, I would sometimes be in the line with B, C, or D, or Battalion Headquarters. Each station had its D3 telephone, which was a small portable instrument which could be used for speaking or sending Morse. We sent all our messages in Morse, which was quicker and more accurate than speaking them. In standing trenches our telephone lines generally ran down the communication trench from Battalion Headquarters to the front-line companies and then along the front-line trench. All companies and Battalion Headquarters were linked up. A signaller could wander around the front line and no questions were asked. In sectors where there was plenty of straffing the lines would often get broken and many a good signaller went West in the act of repairing a broken wire. Signallers also got to know when something important was coming off, in many instances before the company commanders did. When we were out of the line we formed a unit on our own and were billeted together. A signaller's life on the whole was far more pleasant than a rifle-and-bayonet man's.

We had a young officer named Mr. Graves join the Battalion at this time and he was posted to the Company. He was soon highly respected. He and a sergeant went out on patrol his first night in the trenches with us and brought back a large round bottle in a basket which they had found in an unoccupied German listening post. All sorts of yarns were going round regarding the contents of the bottle which had some chemical liquid in it, supposed to be used for damping German gas-respirators, but we never heard for sure what it was.

We left that sector and marched to Bethune. On the way Lord Kitchener inspected us as we marched by. He looked much better in health than when I last saw him, which was years before in India. We took the place of the Guards' Brigade in the 2nd Division, which had left to join the Guards' Division which was then being formed. Since the Aisne we had been attached to the 6th Division; except for a short time with the 8th in the Laventie sector.

We went in the line at Cuinchy brickfields. There were great brick stacks between twenty and thirty feet high around this part of the line; we held some and the enemy held some. Givenchy trenches were on our left and Cambrin trenches on our right and the whole area was infested with rats. The first rats I saw was in January in the Bois Grenier sector, but this place was absolutely alive with them, and another thing, we were continually stretching our necks looking for trench-mortar shells which came hurtling over in all shapes and sizes. During the day sentries were provided with whistles with which they blew different blasts which informed the men in their part of the trench whether a trench-mortar was coming straight towards him or to the left or right of him and then there would be a scamper; we had necks like giraffes after we had been there a little while. At any moment, too, we might have been blown into the air by an enemy mine: two of the largest mines that I ever saw was exploded by the enemy the following year at Cuinchy and Givenchy. In fact, it was a very healthy part of the Front, what with one thing and another, and anyone who were suffering with their nerves could not have come to a better place for a cure.

The second time we went in Givenchy trenches I was posted to C Company with two others. I tried hard to exchange with a man named Green who was posted to A, though he belonged to B. I much preferred going to my own company where I could have a chat with the Old Soldier and Duffy, but Green wouldn't exchange. Signallers generally went into standing trenches an hour or two before their companies to enable them to go around the telephone wires and see which way they were running. When going into the line we carried the next day's rations with us and distributed them amongst us, each station generally mucking in when in the line. We went down the communication trench and had a rest where the trench branched off in different directions to the front-line companies. Green now said that he was quite willing to exchange with me, but I told him it was too late, as we three had distributed our rations amongst us, and that I wasn't going to take my pack off to get at the rations I was carrying. He said, "It won't take you a minute, Dick," and begged hard for me to exchange, but I wouldn't. There were four signallers posted to A this time—we all wished one another luck and went on our different ways to the front line.

The next morning the enemy were shelling all along our front and their big shells which were said to come from a naval gun mounted on a truck on the railway behind La Bassée seemed to us, in C Company's trench, to be falling most on the extreme left of the Battalion front where A Company was. I called up A. Green happened to be on the phone and said that they were having a very warm time of it and that he wished—but he did not finish his sentence. I called him up again but could get no reply and I knew the lines had gone West. I called up D Company, in between us and A, and they informed me that the lines between them and A had gone too. Shortly after this our line with D went too, so I set off to find the breaks. I repaired them and went on till I reached D signalling station. They told me that they were still out of touch with A and that Battalion

Headquarters could get no reply from A either. They had just sent a man along the A line to find the breaks. The shelling had now slackened and I decided to go along to A myself. I hadn't gone many yards before the news was passed along that the four signallers of A and Captain Thomas's servant who happened to be in their shack at the time had been killed. A Company's signallers were in an upright shack and one of the naval shells had exploded in the trench just outside it. They must have been killed at the moment Green was talking with me. I thought to myself how nearly I had been in Green's place.

I came across Duffy and the Old Soldier. They were both cursing flashes: they had made a brew of tea, cooked their bacon and were just going to sit down to have their breakfast when they noticed a trench-mortar shell dropping straight towards them. They both made a dive around the traverse and hardly had time to flatten themselves on the bottom of the trench before the trench-mortar pitched on the parapet of the bay they had left, blowing it to bits and their breakfast as well. I had lost one or two breakfasts that way and could quite understand their feelings. The Company had many casualties besides the signallers, and the both of them had been very busy bandaging the wounded during the shelling. As I was proceeding back to my own trench the enemy were sending over grenades which were fired from a rifle: they rose to a great height before descending and were difficult to see. When we were in the Bois Grenier sector the enemy often dropped them on our parapet and in the trench, and I remember one dropping in the bay of a trench where there were five men, killing three and wounding two. Our rifle-grenade at that time was a very poor one compared to theirs.

We were back in Bethune and billeted in a girls' school: our billet was in the next room to the Aid Post. I had an attack of fever and ague and went sick: the Doctor ordered me to hospital. Coming out of the Aid Post I met one of our old officers who inquired if I had fever. I replied that I had and was going to hospital. I packed my haversack and returned to the Aid Post: the Doctor then informed me that he had decided to keep me in the Aid Post for a few days to see how I got on. I had a temperature for four days and then got better. The Aid Post Sergeant told me that while I was packing my haversack the officer had come in and had a chat to the Doctor about me and that was the reason I was not sent to hospital. Later in the War it was very nearly impossible for old hands who was sick to get sent to hospital, and during the time that Dr. Dunn was with the Battalion and we were out of action, whenever an old hand went sick he would doctor him himself and do his utmost to keep the man in the Battalion. He knew as well as the Colonel the moral support that the old hands gave to the young soldiers that were then coming out to join the Battalion. During the first twelve months of the War I never remember a man going sick when in the line unless he had a severe attack of fever, which all the old soldiers suffered from who had been any length of time abroad. But when out of action a man would often fall sick to dodge a sloppy parade.

CHAPTER IX

THE BATTLE OF LOOS

We went in the Cambrin trenches about the 19th of September and I was posted to C Company. Our artillery were bombarding the enemy's trenches for days, and night after night our carrying parties were bringing gas cylinders and scaling ladders up to the front line. There were rumours going around that a large attack was coming off but nobody seemed to know anything definite. On the night of the 22nd I was conversing with some old hands: there was a lull in our bombardment and it was pretty quiet at the time. Suddenly a German from the trench opposite shouted across in English: "You can come over on the 25th, you English swine, and send your gas over: but we'll smarten you up!" Then our artillery opened out again. During this long bombardment we had a lot of casualties through our shells dropping short and in some cases actually dropping in our own trenches. The Second-in-Command of the Battalion, Major Clegg-Hill, was severely wounded in the head in this way. Some of the old hands swore that all the shells that were dropping short were being fired by the Territorial batteries: which was very unfair—only a couple of days before one of our signallers had overheard a conversation between the Adjutant and an artillery observation officer who complained very bitterly about the bad shells the artillery were now receiving.

On the morning of the 23rd I came across the Old Soldier and Duffy: I had paid a visit to the Company to borrow some candles. With them was a young soldier who had only been with the Battalion a few months, but he had been out on patrols with the Old Soldier, who thought very highly of him. I sat down and gave them the news: that there was going to be a big attack on the 25th and that we were going to send our gas over. "Where did you get that from?" enquired the Old Soldier. "From the Germans," I said, and told him what the man had shouted over the night before. "Then it's bound to be true, man," said Duffy, "the Jerries always gets to know things before we do." The three of us discussed the attack from all points of the compass and arrived at the same conclusion, which was that we didn't have a dog's chance. The enemy trenches were about three hundred yards away and we knew that the men in front of us were good soldiers and excellent shots and could do without the aid of machine-guns to mow us down advancing from that distance; as surely as if they were attacking us we could have done the same to them.

The Young Soldier called us three bloody old pessimists and said that if the attack did come off on the 25th there couldn't be many Jerries left alive after our bombardment had finished with them, and what was left our gas would soon polish off. The Old Soldier then had a fit of swearing and wound up by calling upon

J.C. and his Angels to knock a bit of sense in the Young Soldier's pound. He then said, "Look here, youngster, it's quite possible that not one shell in six is dropping on their parapet or in their trench and I wouldn't mind betting that they have plenty of deep dug-outs which the majority can get into, just leaving a sentry here and there in the trench. In fact they don't want a sentry whilst our bombardment is on, because we can't move over until it stops. And just glance your eye through that periscope and see how much of their barbed wire have been cut. My old granny in one hour with a blunt scissors could cut more wire than what our shells have cut these two days." The Young Soldier had a look through the periscope and admitted that up to now the enemy's wire had hardly been touched.

We discussed the gas, wondering whether the men who were going to send it over had ever been in a bombardment before: if they hadn't it was quite possible they might get the wind up and make a proper box-up of things. We also thought, "Suppose the cylinders get smashed and the gas settles in our own trenches." For we old hands knew that if the attack was to come off Old Jerrie would blow hell out of our trenches before it commenced. He hadn't been sending many shells over for the last few days and we guessed we was saving them up for the Grand Slam which he seemed to know all about and of which we knew nothing except what he had told us the night before. We all took it for granted that this was genuine information.

In May we had been issued with a respirator which we tied over the mouth and nose, and we now had a gas helmet with a teat which we pulled down over our heads; it was proof enough against cloud gas which was used at this time but it was impossible to walk many yards with it on owing to the eyepieces becoming obscured. (In 1916 we were issued with the box-respirator through which we breathed oxygen but still had the same difficulty with the eyepieces and had to be continually cleaning them when we were walking with them on; the eyepieces in the German gas helmets were a hundred per cent better than ours.)

Some of our eighteen-pounder shells were now coming over and Duffy said that we might as well send over a bloody bag of f——ts at the enemy trenches for all the damage they were going to do. Eighteen-pound shells which we called whizz bangs were all right when fired at advancing infantry and would make a man duck his head quicker than any shell that was sent over; but they were no good against good trenches: it wanted a heavier shell to inflict any damage on them. Both sides used a lot of them, the Germans' being a little lighter than ours. Just as I was leaving, the Old Soldier said: "You mark my words, Dick, if this attack does come off on this particular part of the Front it's going to be the biggest balls-up ever known, and unless J.C. is very kind to us the majority of the Brigade will be skinned alive."

We were relieved on the night of the 23rd and went back to Montmorency Barracks in Bethune; the following day we were definitely told about the attack. Signallers were then posted to companies: I was posted to B, and paraded with them to hear all about it. We were going over first, with the Middlesex in support, and after taking so many lines of trenches we would push on and take the village of Haisnes where we would breakfast.

(This village was taken three years later.) The gas would be discharged for forty minutes, to be followed by a short artillery bombardment before we left the front line. Men would carry two hundred rounds of ammunition, signallers one hundred and fifty and bomb-throwers fifty. Packs and greatcoats would be dumped in the Barracks and the Company would parade at 9 p.m. that evening to move off. The way the Company Commander was speaking anyone would think we were going to have a cake walk, and when we were dismissed off parade one old hand remarked that if the Captain had said we would breakfast in Hell he would have believed him just the same, or better. About an hour later I was warned to parade with my own company in the evening and told that I would be with them in the attack.

We were paid out that day the usual five francs. The Old Soldier who had got a decent bit of money from somewhere said, "Let's go out and have a beano as it's probably the last day we will spend on this Ball of Clay." Bethune was congested with troops: new divisions that had just arrived in France being billeted in the surrounding villages. There was a Red Lamp in Bethune situated about five yards off the main street. Only once had I been in it: the first time we were in Bethune the three of us had walked in there one evening to have a look around. There were four women on the stairs and if a man wanted to go with one of them he paid two francs to the landlord behind the bar. We had a drink and left at once, the Old Soldier remarking that if we three old birds couldn't find something better than this it was about time we packed our traps and went

West; and sure enough, forty-eight hours later in a village not far from Bethune each one of us had picked up with a respectable bit of goods. It was these ladies whom we were now going to visit, and later on at a fixed time to meet at a certain café where we would spend the remainder of the evening before returning to barracks.

Passing through the town, we saw stretching from the Red Lamp and down the street towards the rue de Aire about three hundred men in a queue, all waiting their turns to go in the Red Lamp, the majority being mere lads. Duffy said, "I expect they are determined to have a short time before they go West to-morrow." We very nearly had a fight with some of them through the Old Soldier stopping and telling them that it would pay them far better if they jumped in the canal and had a swim around to cool themselves. The Old Soldier was very indignant at the men in the queue, as he considered they were showing up the British Army. When I remarked that they were no different to us, as we were going on the same errand, he looked at me in disgust and told me I was fast developing into a bloody Bible-puncher. Any man who was a bit religious was known as a "Bible-puncher" or a "man that's carrying the brick"; if a teetotaller he was known as a "char wallah", "bun-puncher" or "wad-shifter".

So later we met in the café where we found two old soldiers of B Company whom we knew were about time-expired. In the Regular Army a man enlisted for seven years with the Colours and five on Reserve; if abroad or on active service an additional twelve months had to be served. When the War broke out some reservists only had days, weeks, or months, as the case may be, to com-

plete their time and some of these had now finished the
additional twelve months. All time-expired men had to
leave their units fourteen days before their time was up
so as to enable them to land in England before they were
time-expired and not after. Later in the War, when the
Conscription Act came into force, time-expired men
were forced to stay in the Army for the duration of the
War and compensated to the tune of £20 and a month's
furlough. The two men of B told us that they were time-
expired and had been warned that morning that they
would leave the Battalion to proceed down the line on
the evening of the 25th, and they had appeared in front
of the Colonel to ask his permission if they could be left
out with the transport instead of going in the line that
night as they were leaving the Battalion the following
evening to proceed home. He told them that they
would proceed with their company to the front line and
dismissed them. They were both married men and both
were killed the following morning. (A few weeks before
the Colonel had some time-expired men in front of him
and expressed his surprise that they wanted to go home
when the Country needed men so badly. One of the
men informed him that he had every intention of still
serving his Country but in a safer place and with no
hardships to endure, also with better pay and rations
than what he was getting now; he said he had been told
that men were being enlisted at home simply for working at home and down the Bases, and receiving four
shillings a day. A first-class soldier's pay at this time
was eighteen-pence a day: some were receiving fifteen
pence and some a shilling. A few of us were on nineteen
pence. The latter end of 1917 a first-class soldier's pay

was increased to two shillings a day and the others in proportion.)

We arrived back in Barracks and paraded about an hour later and marched to the assembly trenches in front of the village of Cambrin. We must have taken a roundabout way, the hours we took to get there, and the La Bassée Road was congested with troops and guns. We were now told that the Argyles and Middlesex were going over first, the Cameronians supporting the Argyles and we supporting the Middlesex; the 5th Scottish being in reserve. The weather had been glorious during the last ten days but during the night a drizzly rain set in and we were soon shivering in the trench we were in. Some of the men had to carry tools for digging-in purposes and an N.C.O. informed me that I would have to carry one as well. I told him that I and the two signallers with me were not going to carry tools for him nor for J.C. either, as we were loaded up sufficiently and would have a bloody hell of a job to carry what we got. Captain Thomas then appeared on the scene as we were arguing the toss and told him that signallers were not to be given tools. During the twenty-four hours we were back in Bethune either the Divisional or Brigade Signalling Officer had received a brainwave and orders were issued that all company signallers taking part in the attack would, in addition to their D3 telephone, carry one reel of wire, one large and one small signalling flag, also signalling blinds; and each company to also carry a roll of rabbit-hutching wire which with our full fighting order made each of us look like Father Christmas. We were wondering how the hell we were going to get over the top with all of it. The rabbit wire was a new one on me. I had never seen it before and I never saw it again. The idea was that after we had got over the top we would unroll the rabbit wire out and hitch our telephone wire on to it which we would run out with the Company; then Battalion Headquarters behind, instead of joining up with our lines, would simply have to hitch their lines on any part of the rabbit wire and establish communication straight away. It had been tried out umpteen miles behind the front line where there were no shells and bullets flying about and had proved a great success.

Many signalling stunts tried out in this way were an absolute washout when used in attacks. The truth was that we were very lucky if Battalion Headquarters could keep up communication with Brigade and always, with the exception of one case, had to depend on runners for taking company messages back from any captured position to Battalion Headquarters. I could never make out why signallers were not issued with revolvers instead of rifles. A rifle was very cumbersome when carrying signalling gear and a revolver was far more handy. After July 1916 I always carried one, in addition to my rifle. A man could easily get one in action from some dead officer or other and it came in very handy.

I was trying to snatch an hour's sleep and had just dozed off when I was woke up by Dann, one of our signallers, who said, "Have a drink of this." He had about half a pint of rum in his canteen. He told me that he had come across the storeman who the Company-Sergeant-Major had left in charge of the rum, about three sheets in the wind and giving some of the rum away to his pals; so he thought he might as well have a drop himself and being a bit pally with the storeman had coaxed a drop out of him. I was wishing the Old Soldier and Duffy was near to have a swig, but their platoon was some distance away, so we three signallers had a good swig each and passed the canteen around to a few men who were by us. We at least were making sure of our rum-ration beforehand.

Dawn broke at last and we were anxiously waiting for the time when the Grand Slam commenced. The assembly trenches were about seven hundred yards behind our front line. Dann and I were closely watching to see our gas going over, which we were told would kill every German for over a mile in front of us and which none of us believed in. Our artillery were still sending them over and also the enemy's artillery had opened out and some of the shells were falling around our front line. At last we saw the gas going over in two or three places: it looked like small clouds rolling along close to the ground. The white clouds hadn't travelled far before they seemed to stop and melt away. I found out later that the wind that should have taken it across no-man's-land hadn't put in an appearance and the gas had spread back into our trenches. Shortly after machine-gun and rifle-fire rung out and we guessed that the Argyles and Middlesex had begun the attack without waiting for our intense bombardment.

We were now told to hold ourselves in readiness to proceed to the front line. I told Dann we wouldn't carry that rabbit wire any further, so we dumped it in a shell hole. I heard someone say that Captain Thomas had gone down the communication trench, which was now being shelled by five-point-nines; so I went after him in case he had a message to send back to the Company—I was not aware that he had taken an orderly with him. I was also under the impression that he had gone to the front line, so I made my way there. (I found out later that he had gone to Battalion Headquarters which was about halfway between the assembly trenches and the front line.) I met some of the lightly-wounded men of the Middlesex and enquired how the show was going. "A bloody balls-up" was the reply. One man said that as soon as Old Jerrie commenced to shell the front line the gas-wallahs vanished. The trench was soon full of gas, and that was the reason they went over the top before the bombardment commenced. The enemy were now shelling all along our front and the communication trench was congested.

I found myself along with C Company and we could only proceed at a snail's pace owing to the dead and dying that were laying about and the wounded that were coming back. We reached the front line and found that half of B Company had gone over and the Company Commander, Captain Freeman, was laying dead on the fire-step: he had died of heart failure. C and the remainder of B were now preparing to go over. A platoon officer of C was as drunk as a lord and was making a mug of himself: he had formerly been a non-commissioned officer in the Guards but had been granted a commission in the Royal Welch Fusiliers and had joined the Battalion at Bois Grenier. Major Samson who was Company Commander of C noticed him and told him to remember that he was an officer and to try and behave like a gentleman. The trench was reeking with gas and we were wearing our tube helmets rolled up on our heads; if we pulled them down over our faces we wouldn't have been able to see anything. The scaling-ladders were not much good; when rested on the bottom of the trench or against the back of a traverse they were too short, and when rested on the fire-step they were too long. C and the remainder of B now went over, the majority climbing over the parapet from the fire-steps, to be met with heavy machine-gun and rifle-fire, some of them falling back in the trench killed or wounded as they were climbing over the parapet. Not a man in either company got more than thirty yards from his own trench. The officer that was drunk was shot through the thigh but he managed to scramble back in the trench without any further damage; he was very lucky. Major Samson was laying out in front mortally wounded: three men, one after the other, sprung over the parapet and made a rush towards him with the intention of bringing him in but they were bowled over by rifle-fire.

Captain Thomas and A Company then arrived and we were just about to go over to be slaughtered when the Adjutant, who was now in command of the Battalion, came hurrying up to tell Captain Thomas that he was not going to have any more losses and ordered A and D Companies to stand fast and await further orders. He sent a signaller back with a message to advanced Brigade Headquarters, which was about six hundred yards behind the front line, and from where I expect the Brigadier-General had witnessed the massacre of half his brigade. All our telephone lines had gone West just after the attack commenced, and the Colonel had been slightly wounded on the back of the hand and had gone back with the wounded.

Orders came from Brigade that the attack was suspended for the time being and we were to hold the trench. Our artillery now commenced to shell the enemy's trench, but a lot of the shells were falling short again and exploding amongst the men laying out in the open. Some of these men were not hit but if either they or the wounded attempted to return they were immediately fired at. Some of the wounded were crying out with their pain but we could do nothing, only wait for the night when we would be able to bring them in. The enemy in front of us now put up a cross-fire on our troops attacking on our right and several of them jumped up on the parapet directing the fire. We could have shot them down but we were ordered not to fire in case we might hit some of the wounded Middlesex men laying a long way out in front. There was not much danger of us doing that, especially amongst the old Expeditionary Force men, but orders were orders and had to be obeyed. In less than an hour from the commencement of the attack the Brigade had lost fifteen hundred men, the majority being killed. Argyles and Middlesex were the worst sufferers. If our Adjutant hadn't stopped A and D from going over, in a few minutes most of them would have been kicking their heels up in a different world from this one.

From the time I had arrived in the front line I had been looking through a trench periscope. Some of the Argyles and Middlesex had very nearly reached the enemy's barbed wire: I don't think any had got any further. But if the whole Brigade had reached the enemy's barbed wire without any casualties they would have been skinned alive trying to make their way through it, as hardly any damage had been done to it by our shelling. As the Old Soldier had truly remarked some days before, it was a glorious balls-up from start to finish; and J.C. had not been very kind to our Brigade.

We were all coughing and sneezing and some of my Company were soon gas cases. One of my old platoon, Private Dale, was coughing very badly and also vomiting: a man by the name of Morris was ordered to assist him down to the Casualty Clearing Station. Two months later Dale rejoined the Battalion and told me that when they arrived at the Casualty Clearing Station Morris dug up a cough from somewhere that would take some beating and the Doctor, who was very busy, evacuated the both of them as gas cases. Travelling down to one of the Base hospitals Morris told Dale that he was not gassed but he was going to try and work it to get home. On arrival at the Base hospital Morris dug up a series of coughs that were as loud as high shrapnel exploding, and also commenced retching. In less than twenty-four hours he was in England as a bad gas case. Dale himself had not been further than the Base hospital and the Base camp before being sent up the line again. Four months later he was severely wounded at Givenchy.

Dann told me that the Company had moved off without receiving their rum issue; just before they moved off from the assembly trenches Deadwood Dick gave orders for the storeman to bring it along so that he could see it issued. The storeman was a long time arriving and Deadwood Dick commenced to swear; the storeman appeared on the scene and as drunk as a broken cart-wheel.

As he handed over the jar he dropped face downwards in the trench and Deadwood Dick trod him into the mud; there was no time to issue the rum that was left, as orders then came for the Company to move off. (The storeman was forgotten lying there face downwards in the mud and that was the last we heard of him.) Coming up the communication trench the Company had some casualties through shelling and one minute they were advancing and the next minute retiring: no one knew where the orders were coming from and they had been lucky to reach the front line when they did. The both of us went along repairing the telephone lines, leaving the other signaller to fix up things in the dug-out: in a few hours' time we were in communication with all front-line companies and with Battalion Headquarters. During the afternoon a message came through that sixty thousand French troops had broken through the enemy's front in the Champagne district. Passing along the trench to deliver the message to Captain Thomas I came across the Old Soldier and told him about the break through of the French. His only comment was "Bloody B.S." The message was read out to the Company but the old hands took it with a grain of salt: they had heard yarns like that before. One old hand said that if it was true that sixty thousand Froggies had broken through it would be the bloody last that we would hear of them, as Old Jerrie had simply let them through, closed the gap up and roped them all in. We never had no more news of that break through by the French. Ever since the War commenced we had been dished up with yarns of that description. (The best yarn of all was one we had on the Retirement: we were then informed that a huge Russian army had invaded Germany and surrounded Berlin, giving the German Government twenty-four hours in which to accept their terms, failing which Berlin would be blowed to bits.) I expect yarns like that were dished up to buck up the spirits of the troops and we had now got so that we didn't believe anything; we would have been the dullest and most ignorant of men if we had believed some of the B.S. that was dished out to us.

During the whole of that night the Company were employed bringing in the wounded and dead and the enemy didn't fire a shot during the whole of the night. The dead that were too far out were left. Young Mr. Graves worked like a Trojan in this work and when I saw him late in the night he looked thoroughly exhausted. He was helping to get a stretcher down in the trench when a sentry near him forgot orders and fired a round. Mr Graves called him a damned fool and wanted to know why he was starting the bloody war again. He told a few of us outside the signallers' dug-out in the trench how bravely Major Samson had died. He had found him with his two thumbs in his mouth which he had very nearly bitten through to save himself crying out in his agony, and also not to attract enemy fire on some of the lightly-wounded men that were laying around him. Some of the men as they died had stiffened in different attitudes. One was on his knees in a boxing attitude and another had died with his right hand pointing straight in front of him. (I remember a man on the Arras front in 1917 who was down on one knee with his rifle at his shoulder as if he was about to fire. He must have died at that moment and stiffened in that position. One side of his face had been cut away by a piece of falling shell, leaving the teeth showing. He looked like a man who was doing a fiendish grin as he was taking aim with his rifle.)

Just after stand-to on the morning of the 26th I decided to have a scrounge around the trench of the battalion on our right: they were the Highland Light Infantry, a service battalion of one of the new divisions that had just arrived in France. I went along their trench a considerable way and was surprised not to find a sentry anywhere; they had lost heavily the day before, having over six hundred casualties, the majority being killed. There were dead and bandaged wounded men in the trench and men sleeping on the fire-steps dead-beat to the world. I woke one or two of them by shaking them, but they were so dead-beat that they instantly dropped back to sleep as soon as I ceased shaking them. In the Royal Welch, if every officer and N.C.O. had been casualties the oldest soldier that was left would have posted his sentries and seen for himself that they were keeping a sharp look-out. Proceeding along the trench I met the Old Soldier and two other men of ours: one of them was carrying a rum jar which the Old Soldier said was three-parts full. So I didn't go any further but returned back with them. Before we arrived back in our trench we filled some spare water bottles with the rum and I took one of them back to my dug-out. During the next forty-eight hours there were no more cheerier men in France than some of the old hands of my platoon and more brews of tea were made than what had been known for some time.

Shortly after I delivered a message to Captain

Thomas whom I found standing on the fire-step looking through his field glasses at something on our right front. He got down from the fire-step and read the message, then got back on the fire-step, his head and shoulders being fully exposed. I told him that he had better keep his head down, as only a few minutes before a man had been sniped through the head in the bay on the right of him. "Thanks very much," he replied, "I am watching the show over on our right." Some of our new divisions in the direction of Loos had advanced through a gap that had been made but were now retiring in disorder. A few minutes later Captain Thomas was killed: a sniper had spotted him and the bullet had entered the side of his neck. We were very cut up over his death: he was a soldier to his finger-tips and a very brave and humane man. He always treated us as men and not as machines.

On the night of the 26th all the good gas cylinders were carried to the left flank and if the man who invented them had all the good wishes of the men that were carrying them he would have been in untold agony both before and after his death. The Old Soldier was in magnificent form and going around the trench during the night I met him and the young soldier carrying one of the cylinders. They had a rest and he swore for some minutes, hardly using the same word twice. After he had calmed down a bit he asked me if I had any idea for the reason of carrying the blasted cylinders to the left flank. I replied that I had not. It was a hundred-to-one that they were going to send the stuff over again before long; but I had no news over the telephone about it. "Well," he replied, "If they do send it over

again it won't do no good. The Jerries will simply inhale it and think they are having a champagne supper."

There was going to be another slam on the 27th and
we signallers got to know all about it before some of the
platoon officers. Of course we handed over the information to some of our pals, though the men were not supposed to be told until shortly before the attack. At 4
p.m. the gas would be discharged, then a fifteen minutes'
bombardment by our artillery, to be followed by the
attack. The enemy seemed to know all about this attack: at 4 p.m. there were fires all along their parapet
which would send the gas up over their trenches. This
time the gas went over all right and our artillery carried
out their bombardment. The enemy did not reply with
any shelling or even fire a rifle shot. Orders now came
to stand fast, and at twilight a patrol of Cameronians
consisting of one officer and twenty-five men were sent
out. They reached the enemy's barbed wire and then
machine-gun and rifle-fire rung out from the enemy's
trench: only two wounded men returned from that
patrol.

A drizzly rain was now falling and after being hours
on the fire-step orders came that the attack was cancelled.
We were not sorry as we all knew that it was a fifty-to-
one chance against any man getting in the enemy's
trench. In the dark we might have got to their wire
with a small number of casualties but we would have
been skinned alive trying to get through it; the small
amount of damage that had been done to it before the
25th had been repaired during the nights of the 25th
and 26th.

A few days later I visited Duffy in his dug-out: he was

now a company stretcher-bearer. There were good dug-outs in some parts of the Cambrin trenches which had been made by the French when they occupied this part of the line. Some were down twelve or fifteen feet in the earth and some had two outlets. Duffy's dug-out only had one outlet: he always kept a supply of dry and wet wood and even with a dry-wood fire burning in the bottom of the dug-out a man would have to go through a strong smoke barrage before he reached the bottom, but the men sitting around the fire-bucket on the ground were quite free from the smoke which would be above their heads and going up the outlet. When any unwelcome visitor attempted to come down the dug-out, wet wood was put on the fire and before he had come two or three steps he would be very nearly suffocated and would generally retire cursing, coughing and wiping his eyes. I found Duffy making a brew of tea and the Young Soldier was laying on his back reading aloud a newspaper to the Old Soldier and him. French newsboys used to come up, even under shellfire, from Bethune to the mouth of the communication trenches in this sector, selling English newspapers.

The Young Soldier was reading out an account of the attack on the 25th which had been written by a well-known war correspondent who had been donkeys miles behind the front line at the time: how the troops had gone over the top laughing and joking as if they had been on a joy-ride back in Old England. The tea was made and with a drop of rum to go in it we gave full vent to our feelings: if that well-known war correspondent whose dispatches were read by millions in England had been in that dug-out he would have heard something about himself that would have surprised him. Ever since the War commenced these men had been writing the biggest B.S. imaginable about the Germans being no good, how they couldn't shoot, they couldn't do this and that, and in fact were no good at anything; if all that these men wrote was true we simply had to leave our trenches and walk through them.

This particular well-known war correspondent was the top of every soldier's roll: he was a great romancer and wrote the biggest B.S. of them all—even the young soldiers that had lately joined the Battalion had him in line. In May 1917 we were in reserve, in a sunken road about a mile behind the front line; one afternoon three civilians passed us and we mistook one of them for him. We called out his name and gave three cheers for the Biggest Liar on the Western Front; the three civilians laughed most heartily and we found out later that they were big pots from England, Members of Parliament or something, who were paying a visit to the Arras front. We had never seen our hero in person and we were going by his photograph which closely resembled one of these civilians. War correspondents in front-line trenches or attacks were rarer than full generals. The Old Soldier was always threatening to draw up a petition signed by front-line troops asking the Government to strike a special medal with the words inscribed on it: "For Distinguished Lying off the Field," which was to be awarded to all Western front war correspondents, as soon as they arrived at Army Headquarters.

CHAPTER X

WINTER IN THE BETHUNE SECTOR: CAPTURE OF R.W.F. CRATER

We were relieved the first week in October and went back to Sailly La Bourse where our Colonel rejoined us, and a few days later went back to Annezin where we had reinforcements of officers and men. Since the death of Captain Thomas, Deadwood Dick had been our Company Commander. We worked the Cambrin and Givenchy trenches until December and then went back for a three weeks rest to a place named Busnes. The signallers were billeted in a barn which was also the guard-room, and I volunteered to do the cooking for us while we were out of action. Whilst we were there Private Jones of my company arrived back with an escort. He had been a deserter since the 24th September. Jones was a grand front-line soldier, but when out of action was continually in trouble; a few days before the 24th he had the whole of his field punishment washed out for gallant work on patrols. A man doing field punishment never received any pay, and when the company were paying out Jones went in front of the young officer who was paying out to receive his, but was refused. Jones said: "I beg your pardon, sir. I am not now on Number Ones and I am entitled to pay, the same as the remainder of the company." The young officer, who was not a Royal Welch Fusilier, but attached to us from the East Surreys, replied: "I know that, Jones, but I am afraid if I give you any pay you will be getting in trouble again." Jones then told him that he hadn't received any pay for twelve months and that it would be impossible for him to get in any trouble with five francs. But the officer wouldn't give him any. "All right," said Jones, "no bloody pay, no bloody fighting." Jones spent the remainder of the day in the guard-room until he paraded that night to march off with the Company. Going down the La Bassée Road Jones fell out and when the roll was called in the assembly trenches he was absent. We old hands who knew him very well knew when he said to the officer "No bloody pay, no bloody fighting" that he would keep his word. There was only one penalty for being absent from an attack, and that was death.

Whilst Jones was awaiting his court-martial he told me of his wanderings in Back Areas during the three months he had been away, and how he could have still been away if he hadn't got fed up and given himself up. He had gone back to Bethune and in two days was in Boulogne: he had a good time there and then went to Calais. He never walked far, always getting lifts with motor lorries and got more food than what he had had since he landed in France. He also had some glorious drunks with some of the men he had met and nobody ever pulled him up or questioned him. He made his way back up country to Bailleul and one night when passing through that town an Assistant Provost-Marshal of police called upon him to assist two of his men to take an obstinate soldier to the guard-room. He gave the assistance and the A.P.M. told him that he would be delighted to have a man like him on his staff. Jones then asked the A.P.M. if he would do him a favour. "Certainly," replied the A.P.M., "if it's in my power." "Well, bloody well put me in the clink with the man I have just assisted your men to put there. I have been a deserter from my battalion for the last three months and I want to give myself up." He had a job to convince the A.P.M. that he was a deserter, who said at last that he would put him under lock and key pending enquiries. I told Jones that, as sure as God made both the louse and the lark, he would be put up against the wall and shot. I said also that I had better fatten him up a bit before he faced the firing-squad. He said he didn't care a damn about being shot, but on the other hand he didn't mind being fattened up a bit.

During the time he was awaiting his court-martial he lived like an owl and drank like a lord. He was sentenced to death, but owing to his gallant conduct on numerous occasions in the line and other extenuating circumstances in his case, the sentence was altered to ten years imprisonment. Jones was one of the few men that were sent away to serve their sentences. Seven months later one of our chaps met him on the Somme: he was then a full sergeant in one of our service battalions. He had been sent to England to serve his sentence and after being three weeks in prison was took in front of the Governor, who asked him if he would like to go back out to the front. "I don't mind," said Jones, "as long as I don't have to go back to my old battalion." Three days later he was released and sent back out with a draft to one of our service battalions where he was made a full sergeant two months later. I knew several cases like this. Good soldiers were not kept very long in prison after the year 1915.

We had a grand Christmas dinner. We bought two chickens and pinched seven. We eighteen signallers had plenty to eat that day. A few days later we were back in the line and for the next six months did spells in the front line between Givenchy and Hulloch. The 1915-1916 winter was hard enough, but we were getting more time out of the line than the previous winter. We were up at the front for sixteen days: eight days in the front line and eight in supports, and then back out to Bethune or one of the neighbouring villages for an eight days rest. I have seen the Battalion arrive at Bethune plastered in mud from head to feet, and twenty-four hours later turn out as clean as new pins. Long waders were issued to the men going in the front line, which reached to the top of the thigh. They were all right for walking through water but were a nuisance when the trenches were very muddy; often when walking down a communication trench a man would sink in mud above the knees and in trying to get one leg free the other would be sinking deeper. He generally released himself by pulling one leg out of the wader and putting one of his boots on, which we carried with us tied around our necks, and then doing the same with the other leg; and against he had pulled and tugged to release his waders, and fell on his backside in the mud, his curses would be loud and deep enough to blow up every wader factory in the world.

The Machine-Gun Corps was formed during this

winter, and our machine-gunners left us. Each company now had Lewis guns. The Mills bomb was also introduced: it was the best bomb on either side that was invented during the whole of the War. The German bomb was a stick-bomb and looked like a swede-masher.

During a spell in Givenchy I was posted to Battalion Headquarters. One afternoon I and a young signaller, a little fellow called Tich, had to take some orders to front-line companies. A hundred yards of the communication trench was waterlogged, being four feet deep in some parts. Tich was exactly five feet high, and in these parts, being a very poor swimmer, he walked carefully. But at last his feet shot from under him, and when I fished him out he looked like a young walrus. He had only been out in France a month and was getting a good breaking in. If it had been night we would have walked over the top, but we couldn't chance it in the daytime. Returning back he wanted to chance it over the top, saying that he might as well be bloody well shot as drowned, but I made him listen to reason, and against we arrived back at Battalion Headquarters his language had improved fifty per cent.

In January 1916 I went on my second leave. Leave had now been increased to seven days and there were also rest-camps at the ports. My second leave was similar to my first. They made as much of me as before, and if I wanted a quiet drink with my friends I had to go to another village to get it, everyone crowded about me so, asking questions. A smoker was held at the Castle Hotel at Blaina, and I and an old soldier called Tiny, who was also home on leave at the time, were the guests of honour. I was presented with a pipe and pouch, and suitably responded. Tiny, who was three sheets in the wind, was presented with a wristlet-watch, which was the last thing in the world he required. He responded in this way: "Well, Mr. Chairman and gentlemen, I thank you very much for this magnificent present, but I can honestly assure you that I have pinched dozens of better watches than this one from the dead Jerries laying out between the lines. And [here he pointed at me] my worthy friend Private Richards can bear me out in my statement." The majority of the company took it in good part: they knew Tiny very well.

I picked the Battalion up in a little village behind Cambrin, and met Duffy who was looking pretty glum; he told me that one of his pals had been killed and the Young Soldier had been badly wounded and gassed. But the Old Soldier was safe. I had left the Battalion in the trenches at Givenchy with two more days to do before they were relieved; on the last day the enemy had shelled hell out of our front line and some of the gas-cylinders, which were still there, had been smashed. The Company had many casualties from gas. We thoroughly hated the sight of these cylinders and knew the danger we were in when the front line was being shelled. Some time later they were all removed, and our artillery sent over gas shells instead; but as yet this was only tear-gas, not poisonous.

On the night of the 4th February, C Company, made up to two hundred men, were sent in the line between Cuinchy and Cambrin to capture a large crater which was about sixty yards from our front-line trench. In the first place the enemy had exploded a large mine and had rushed and occupied the crater. They had been driven out of it the following night but had recaptured it two nights later. During the last fourteen days three separate attacks had been made on the crater but each one had failed. We could not afford to let the enemy hold the crater that distance from our front line: they would have been able in a short space of time to have driven mine galleries from there in under our front line and blown up hundreds of yards of our trenches. Four signallers were told off for the attack—two with the attacking party and two to remain with Lieutenant Stanway who was in charge of operations and who would be in the front line trench. We were issued out with steel helmets, the first we ever wore, and arrived in the front line at 10.30 p.m.

I and a signaller called Paddy were going over with the attacking party, and our orders were to run a reel of wire out and endeavour to keep up communication if the crater was taken. There was to be no bombardment by our artillery, and men were to leave the front line as silently as possible; each man was to carry as many bombs as he could and a number of men were told off as bomb-carriers. The attack would be made at 11 p.m. The 2nd Worcesters holding the front line thought we had come up to relieve them, and were surprised to learn that we had come up for an attack on the crater. There were very few old Expeditionary Force men left in this battalion. One man said: "I don't envy you your job: only two nights ago two hundred men came up to do the same job and failed, and two hundred didn't get back, not by a big number. And the other night we had a try at it too, but we got more than we bargained for, just look over the parapet and see for yourself." I got up on the fire-step and although it was very dark I could see little heaps dotted here and there which I knew were dead men. I told him that we were having no artillery bombardment before going over. "All the better," he replied, "you are more likely to surprise them, but you'll surprise me greatly if you do capture that crater: there are good men holding it and they are very wide awake as well."

He was such a cheery individual that I was delighted when 11 p.m. arrived. We left our trench and dashed silently for the crater, we signallers running our wire out; we could not keep pace with the rest of the company, who were soon ahead of us. They had reached over halfway before they were spotted. Then the enemy opened out with machine-gun and rifle-fire and bullets were now zipping around us. We had made it up before we left the trench that if one of us fell the other would carry on the best way he could; but luck was with us and we got safely across to the lip of the crater. The scrap was well in progress and I covered Paddy whilst he was fixing the lines to the instrument and establishing communication. At 11.30 p.m. the whole of the crater was captured, and we were consolidating our position. Half of the men were digging in, the other half covering them. The officer in charge now got on the phone to Stanway, reporting the complete success of the attack. But five minutes before that Paddy had privately sent the news by Morse to our signallers at the end of the line. I don't remember this officer's name. He was a tall, big-limbed, young man, inclined to be sandy, with a small sandy moustache, and

was awarded the M.C. for his night's work. He
was killed on the Somme a few months later.

About twelve o'clock the enemy commenced shelling
our position and by 12.30 a.m. they had put up an intense barrage between us and the front-line trench. It
was impossible to get our wounded back, and our lines
also went West. Paddy and I decided to try and keep
the line going and go back, every other time, when there
was a break; and if one did not come back within a
reasonable time the other would go out to look for him.
Paddy went first. I didn't expect to see him come back,
but he did. I went next. I don't know how many times
we repaired that line, but during the whole of the night
we managed to keep up communication, which we were
afterwards told was of the utmost assistance to our officer and Lieutenant Stanway. About 2.30 a.m. the
shelling ceased and we were expecting a counter-attack,
but none came. The men in the front line began hurriedly to sap out to us, and at 5.30 a.m. we were relieved
by a company of our own battalion. During the night
our casualties were sixty killed and wounded. The
crater was afterwards named the R.W.F. Crater. For
our night's work Paddy, I and two sergeants were
awarded the D.C.M. We had did no more than the
other men; we were the lucky ones. In a successful stunt
a man who got recommended had far more chance of
receiving a decoration than a man who had been recommended in an unsuccessful stunt.

CHAPTER XI

THE BANGALORE TORPEDO AND A
DECORATION CEREMONY

We were in the Cambrin trenches and a Bangalore Torpedo was sent up to the Battalion, which had to be taken out and attached to the German barbed wire. This torpedo had been tried and proved a great success in some Back Area or other where there were no shells and bullets flying about and also no enemy waiting to ram a foot of steel through a man's chest. It was claimed that this torpedo would destroy more barbed wire than a battery of artillery would, firing for a week. Our comments were that if the inventor and the men who had tried it out in the Back Areas had the job of hitching it on the enemy's wire here at Cambrin they'd not reach halfway across no-man's-land before they'd be returning to change their under-pants.

Volunteers were called for from C Company: which met with no response. Everyone knew that the men who went out with the thing would be extraordinarily lucky to get back. There was every prospect of being spotted by a German patrol or listening-post and even if they escaped these, there would probably be German working parties busy on the wire. There was also the danger of the torpedo being struck with a bullet as they were carrying it and blowing them to pieces. A second call came for volunteers, and three old soldiers, as a matter of Regimental *esprit de corps*, said that before anyone should be warned for the job as a duty, they'd volunteer. One of the men was called "Freezer": I knew him very well, having soldiered with him in India, and he was a hard case. He was continually being awarded Field Punishment Number One and getting the sentence washed out for some daring deed or other. What he didn't know about patrols and trench warfare in general was not worth knowing. The volunteers were shown how the torpedo was to be fixed and where to fix it, and before they left the trench it was set ready to explode at 1 a.m. that night. They went out at midnight with Freezer in charge, and perhaps forty minutes later we were glad to have the message passed along that they were safe back. A little group of officers was now in the front trench. They had their watches out and were anxiously studying the luminous hands. One of them commenced to reel the seconds off: five seconds to go, four, three, two—CRASH! This was a German shell exploding five yards from them. But the Bangalore Torpedo failed to explode.

When day came and we stood-to, the torpedo could be distinctly seen where Freezer and his chums had put it on the enemy's wire. Some very beautiful remarks were made about it. One old soldier told a few young soldiers that the torpedo hadn't finished yet. It was liable to go off and when it did it would travel up and down the German Front, with a rage against barbed wire, blasting it all away without missing a single strand; after which it would turn its attention to the barbed-wire dumps in Back Areas, and finally make for Germany where it would destroy the factories where the barbed wire came from until there wasn't a strand of barbed wire left in enemy territory large enough to stick a louse with.

It lay out on the wire all that day but a message came through from Brigade Headquarters that it must be retrieved without delay. We all wanted to know what they wanted the thing back for, after calling for volunteers to get rid of it. I heard an officer remark that the reason was so as the enemy would not be able to get the Secret of it. So volunteers were again called for. The first journey had been dangerous enough, but this would be doubly so: the enemy would be on the watch, and have their machine-guns set. The same three men volunteered.

It was a quiet night. The Germans were not firing a shot in front of C Company, which made us think that they were waiting for whoever might come to fetch the thing back. But the men crept out, unhooked the torpedo and brought it back, much to everyone's surprise, without themselves or it being hit. Freezer, safe home in the trench, remarked that the torpedo seemed a damned sight lighter than when they took it out. He was right. Either that night or the night before the Germans had got hold of it and brought it into their trench. They had taken it to pieces, removed the mechanism and hung the empty thing back on their wire for us to retrieve. That was why they had not fired—to invite us to come and fetch it. I expect they did a good grin over the Secret of that torpedo. It was the first and last Bangalore Torpedo that I ever saw come up the line. The three men were not even recommended for medals, let alone get them, for this daring job they undertook. But they did get an extra drop of rum when they returned from the first journey.

In our next turn in the Cambrin trenches, after he had taken out the Bangalore Torpedo, Freezer formed one of a patrol of three who had a running fight with a German patrol of six. They both spotted one another simultaneously and the enemy patrol opened fire, which was a very unusual thing to do. If patrols ever clashed it was generally settled by the bayonet. Our patrol returned the fire and the enemy then began to run back to their own trench, turning around now and again to fire. Our patrol chased them back to their barbed wire and then had to give it up. Once the enemy patrol were safely in their trench the whole of the German front line opened fire, which they kept up for a considerable time, but Freezer's patrol was under cover in a large shell hole where they stayed until the firing died down. For this and other patrol work and the Bangalore Torpedo job, Freezer had a lot of twenty-eight days' Number Ones washed out.

We were back in billets in a village five miles behind. The Regimental-Sergeant-Major's batman, who was time-expired, invited me to his billet to spend an enjoyable evening the day before he left the Battalion. He informed me that he had roast ducks and all kinds of vegetables, four bottles of champagne and two charming young ladies who were refugees from one of the villages closer to the line. The batman was called "Nutty" and he *was* a nut. He was a proper Don Juan among the ladies and there wasn't a feathered fowl from Houplines to Bethune but what wouldn't attempt to rise on the wing and fly away in terror at the sight of him. Also we had some first-class scroungers among the old soldiers but he was the greatest of them all. The supper and champagne were excellent and so were the ladies. Late in the evening Nutty and one of the ladies retired into an adjoining room leaving me with the other in the dining room. After a few minutes the enemy commenced to shell the village and one shell exploded in the yard of the house we were in. We could hear the lady with Nutty exclaiming, "Oh, Monsieur Nutty, Allemenge Boko Bombard.""Yes," replied Nutty, "and in one minute Monsieur Nutty Boko Bombard too." I and the young lady with me burst out laughing. Nutty called out to us to keep quiet. About an hour later the enemy packed up shelling and I spent one of the most enjoyable evenings, and nights, that I ever spent in France. It hadn't cost Nutty a cent. He wasn't the Regimental-Sergeant-Major's batman for nothing.

In Bethune and some of the mining villages around, the men used to spend their Sundays in a way which we old soldiers considered a hundred per cent better than the way our folks spent theirs in England and Wales. The general rule around these places was church in the morning, and after church the men went to the cafés for a drink and a game of cards, then in the afternoon cock-fights were held in the back of the cafés. There was still a lot of miners working in the pits around here and Sunday was the only day when they could get a bit of pleasure. I saw some wonderful cock-fights around this area and thoroughly enjoyed them. About the middle of 1916 cock-fighting was prohibited until the War was over. It went on just the same.

In a café in one of these mining villages was a fine stuffed cockerel. I had never seen a stuffed cockerel before, so I asked the landlord the reason of it. He burst out crying! I asked his wife. She burst out crying too, and so did their eldest daughter, a young lady of about nineteen summers, going at it as if tears were her life's profession. Though I knew full well that most ladies are born with a well in their heads, I thought it strange that they and the landlord too, a big strong man, should begin crying over a stuffed cockerel. After they had calmed down a bit the landlord explained in French and bits of English that the bird had been the champion fighting-cock of the whole of the La Bassée district, and undefeated for three years. Every Sunday afternoon, when it was fighting, crowds of people used to visit the café and much champagne and other wines were drunk. He had won thousands of francs on that cock's matches. Then one morning he had found him dead in his cot. At this point they all started crying again. Both he and his wife then told me that they would have parted with one of their children sooner than lose that bird. And knowing the fondness for shekels these people all had I quite believed him.

The latter end of March we were in the Cuinchy trenches between the brick stacks and the Bethune-La Bassée Canal. We had waders issued but were in a sorry state, the weather having been very bad for some time. A message came through that I, Paddy and Sergeant Aston of A Company were to report ourselves at once at Battalion Headquarters. We arrived there about 1 p.m. and were told that we were due at Montmorency Barracks in Bethune at 2 p.m. We were to be decorated with the D.C.M. ribbon by General Munro who had lately come to France from the Dardanelles and was now in command of the First Army. Sergeant Aston was from Burnley, Lancashire, a short, wiry, hatchet-faced man with sandy hair and blue eyes and as gutsy as a bull terrier. On the night we took the R.W.F. Crater he seemed to be here, there and everywhere during that little show, and after the crater was taken but bombing still had to be done, was continually dancing round the crater and yelling for more bombs. He did the work of three men and set a wonderful example to the men alongside him. Another sergeant, Sergeant Bale of D, had also been warned for the Decoration ceremony.

It was impossible for us to arrive in Bethune in an hour on foot, but the Brigadier's car was waiting for us at the mouth of the communication trench and in it we piled. Bethune was about six miles behind the front line, and the main road was being heavily shelled. I believe our driver broke all records along that road and arrived at Bethune before we hardly had time to settle down in the car. Montmorency Barracks was situated off a small narrow street adjoining the Fish Market and the car had to proceed very slowly when going down this street and around the corner into the Barracks. Every general's car carried a small flag in front and outside the Barracks the sergeant of the guard had posted a scout who would shout to the sentry when General Munro's car was approaching. The scout seeing our car approaching warned the sentry, who turned the guard out, being under the impression that General

Munro was in it. The Sergeant gave the order, "General Salute! Present Arms." As the car passed slowly by I popped my head out of the window and rose my hand to acknowledge the salute. "All right, Sergeant," I said, "you may dismiss the guard!" We could still hear his language after the car had driven into the Barracks. It was the first and last time I was ever given a General Salute by a guard.

Inside the Barracks about thirty men were on fatigue with a sergeant in charge: they were picking up fag-ends and matchsticks and cleaning the place up. As the car stopped the Sergeant sprung the men smartly to attention and stood at the salute. Paddy was the first to step out of the car and he returned the salute this time, but this sergeant was different to the other and took it in good part.

Troops were lined up on the square and with brasses polished they looked clean enough to have mounted guard at Buckingham Palace: they had been warned for this show three days before, whilst we who were the principals had only been warned during the last hour. We looked at ourselves: we were in fighting order and I and Paddy were as black as two sweeps. Not one of us had washed or shaved for the last three days and we must have been the four most dirty men in Bethune. We were wondering whether we would have time for a wash and shave when a sergeant-major approached us and lined us up in the square in front of the troops. A few minutes later General Munro and his staff arrived. He gave a lecture on the spirit of self-sacrifice; afterwards each one of us marched up to him and it was read out what each man had did to win the D.C.M. After pinning the ribbon on our breasts he shook each man heartily by the hand and wished him the best of luck to live and wear it. When I was in front of him he asked me where I came from. I replied that only an hour before I had left the Cuinchy trenches. He said it must be very dirty there, I told him it was, and in more ways than one; and a good honest grin swept over his face. We were took back by the car and were in the front-line trench in no time.

All parades for the distribution of decorations were afterwards held when troops were out of action and warning was generally given a few days before; then it was spit and polish until the parade came off. We always made it a rule now to wash and shave on the day we were relieved in the line; we would boil a pint of shell-hole water and about a dozen men would have a shave and a lather-brush wash in it.

About this time a new decoration was introduced which could only be won by officers and warrant officers; it was called the Military Cross. I overheard one of our old officers say that it had been simply introduced to save awarding too many D.S.O.s. All officers thought a lot of the D.S.O., and all men thought a lot of the D.C.M.; both decorations ranking next to the Victoria Cross. In the spring of 1916 another decoration was introduced which was called the Military Medal. It was a decoration for N.C.O.s and men and in order of merit ranked below the D.C.M. There were no grants or allowances with the Military Medal, which without a shadow of a doubt had been introduced to save awarding too many D.C.M.s. With the D.C.M. went a money-grant of twenty pounds, and a man in receipt of a life pension who had won the D.C.M. was entitled to an extra sixpence a day on to his pension. After the new decoration was introduced, for every D.C.M. awarded there were fifty Military Medals. The old regular soldiers thought very little of the new decoration.

CHAPTER XII

THE CORPS COMMANDER AND
QUICK FIRERS

During the latter end of 1915 the 19th Brigade were transferred to the 33rd Division, the Middlesex and Argyles were transferred to the 99th or 100th Brigades, and we, the Cameronians, 5th Scottish Rifles and 20th Royal Fusiliers now formed the 19th Brigade. The 20th Royal Fusiliers were a Public Schools battalion who had arrived in France about November 1915. They were very decent chaps but hopeless as soldiers; the only thing they ever became proficient in was swearing. Their mail was always twice as large as the rest of the Brigade's put together. We old hands were sorry that the Brigade had been split up and would have much preferred for it to remain as it was. Young Mr. Graves had been transferred to the First Battalion: he rejoined us on the Somme but was soon wounded in the chest, and again in 1917, but only lasted a few weeks before he went sick and did not return. Deadwood Dick had also left us and our Adjutant had been given the command of a Territorial battalion. We had a new medical officer, Dr. Dunn. He was the bravest and coolest man under fire that I ever saw in France. Whilst serving as a yeomanry trooper in the South African war he had won the D.C.M. I always thought he was more cut out for a general than a doctor and that he certainly would have made a better one than most of those who were in France. The Old Soldier had also left us—he had been transferred to the sappers and miners—and I missed him very much.

On this part of the Front on both sides trenches would be sapped out from the front line towards the enemy. Some of our sap-heads were only fifteen yards from the German sap-heads. Generally an N.C.O. and three men were posted in the sap-heads. Each side could have easily thrown their bombs into one another's saps, but this was very rarely done and they generally lived in peace with one another; sometimes they held conversations. In some parts of the front line and up the saps mine shafts were sunk and galleries driven forward at various depths until they reached under the enemy trenches, and then mines were exploded. Sometimes both sides would knock loose into one another's galleries and many a scrap took place in the bowels of the earth. The miners on both sides were often blowing one another's galleries in and many a good man was buried alive. In the galleries a man was always posted as a listener with a listening apparatus in his ears which would record any sound within reasonable distance in the earth.

We were in the trenches at Hulloch, and a Battalion Headquarters' signaller came in our dug-out and handed me Battalion Orders to give to the Company Commander; of course Dann and I read it before handing it over. It consisted mainly of orders sent by the Lieutenant-General commanding the corps we were now in, and ran something like this: "It has been brought to my notice that a pessimistic feeling prevails amongst the officers, N.C.O.s and men in my Corps; such expressions as 'We will never shift the enemy out of their entrenched positions' and 'The War has now become a stalemate', are frequently made. Officers must eradicate this feeling from their minds and from the minds of the men serving under them, and remember that it is only a question of time before the enemy will be driven headlong out of the lines that they now occupy." There was also too much swearing in the corps for his liking, and the officers were worse than the men: "This practice must also cease." I took the message to the Company Commander, and his language for the remainder of the day was delightful to listen to: it would have done that Lieutenant-General a heap of good if he could have heard it.

The Corps Commander was right about the pessimistic feeling prevailing: all along this front from Cambrin to Hulloch and as far as the eye could see, our dead were still lying out in front of us, and looking through the periscopes by day we could see the rats crawling over their bodies. They had a good picking along this front and were as fat as prize porkers. We also knew that from now on any attack that was made by us would involve huge casualties. We old hands were always hoping that the enemy would attack us, so that we could get a bit of our own back for the Loos battle. It was all very well for the Corps General to be so optimistic: he was living in a château or mansion many many miles behind the front line from where he issued his orders, which went from him to Divisions then to Brigades then to battalion commanders, from them to company commanders and platoon officers who with the men had to do the real dirty work. If he had been in a front-line trench on a dark or dirty night, and going around a traverse had been knocked head over heels on his back in the deep mud by someone carrying a roll of barbed wire, or by the burst of a shell, I expect his language would have been a little stronger than what he used back in his abode of luxury. A few weeks previously he had inspected the Battalion in Montmorency Barracks and noticed that the men's brasses were not polished. He gave orders that all men in his corps when out of action must polish their brasses the same as if they were at home. Up to this time it had been a standing order in the Battalion to keep the brasses dull, but after that inspection our brasses were polished good enough to shave in. Many prayers were offered up for his soul, and a few days later when we marched down the main road towards the line, with the sun shining brightly and striking on our polished brasses, the enemy in their observation balloons must have thought that hundreds of small heliographs were moving into action. Duffy swore that the Corps Commander was a chief director in one of the large metal-polish companies and another man remarked that the old bastard would sooner lose his trenches than his button-sticks.

During one spell in the line at Hulloch, Dann and I came out of our little dug-out, which was about fifteen yards behind the front-line trench, to clean our rifles and bayonets. We were just about to begin when there appeared, on the back of the trench we were in, the largest rat that I ever saw in my life. It was jet black and was looking intently at Dann, who threw a clod of earth at it but missed, and it didn't even attempt to dodge it. I threw a clod at it then; it sprung out of the way, but not far, and began staring at Dann again. This got on Dann's nerves; he threw another clod but missed again, and it never even flinched. I had my bayonet fixed and made a lunge at it; it sprung out of the way for me all right, but had another intent look at Dann before it disappeared over the top. I would have shot it, for I had a round in the breach, but we were not allowed to fire over the top to the rear of us for fear of hitting men in the support trench; one or two men had been hit in this way by men shooting at rats, and orders were very strict regarding it. Dann had gone very pale; I asked him if he was ill. He said that he wasn't but the rat had made him feel queer. I burst out laughing. He said: "It's all right, you laughing, but I know my number is up. You saw how that rat never even flinched when I threw at it, and I saw something besides that you didn't see or you wouldn't be laughing at me. Mark my words, when I do go West that rat will be close by." I told him not to talk so wet and that we may be a hundred miles from this part of the front in a week's time. He said: "That don't matter: if it's two hundred miles off or a thousand, that rat will still be knocking around when I go West." Dann was a very brave and cheery fellow, but from that day he was a changed man. He still did his work, the same as the rest of us, and never shirked a dangerous job, but all his former cheeriness had left him. Old soldiers who knew him well often asked me what was wrong with him. But I never told them; they might have chaffed him about it. Neither I nor Dann ever made any reference about the rat from that day on, and though we two had passed many hours together shooting at rats for sport in those trenches, especially along at Givenchy by the canal bank, he never went shooting them again.

We had one platoon officer who was very thick in his speech. He was constantly going out on patrols, sometimes alone, sometimes with a sergeant, and he always looked three sheets in the wind. Out in no-man's-land he would commence shouting and cursing the Germans in their own language. One sergeant who had been out with him on two occasions told me that he had to clap his hand over the officer's mouth after he had been shouting and cursing for some time. At the time they were not very far from the enemy's wire. This officer had only been with us six weeks, and the last time we were in the Hulloch trenches one of our sergeants, who was an old crony of mine, came up and asked me what I thought of this officer. I told him that I didn't think very much of him and that I wouldn't go out on patrol with him, not for a gold cow. He then told me in confidence that he had been detailed off to watch him, and if he caught him acting in a very suspicious manner his orders were to shoot him on sight. The same night the officer went out on patrol, and when lying about fifty yards from the enemy's wire was shot through the backside. The shot must have come from further along the enemy's front as the enemy were not firing directly in front of him and we were not firing because the patrol was out. After he was shot he began to shout and curse louder than ever and the sergeant who was with him had to very nearly strangle him before he could make him shut up. They arrived back in our trench and he was carried away on a stretcher, one old hand remarking that if he had received such a beautiful wound as that he would have run all the way to the bloody dressing-station. We always thought that he was imparting information to the enemy when he was out shouting and cursing them, and it was evident that the senior officers had their suspicions, otherwise they would never have detailed a sergeant to watch him. Of course it may have been the sergeant himself who fired that shot from just behind.

We were in supports in a little village, and early one morning the enemy sent a lot of gas over. I had just finished cooking the breakfast, and our buttons and badges and the bacon and tea and everything else turned as green as grass. We had no breakfast that morning and some of the men were vomiting very badly. When we moved back into reserves Paddy and I decided to celebrate our winning the D.C.M. by going to a certain café where we were well known and which was standing alone about two hundred yards from the village we were in. No one was allowed in a café after 8 p.m., and at 8 p.m. we were the only two men in the café; with ving blong, the gramophone playing, and two fair damsels to dance with, we were celebrating very well. About 9.30 p.m. the door was thrown open and in walked two military policemen. I was at that moment pouring out some ving blong. They seemed two decent chaps, so we asked them if they could overlook it: we were not thinking of ourselves, but we knew very well that the two young ladies and their mother who owned the café would get into trouble over it.

They said that they would like to, but their Assistant Provost-Marshal was just up the road and they would have to take our names. They took our names from our pay-books—otherwise we could have given any name and a different battalion of the regiment we belonged to, and they would have never found us when they sent the crime in. Some time later our crime came through, with also a postscript from the Divisional General informing commanding officers that they had been too lenient with this kind of crime, and that the punishment these two men were awarded should be sent back to him. I appeared in front of my young Company Commander, Captain Higginson, who was one of the Artists' Rifles men, and my crime was read out, which was "Found drinking after hours in a café". He tried to be serious but failed, and burst out laughing. He then said that if he had his way he would tear the bally crime up but that he had no option in the matter and would be bound to put me back for the Commanding Officer to deal with. Paddy's Company Commander had also dealt with him in the same way. We both had a lovely yarn to tell the Colonel, which any judge in the land would have accepted as the truth, and he awarded us eight days Number One Field Punishment, which was twenty days less than we expected. There's no doubt but that no two men could have celebrated their winning of the D.C.M. better than what Paddy and I did, tied to those G. S. waggon wheels in the transport lines. The Provost-Sergeant was allowed to use his discretion as to whether he tied us by our ankles and our wrists or only by our wrists; and in this case he left our ankles free. We were lucky.

All our letters home were censored by platoon officers: we were not allowed to mention what part of the Front we were on, or casualties, or the conditions we were living in, or the names of villages or towns we were staying in. Green envelopes for private correspondence were introduced, which platoon officers did not censor, but they were censored by the Base Censor who I expect opened one here and there. When we had no time to write letters we sent field-service post cards which we called "quick-firers". We simply wrote the address on them and signed our names and dates of sending on the backs; there was some printed matter on the backs, such as "I have been wounded" or "I received your parcel", which we crossed out if it did not say what we wanted, simply leaving the words "I am all right". A private called Tim went on leave, and a few of us for a lark decided to send him half a dozen quick-firers and sign each with a French lady's name, with kisses; and one which we signed Mdlle. Yvonne had three times more kisses than the others. We judged the cards to reach him about three or four days after he was home. Tim was a married man and thought the world of his wife and children, and little did we think when we sent the cards how disastrous they would be. If we had known we wouldn't have sent them: we all liked Tim very much. We were in the trenches when he returned. He was posted to a different company than I was; so I took a stroll around to his trench to ask him if he had received the quick-firers. On the way I met one of the signallers of Tim's company, who inquired if I had seen Tim since he arrived back off leave. I replied that I hadn't but was now on my way to see him. He said: "I advise you to keep away. Last night he called in our dug-out breathing fire and blood and swearing that if he found the men who had sent him those quick-firers he would bloody well bayonet them. We asked him what was the matter and he said that his wife had received the cards from the postman and had raised holy hell when she saw the senders' names. We assured him that it wasn't us who had sent the quick-firers, we were quite innocent. When he left us he said it was either a signaller or a policeman that had sent the cards and that he would find the man out before he was many days older." I then decided not to see Tim and to let him cool down a bit before explaining things to him. When we were out of the trenches he was cook for the regimental police who were generally billeted by the signallers.

Ten days later we were back in Bethune and Tim asked me if I had sent any of those quick-firers to him; I admitted that it was at my suggestion that the lot were sent and that they were only sent for a lark. "Yes, I know that," he replied, "but they made me the most miserable man in England for the last few days of my leave. Just listen to me for a bit and you'll be able to understand the damage you have done. It was like this: on the evening of the third day of my leave a smoking concert was held in my honour, and the following morning I woke up with a very fat head. The wife went downstairs to make a cup of tea, and while she was making it I heard the postman knock at the door. A few minutes later she rushed up the stairs taking two steps at a time. I was wondering what was the matter for her to come up the stairs at such a rate, when she burst into the bedroom, threw those cards in my face, and called me all the filthy names imaginable. 'You!' she cried. 'Pretending you have been fighting with the Germans and up to your waist in blood and mud in the trenches, when all the time you have been in France you have done nothing but carry on with a pack of mucky French girls. And now they have the cheek and impudence to send you cards with kisses on, the dirty cats! I am going to leave you now and take the children with me and I never want to see you again.' She then began to pack a box and I picked up the cards to see what had caused all the mischief. The first signature I read was 'Mdlle. Yvonne' with a whole row of kisses, and although my head was bad I burst out laughing. She turned on me like a flash and said: 'You laugh, do you, you filthy old Mormon! You are worse than the girls that sent the cards.' I tried to explain to her that the cards must have been sent for a lark by some of my pals and that I knew no Mdlle. Yvonne nor none of the other ladies, but she wouldn't listen to no such explanations. She said that if my pals was anything like me they were a bad dirty lot and she hoped they were not married men. That day she went to her mother's and took the children with her.

"I thought she would return in the evening, but she didn't, so the following morning I took a stroll around to my mother-in-law who lived about a quarter of a mile away. As I approached the house the door was opened and my mother-in-law appeared in the doorway, and I could tell by the look of her that she was out for blood. I was a good ten yards from her when she commenced, and for the next fifteen minutes I couldn't get a word in edgeways. She finished up by telling me that I was Brigham Young and Henry the Eighth and the Sultan of Turkey rolled into one. By this time a lot of women in the street had gathered around and I overheard a few of them saying what they would do to me if I had been their husband. I tried to explain to my mother-in-law, but she cut me short and ordered me from her house, saying that she always knew I was a wrong 'un. My wife and children stayed with her for the remainder of my leave, and the only time I saw them again was when I was waiting to catch the train returning from leave. My wife's last words to me were: 'I hope Mdlle. Yvonne will be waiting for you with all those kisses when you land back in France.' "

I told Tim that I and the other two men were very sorry for the mischief we had done but that I would write a letter to his wife explaining everything, and the three of us would attach our names and addresses to it. I sent the letter, but not one of us received an answer. Instead she wrote to Tim, informing him that she had received the letter but that she had no doubt in her own mind that we had wrote the letter to screen him. Two months later Tim was lightly wounded and was lucky enough to be sent home, and I have heard since the War that he and his wife are living happily together.

CHAPTER XIII

THE RED DRAGON MINE AND A RAID

Late in June we relieved a battalion of the Hertford-shire Regiment in the Givenchy trenches. One of their signallers informed me that they had a very quiet time and that during the last four days there hadn't been a dozen casualties in the whole of their battalion. I thought it very strange and knew that any battalion holding this part of the line was extremely lucky if it had under fifty casualties in that period. Some months previously we had been relieved in Cuinchy by the Argyles after spending four of the quietest days that I ever remembered; a few hours after we were relieved the enemy exploded a mine under the front-line trench and blew up one hundred and thirty men—mostly Argyles, but a lot of sappers and miners amongst them. I was posted to my own company on the left of the Battalion's front. D and C were in the centre and B on the right. About 11 p.m. I strolled along our front line and arrived at B Company trenches. All company signallers with the exception of B had dug-outs and I found the three signallers of B sitting on the fire-step with their D3 telephone, doing a good old soldiers' grouse, saying that they were the only signallers on the whole of the Western Front without a dug-out. I made them grouse a bit more when I told them what a grand dug-out we had, with two outlets to it and enough of dry wood to last us the whole of the time we were in the line. I pulled their legs to some order and when I left them they cursed me until they were blue in the nose. Old hands were continually pulling one another's legs: our dug-out was really a poke of a hole. It was a glorious summer's night but much too quiet for my liking. All along our front the enemy were not hardly sending a shell over or firing a shot and the stillness was uncanny. Several old hands that I stopped to talk with didn't like it no more than I did; we knew that something was going to happen.

I arrived back in my dug-out and about 1.30 a.m. was woken up by a terrific explosion on our right front. The ground shook and rocked as if an earthquake had taken place. The enemy's artillery had also opened out and they were bombarding our right front, the majority of the shells being five-point-nines. The company stood-to: we knew that the enemy had exploded a mine on our extreme right but were not sure whether it was in our Battalion's area or not. All communication with the exception of D on our right had broken down. A little later the enemy shells began falling all along the Battalion's front and the lines went between us and D and also we lost touch with Battalion Headquarters in the rear. I made my way along the trench to D and met one of their signallers who told me that he had just repaired two breaks in the line. I asked if they were in touch with C or B. He replied that they hadn't received a sound since the mine went up. Word was now passed along the trench that the enemy had set off a mine under B Company. A and D were now being heavily bombarded and about an hour later word came that with the exception of eight men the whole of B had been blown up by the mine and that the enemy had made a rush to occupy the crater, but had been repulsed by C Company and the eight survivors of B.

Dawn was now breaking and I made my way to C. Passing along the trench I came across the headless body of Sergeant Bale, one of the two sergeants who had been decorated with the D.C.M. by General Munro the same time as Paddy and me: as he was standing on the fire-step a piece of shell had took his head clean off and deposited it on the back parapet in such a way that it now seemed to be looking down at the body. He was an old Expeditionary Force man and one of the best N.C.O.s in the Battalion. The part of the trench near the mine-crater was now only between three and four feet deep because of the showers of earth that had fallen into it, and there I found the survivors of B with "Hammer" Lane, an old soldier, in command. There wasn't a lance-corporal left.

One of the men gave me a full account of it and said that after the mine went off the enemy bombarded their lines with five-point-nines, and when they switched the barrage to the left, right and rear of them he had a pretty good idea that they were coming over to try and occupy the crater. Soon they did come over and into the trench. Some got around the rear to their left and there was some hand-to-hand fighting. A platoon officer of C lost his head and shouted, "We'll have to surrender! They've got around the back of us." "Surrender my bloody arse!" shouted Hammer Lane. "Get your men to meet them front and rear." Captain Stanway with the rest of C Company then made a counter-attack and the show was soon over. One young officer of B who had escaped the mine had been killed in the fighting; a dagger had been driven up to the hilt in his belly. A young German officer and some of his men had been killed in the trench and a few prisoners had been taken. It was a big mine and the crater must have been a hundred feet across from lip to lip. The company commander of B, Captain Blair, was dug out alive on the lip of the crater, where he had been buried up to the neck. He was a man with many lives: he had been in the South African War, had been severely wounded on the 25th September, when serving with the same company, and had only lately rejoined the Battalion. If the signallers of B had had a dug-out I might have stayed with them a couple of hours swopping yarns and brewing tea and would have gone West with them. Captain Stanway was awarded the D.S.O., which he had thoroughly earned before this affair. The platoon officer who shouted "We'll have to surrender" was awarded the Military Cross. He really deserved something different. Lane was awarded the D.C.M.

It was a glorious summer morning the next day and anyone who had visited this part of the Front would have thought it was the most peaceful spot in France. No shells coming over, no reports of rifles, and the larks were up singing beautifully. It was generally like this after a show. A Staff Colonel from the Corps visited the front line to see the crater, and a few old soldiers put the dead German officer on a fire-step, fixing a lighted candle in one of his hands and a small pocket Bible in the other. Just as the Staff officer approached them they fixed a lighted cigarette in his mouth. The Staff officer didn't stay long in that part of the trench. This was done out of no disrespect to the dead German officer, but just to give the Staff officer a shock; who I don't expect would have come up to the front line if the enemy had been shelling it. We all hated the sight of Staff officers and the only damned thing the majority seemed to be any good at was to check men who were out of action for not saluting them properly. The big mine-crater was afterwards called Red Dragon Crater, after our Regimental badge. A prisoner told one of our chaps that the German officer was the bravest and most popular officer in the whole of the Jaeger Battalion to which he belonged. The same chaps that had propped him up on the fire-step also gave him a decent burial about thirty yards behind the back of the trench.

During the day one of the men of the 5th Scottish Rifles on our right noticed a wounded man of ours lying out in front who was trying to crawl back to the trench. He jumped over the parapet and ran towards him and under a heavy fire of rifle-bullets safely brought him back to his trench. He was awarded the Victoria Cross for this but was killed on the Arras front in 1917.

We were relieved and went back to a delightful little village called Le Prele (I don't think this is the right spelling) by the side of the La Bassée Canal. Paddy and I had bought some cheap rods and lines and went for a day's fishing, also taking a couple of Mills bombs in case we met with no success. After three hours fishing not one of us had caught a tadpole. An elderly Frenchman then commenced fishing by us and in no time he had caught half a dozen lovely fish. We stuck it another hour but with no results. We then gave it up and walked a couple of hundred yards down the Canal, and after a careful look around pulled the pins out of our bombs and dropped them in. Ten seconds later we had more fish than what we could carry back. This was a favourite method of fishing with some of us although strictly prohibited: if a man was caught the least punishment he could expect was twenty-eight days Number Ones. When the Old Soldier was with the Battalion he always went fishing in this way: he often used to say that a man who shot, bayoneted or bombed a dozen Jerries was complimented on his gallant deed and perhaps given a decoration, but if the same man stunned one fish with a bomb he was given twenty-eight days Number Ones. "That's what they call civilization," he would finish up.

Our next spell in the line was a little to the left of where the mine exploded but still in the Givenchy area and a big raid had been planned for the night of July 5th in retaliation for the mine, in which A Company was to take part. There was always an element of luck with night raids: we had made one three months previously when we were in the line at Cuinchy. Our artillery and trench-mortars had been blowing up the enemy's wire, and looking at it by day it seemed to be levelled to the ground, yet when the raiding party from B Company went over they found that not a quarter of it had gone and they were soon entangled in it. That raid was a washout, not a man getting in the enemy's trench, and we had many casualties, amongst them being Sergeant Joe Williams, a Liverpool man with whom I was very pally. In addition to the ordinary barbed wire, both sides used trip-wires, concertina-wires and other varieties. For a night raid to have any hope of success it was essential that the enemy's wire should be very nearly obliterated, and this was no easy matter. On both sides, on some parts of the Front I had been in, the barbed wire was between thirty and fifty feet in depth.

The raid on July 5th had been carefully thought out and our artillery and trench-mortars had sent enough of stuff over to level all the wire in front of us—at least we hoped so. Four signallers were detailed off to go with A Company and it was hoped that we would be able to establish communication as soon as we arrived in the enemy's trench and so save sending runners back. Two would run a line out with the Company and the other two, who was Tich and I, would run a line out by ourselves, about one hundred yards to the right of where the Company would leave the trench; so in case one line went West we would have the other to fall back on. During the day Captain Higginson pointed out the way we should run our line and hoped we would have the luck to pick up the Company just before they entered the enemy's trench. D Company, under Captain Moodie, were going over on the right without signallers and with them were men of the Royal Engineers, who if the raid was successful would blow in the enemy's mine-shafts and concrete dug-outs.

On the morning of July 5th I went back to Battalion Headquarters for a reel of wire. For the last two days and nights their linesmen had been very busy running out spare lines along the communication trenches and over the top. These lines were looped and laddered and with them done this way it was quite possible to have many breaks and still keep up communication. If we signallers going over with the raiding-party failed to establish communication with the front-line signal stations, it was arranged that runners would have to be used who would hand their messages in to one of those stations, from where they would be dispatched to Battalion Headquarters. One old signaller wanted to bet that no station would be in touch with any other fifteen minutes after the raid commenced. He wanted to back a cert because we old hands knew that if Old Jerrie did bombard our front all the looped and laddered lines would be blown to the four winds of Heaven. When I arrived back I came across "Fizzer" Green and Seth Elliott, the two sanitary men of the Company, whom I have mentioned before, fixing knives on to a couple of broomsticks which they were going to use in the raid: they had borrowed some sticking-plaster for the job from the Aid Post. They were two old soldiers and two of the greatest scroungers on the Western Front; it was said of them that they would have dug up the body of their grandfather and cut it open if they thought he had swallowed a penny before he died. Elliott once saw a German leg, blown off, lying in front, but remarked that it still had a trouser-pocket, and the same night went out and found a purse of gold marks in it. Fizzer was a steeplejack in civil life. Some of the officers were going to carry clubs with spikes on, which were very handy weapons at close quarters in a trench. An order was issued that the raiding party would leave their pay books and badges behind, so in case of a man being killed in the enemy's trench they would not be able to tell what regiment he belonged to. But all men would carry their identity discs. This order created a lot of amusement amongst the raiding party, and no wonder, as each man had stamped on his identity disc his regimental number, rank, name, battalion and regiment. Duffy who was going over as a stretcher-bearer said that the Big Pot who had issued that order in the first place should have been immediately rose to the rank of a Field-Marshal. Each man was issued with a white band to tie on his sleeve and the password after we left the trench would be "Welch". The Company Commander informed me that the Company would leave the trench at dusk and get out as far as they could and lie down, and at a given time our trench-mortars and artillery who would still be putting up a barrage on the enemy's wire and trenches would cease bombarding. Our artillery would then lengthen their range and put up a barrage behind the enemy's front, preventing any reinforcements from coming up. That would be the signal for the Company to make a dash for the enemy's trench.

Just before dusk Tich and I took up our position in the trench. Our trench-mortars were Stokes trench-mortars, a very efficient type that had been introduced a month or two previous to this, and could fire extremely fast, being very different from the clumsy ones that we had had up till then which were more danger to ourselves than they were to the enemy, having a short range and the shell often bursting in the gun. These Stokes trench-mortars were still putting up a tremendous barrage on the enemy's wire and trenches, and the enemy's artillery now opened out and commenced to bombard our line with big shells. We decided we would be safer out in no-man's-land and left our trench, running our wire out. The ground over which we had to travel was very uneven and for over an hundred yards we were walking over large shell holes, mine-craters and boggy ground; and what with falling into some of the shell holes and craters and getting stuck in the mud we were soon in a sorry state. No one could have told whether we had a white band on our arms or not, they were caked with mud. Tich sunk to his waist in one place and I had a job to tug him out; we were making very slow progress with running our wire out. Our trench-mortars had packed up by now and our artillery were bombarding the enemy's reserve lines and communication trenches. Looking behind us we saw that the enemy were putting up a proper barrage all along the Battalion's front. Heavy shells were bursting everywhere. At last we got on some good ground and had a rest: we knew that by this time the Company must have entered the enemy's trench, but we were only halfway there. We tried the bolts of our rifles but couldn't move them: they were caked with mud and clogged. On our left front an enemy's machine-gun started traversing; we sprung to our feet and carried on, running our line forward. We stopped about ten yards from their front-line trench and found that our artillery and mortars had done their work very well, the whole of the wire being practically obliterated, with only a post here and there left standing. We tested our lines but could get no reply from our front-line stations; we kept calling for some time and then gave it up. We decided to leave our reel of wire where it was and have no more to do with it. We advanced cautiously towards the trench where we could hear screams, yells, explosion of bombs and louder explosions from the demolitions that the R.E. men were busy doing. It was quite possible that there were stray Germans knocking about who had been missed by the raiders, and we were taking no chances.

When we were a few yards from the trench Tich pulled my sleeve and pointed to his right: a man was approaching us and we couldn't tell whether he was one of our men or not. We stood still and as he came nearer we could see he was a German. We went to meet him but when we were a few paces from him he threw his arms above his head and commenced to jabber in German. He then threw himself on the ground and sobbed like a child, he was absolutely terror stricken. We were puzzled what to do with him. We couldn't very well take him back in his own trench which was now very quiet (our chaps by now had reached their support trenches) because some of his comrades might be still prowling about. Tich then said, "There is only one way out of the difficulty and that's to bayonet him," and drawing his arm back with the words was about to drive the bayonet home; but I prevented him. At the same moment we were challenged with the cry, "Halt! Hands up! Who are you?" I replied: "Welch!" One of our men now clambered out of the trench on our left and approached us; he said that he had spotted us a little higher up the trench and not knowing whether we were friend or foe had advanced along the trench nearer to us and challenged us. He told us that the raid was very nearly over and that the raiding party would soon be returning. He had left the Company in the enemy's second line of trenches and was going back with a message as our two signallers had failed to get any answer to their signals. He was in a hurry and off he went.

We decided to take our prisoner back and we had a job to get him up on his feet. I pointed towards our lines. He nodded his head and led the way to our lines, I behind him and Tich behind me. He seemed to know the ground all right: probably he had done many a patrol over it. When we were about fifty yards from our trench he jumped a large shell hole half full of water and cleared it easily. I followed, but failed to clear it and was over my waist in water and stuck fast in the mud. I gave a quick glance over my shoulder but failed to see Tich: he had lagged a little behind. I shouted at the prisoner, who turned around. I still retained my rifle and menaced him with it. If he had known it was useless for firing, he could easily have got away and hid himself in a shell hole until our raiding party returned and then have made his way back to his own lines. But he stood fast. Tich now came along and seeing my plight went around the lip of the shell hole and made the prisoner, who was a magnificent made man, pull me out. It took some tugging on his part before he released me. Tich said that he wasn't far behind and hearing me shout and seeing the prisoner and not me he thought there was something wrong and put a spurt on.

When we arrived back in our front-line trench we hardly recognized it: it had been levelled to the ground in some parts and the enemy were still shelling. We arrived at the signallers' dug-out which was about twenty yards behind the front line. The entrance to it was three steps down and turn to the left; sitting on the steps were three men who had been over with the raiding party but had returned with messages which they had taken to Battalion Headquarters, and just arrived back. They got up off the steps and stood in the little trench to allow us to enter, Tich now leading the way, then the prisoner and I in the rear. I was on the bottom step and Tich had just entered the dug-out when crash! a large shell exploded just outside. At the same moment I crashed into the prisoner, knocking him and Tich in a heap. The two signallers in the dug-out thought that we were hit, but we had not been touched. I shouted to the three men and, receiving no reply, mounted the steps and found the three of them dead: the shell had exploded on the parapet about a yard from the top step and they were horribly mangled. It was tough luck for them after surviving the raid. The two signallers told us that ten minutes after the raid began they could get no reply from the front-line signal stations or Battalion Headquarters. They had gone to look and found that all the lines had been blown to bits. We took our prisoner to Battalion Headquarters and when we arrived back the raiding party were returning.

The raid had been a great success: over forty prisoners, a trench-mortar and two machine-guns were brought back. Many mine-shafts and concrete dug-outs had also been blown in and the only thing that had been a failure were the signalling arrangements. I don't know how many of the enemy had been killed, but the two sanitary men swore they had killed a dozen each. But going by the display that they spread out the next morning on the fire-step, they did not seem to have had much spare time for killing, they had been so busy with the looting; they had enough of watches to have opened a jeweller's shop. But they were very brave men for all that, and had proved it on many occasions. Looting was universal amongst us old hands, and all prisoners were made to hand over their valuables; if we didn't have them, the men in the Back Areas would before they got in the prisoners' cages, and we always found a ready market for our loot among non-combatant soldiers in Back Areas, such as the Army Service Corps and men on duty at Divisional Headquarters. We never reckoned to keep anything, and the money that was realized in this way enabled us to have a good time when we were out of action. We made merry whenever we had the chance: we knew we might be dead cocks the next time we were in the line. Our casualties for that night were about sixty: the two companies holding the front line had suffered worst than the raiding companies.

I don't know what happened to Fizzer Green and Seth Elliott after Elliott, who had been made a sergeant shortly after this, was badly wounded on the Somme in our High Wood show, and Green got one through the muscle of the arm about the same time. Neither of them returned to the Battalion.

CHAPTER XIV

THE SOMME: CAPTURE OF HIGH WOOD

We were relieved, and some days later we entrained for the Somme. We had a new colonel now, Colonel Crawshay, who proved to be the best we ever had. I had soldiered with him in the Channel Isles and abroad. He was universally liked by everyone, a stickler for discipline, and when in the line, no matter what the conditions were, was always visiting the front-line trenches and seeing things for himself. He had a cheery word for everyone and was as brave as they make them. Captain Stanway had left us to take command of a new service battalion. He and Fox had been the only two sergeant-majors of the Company that never pinched our rum.

It had been very noticeable during the last few months that all old hands were getting killed and youngsters who had only been out a few months were receiving lovely blighty wounds. This had happened so frequently of late that we old hands often used to remark that when we did get hit it would either be a bullet through the pound or stop a five-point-nine all on our own. But we considered that men were very lucky who met their death in this way: they didn't know anything about it and it was the death we all wished for if death must come our way. It was much preferable than to be blinded for life or to be horribly wounded and disfigured by shell splinters and perhaps still survive it.

We arrived on the Somme by a six days march from the railhead, and early in the morning of the 15th July passed through Fricourt, where our First Battalion had broken through on 1st July, and arrived at the end of Mametz Wood which had been captured some days before by the 38th Welsh Division which included four of our new service battalions. The enemy had been sending over tear-gas and the valley was thick with it. It smelt like strong onions which made our eyes and noses run very badly; we were soon coughing, sneezing and cursing. We rested in shell holes, the ground all around us being thick with dead of the troops who had been attacking Mametz Wood. The fighting was going on about three-quarters of a mile ahead of us.

Dann, a young signaller named Thomas, and I, were posted to A Company. The three of us were dozing when Thomas gave a shout: a spent bullet with sufficient force to penetrate had hit him in the knee—our first casualty on the Somme. Dann said: "I don't suppose it will be my luck to get hit with a spent bullet; it will be one at short range through the pound or a twelve-inch shell all on my own." I replied, as usual, that he would be damned lucky if he stopped either, and that he couldn't be able to grouse much afterwards. "You're right enough about that, Dick," he said. A few hours later the Battalion moved around the corner of the wood, the Company occupying a shallow trench which was only knee-deep. The first officer casualty on the

Somme was the lieutenant who got the M.C. for shouting: "We'll have to surrender. They've got behind us." Hammer Lane was next to this officer, deepening the trench, when a very small bit of shrapnel ricocheted off his shovel and hit the officer in the foot. He began to holler like mad and the Colonel who was not far off rushed up and wanted to know if he was badly hit. Lane answered: "No, sir. He's making a lot of bloody row over nothing at all." The Colonel told Lane to shut up and never speak of an officer in that way again. Lane told me later in the day that if the officer had had his bloody belly ripped open he could not have made more row than what he did.

Dann and I were by ourselves in one part of this trench, the Company Commander being about ten yards below us. The majority of the Company were soon in the wood on the scrounge; we had been told that we were likely to stay where we were for a day or two. I told Dann that I was going in the wood on the scrounge and that I would try and get a couple of German top-coats and some food if I could find any. The topcoats would be very handy as we were in fighting order, and the nights were cold for July. Just inside the wood, which was a great tangle of broken trees and branches, was a German trench, and all around it our dead and theirs were laying. I was in luck's way: I got two tins of Maconochies and half a loaf of bread, also two topcoats. The bread was very stale and it was a wonder the rats hadn't got at it. Although gas destroyed large numbers of them there were always plenty of them left skipping about. I returned to Dann telling him how lucky I had been, and that we would have a feed. "Righto," he replied, "but I think I'll write out a couple of quick-firers first."

Enemy shells were now coming over and a lot of spent machine-gun bullets were zipping about. He sat on the back of the trench writing his quick-firers when—zip!—and he rolled over, clutching his neck. Then a terrified look came in his face as he pointed one hand behind me. I turned and just behind me on the back of the trench saw the huge black rat that we had seen in Hulloch. It was looking straight past me at Dann. I was paralysed myself for a moment, and without looking at me it turned and disappeared in a shell hole behind. I turned around and instantly flattened myself on the bottom of the trench, a fraction of a second before a shell burst behind me. I picked myself up amid a shower of dirt and clods and looked at Dann, but he was dead. The spent bullet had sufficient force to penetrate his neck and touch the spinal column. And there by his side, also dead, was the large rat: the explosion of the shell had blown it up and it had dropped by the side of him. I seized hold of its tail and swung it back in the shell hole it had been blown from. I was getting the creeps. Although Mametz Wood was, I daresay, over fifty miles as the crow flies from Hulloch, I had no doubt in my own mind that it was the same rat what we had seen in the latter place. It was the only weird experience I had during the whole of the War. There was no one near us at the time, and men on the right and left of us did not know Dann was killed until I told them. If I hadn't handled that rat and flung it away I should have thought that I had been seeing things, like the many of us who saw things on the Retirement.

For the next couple of days we didn't have much to do; there were batteries of our eighteen-pounders just in front of us and heavier artillery behind us, and there was a proper artillery duel going on. The valley we were in was thick with guns. One afternoon a couple of guns in front of us were blown to bits and two young artillery officers were led past us, hysterical and horribly shellshocked. They were the two worst cases I ever saw, and anyone would have been doing them a kindness if they had put them out of their misery.

Just behind us on a ridge was a battery of small howitzer guns, and as we were watching them, guns, men and everything else vanished. The enemy shells were simply raining on that ridge. It was the most accurate shellfire I had seen, and Duffy who was standing by me said: "If the Jerry gunners were only fifty yards away they couldn't drop their shells more accurately than what they are doing." We both thought it very queer. About a couple of hours later two men of the Middlesex were on the scrounge in Bazentin Le Petit wood which was just in front of us, and happened to see a man dressed in grey disappear in a dug-out. They followed him but on reaching the bottom of the dug-out could see no one. They didn't have a candle and were striking matches to have a look around it. One of the men said that they must have been mistaken, but the other was positive that someone had entered and told his pal to bring along an officer with a pocket torch whilst he kept watch. The man arrived back with an officer who examined the walls of the dug-out with his torch, and found a door in one of the walls that they hadn't spotted because it fitted very close and was covered with canvas, the same as the wall. He said in a loud voice: "No, you made a mistake, there's nothing here;" and they went back out of the dug-out. When outside, the officer said quietly to the men: "Did you see that door? There may be someone behind it. We might have been met by a stream of bullets as we opened it. Now if there is anybody behind it he'll think we've gone away. I want one of you men to stay at the entrance and the other to come very quietly with me back inside." So one man waited outside and the other, with the officer, re-entered the dug-out. Soon the door was quietly opened and a man appeared in the doorway. The officer flashed his torch on him and at the same moment fired his revolver. It was a German officer dressed in his own uniform and the bullet got him in the breast. Behind the door was a neat little dug-out with an underground cable running into it and also two trench telephones. He had been sending back the positions of every one of our batteries that he spotted, and no wonder the German shellfire had been so accurate. He wasn't dangerously wounded; the bullet had entered high up in his breast and he was walking assisted by two men as he passed us. He admitted to the Middlesex officer that he had volunteered to stay behind for this dangerous work, and he was proud he had served his country so well. I heard some officers remark that he was a very brave man. Two days later when digging a trench on the right front of Bazentin Le Petit we came across the cable which must have run right back to High Wood.

On the 18th the Company took over a position on the east front of Bazentin Le Petit; we were in a shallow trench which ran into a cemetery. High Wood was about seven hundred yards in front of us. The following day the enemy shelled us heavily, and by the afternoon they had a nasty barrage extending right down to the valley we had left. In our part of the trench the shells were falling either in front or behind us; but the other end of the Company was not so lucky, the shells bursting right on the parapet, blowing trenches and men to pieces. The whole of a Lewis-gun team was killed. In the cemetery the shells were throwing corpses and coffins clean out of the graves, and some of our killed were now lying alongside of them. We could only sit tight and grin and bear it. One shell burst just outside the trench not far from me, and a man had one side of his face cut clean away by a piece of shell. He was also hit low down but was still conscious. His two pals were deliberating whether they would put him out of his misery or not; fortunately they were spared that, as he died before they had made up their minds. One of our old stretcher-bearers went mad and started to undress himself. He was uttering horrible screams, and we had to fight with him and overpower him before he could be got to the Aid Post. He had been going queer for the last month or two.

Duffy was hit low down on the right side: it was a bad wound and I knew his case was hopeless; but he was still conscious. I asked the Company Commander if I could help to carry him down to the Aid Post. "Certainly," he replied. We had gone halfway to the Aid Post, four of us carrying the stretcher, one at each handle, when as I lifted my right foot in its stride a shell splinter buried itself in the ground beneath it. Although Duffy was dying on the stretcher he noticed it as he hung his head over the side and said: "Hard lines, Dick! If a youngster had been in your place he would have had a beautiful Blighty wound through the foot. We old ones aren't lucky enough to stop one that way. We generally stop one the way I have done." I told him to shut up, saying that he had every chance to get over it. He replied simply: "You know better than that, Dick." We arrived at the Aid Post and I should have liked to stay with him for a little while, but I had to get back to the Company. As I shook him by the hand he wished me the best of luck, and about two hours later I had news that he had died where I left him. No man could wish for a better pal, and I never scrounged much around the Company, when in the line, after he was gone.

We were relieved that evening and went back to Mametz Wood, and during the night we got wind that the Brigade were going to attack High Wood. A message came through that the Battalion would send one visual signaller to Brigade Headquarters who would report himself there at 2 a.m. on the morning of the 20th. I was detailed off for this and as I made my way there was wondering what the idea was. Eight of us and the Brigade Signalling Corporal were detailed off to form a transmitting station between High Wood and Brigade Headquarters which was situated on the fringe of Mametz Wood. No telephones would be carried and our station would receive messages by flag from the signallers with the attacking force; which we would transmit to Brigade by heliograph or flag. The position that we had to take up was by a large mill about six hundred yards this side of High Wood. The mill was built on some rising ground which made it a very prominent landmark. We had a good view of everything from here, but we also found that when we were exchanging messages with the wood, the enemy would have an equally good view of us, especially when we were flag-wagging. An old soldier of the Cameronians who was now a Brigade signaller, an old soldier of the Royal Welch who was now a Brigade runner, and the corporal, were the only ones I knew of our station. I was wondering how the other five would conduct themselves if we were heavily shelled.

The Cameronian and I fixed our heliograph and telescope up, and at 8 a.m. we were in communication with Brigade. Shortly after this the enemy began shelling us and by 10 a.m. they had put up one of the worst barrages that I was ever under. Twelve-inch, eight-inch, five-point-nines and whizzbang shells were bursting around us continually and this lasted during the whole of the day. North, south, east and west it was raining shells, and we seemed to be the dead centre of it all. The barrage of the previous day was a flea-bite to this one. The ground shook and rocked and we were continually having to reset the heliograph. When receiving a message the smoke of the bursting shells and the earth and dust that was being thrown up constantly obscured our vision, and we could only receive a word now and then.

The five men I didn't know were sheltering in a large shell hole by the side of the mill; they were absolutely useless and terror-stricken. We were not able to see our attacking troops who were to advance up a valley to the right of us at dawn, to enter the wood on our right front, but during the afternoon I saw some of our men moving about on the outskirts, and a flag commenced to call us up. I asked one of the men in the shell hole to come and write the message down, but not one of them would budge. The corporal and the Cameronian were busy receiving a message from Brigade at the time. I cursed them until I was blue, but it made no difference. The Brigade runner who was not a signaller then volunteered to write the message down and stood behind me in the doorway of the mill whilst I read it. The message said that the whole of High Wood had been captured. About an hour later I was receiving another message from the wood, the runner again writing it down, standing behind me in the doorway of the mill. When I was about halfway through it, he gave a shout; I turned round and found him groaning on the ground. A shell splinter which must have passed high up between my legs had hit him in the thigh. It was a nasty wound, but he stopped groaning after a bit and said: "Carry on with the message, Dick, I can bandage this myself." I shouted to the Cameronian to come and finish writing the message down. We only received about another six words when the signaller in the wood who was sending the message, and the other with him who was evidently calling it out, both fell; that message was never completed. The message as far as we got with it stated that the enemy were counter-attacking. It was the last visual message that arrived from the wood: every message after this came by runner.

The enemy now turned a machine-gun on the mill, our flag-wagging had attracted their attention. On the right front of the mill a battalion of Manchesters of another division were in some shallow trenches; they had heavy casualties during the day, a number of shells

bursting right among them. One of their captains
ran across to us and asked if it was possible to get a message back to his Brigade Headquarters, as his men were
being blown to pieces. We told him we were very sorry
but we were under orders only to deal with messages
connected with our own Brigade. As we were speaking,
some large shells exploded right on the parapet of the
trench he had left, knocking in a big stretch of it. He
then rushed back there to look after the survivors. He
was a very brave and humane man. But even if we had
been able to send his message I don't suppose our
Brigade Headquarters, being in a different division,
would have known where his Brigade Headquarters was
situated; and even if they had, and transmitted it on, his
Brigadier would have taken no notice of it, for sure.

A number of lightly wounded men from the wood
passed by us on their way to the dressing-station which
was in the valley below. We inquired how things were
going. Most of them said that half the Brigade had been
wiped out before they entered the wood, and that old
Jerrie was counter-attacking when they left. Many of
these men were killed on their way to the dressing-
station. I saw one of our old signallers limping along;
he had stopped one through the ankle. He told me that
if he had the luck to get through the bloody barrage, and
then the luck also to be sent home, J.C. and all his angels
would never shift him out to France again. He was true
to his word. He got through the barrage and was sent
home. His wound soon healed up and he was pro-
nounced fit for the blood-tub. Draft after draft going
overseas he was absent from, and he was finally sentenced to six months imprisonment. After a week in

prison he was taken in front of the Governor, who informed him that if he volunteered to go back out to the Front he would be released. He informed the Governor that he had done close on two years active service, and that he considered he had done his whack, and that he didn't mind if he was kept in prison until the bloody War finished. The last I heard of him was about a month before the War finished, and he was still in England.

We received a message that no more visual signalling would be carried out, and that we would be employed as runners between Brigade and High Wood. Down in the valley below us a company of Argyles were occupying some shell holes and shallow trenches: they seemed to be just outside the barrage. I had to pass by them when I was taking back a message to Brigade Headquarters, about a hundred yards beyond. I had just reached Brigade when it seemed that every German artillery gun had lengthened its range and was firing direct on the Argyles. This lasted about fifteen minutes, and then the shelling slackened. I waited awhile before making my way back, and when I did pass by the Argyles' position I could only see heads, arms, legs and mangled bodies. I have often wondered since then, if all the leading statesmen and generals of the warring countries had been threatened to be put under that barrage during the day of the 20th July, 1916, and were told that if they survived it they would be forced to be under a similar one in a week's time, whether they would have all met together and signed a peace treaty before the week was up.

The Brigade, which was still hanging on to three parts of the wood, was relieved at 10 p.m., three-quarters of them being casualties. The Public Schools Battalion was practically annihilated, and the Royal Welch were not much better off. We had lost ten of our eighteen signallers; but Paddy and Tich were safe. Half the Brigade had been knocked over before they ever entered the wood. It was the custom that all parcels that arrived for men who were casualties should be distributed among the survivors. The Commanding Officer of the Public Schools Battalion kindly sent a number of mail-bags full of parcels for distribution among our men. We lived on luxuries for the next few days.

CHAPTER XV

TRENCHES IN HIGH WOOD

We went back to a village the other side of Albert to reorganize. We were sent drafts of officers and men, but a lot of the men belonged to other regiments. During this time men at the Bases were lucky if they were sent to one of the battalions of their own regiment. In 1917 this practice was stopped: if a man was sick or lightly wounded and got no further than the Base he was generally sent back to his own battalion. A lot of the men that joined us did not know the way to load their rifles. Any old hand could have been given a stripe or two if he wanted them, and Freezer, who had just had a lot of Number Ones washed out as usual, told me that he had been offered to be made a full corporal but had refused. He would either be a sergeant or nothing. Two days later he was made a sergeant.

Apart from the transport, there were not fifty men left now in the Battalion of the old Expeditionary Force men, and most of these had been wounded once or twice. Yet, if we had known, we had not yet reached half-way in the War, and the conditions and casualties in 1917 and early 1918 were worst than what we had yet experienced. There was a big concentration of troops around this village and the cafés were always full of troops. It was no uncommon sight to see a dozen Crown-and-Anchor boards outside each café, and one evening Paddy and I won over a thousand francs— about £40—which we invested in champagne, buying fifty bottles at twelve francs a bottle. The remainder of the money we kept until next day. We were making sure of something. The old signallers had a muck-in with that lot of champagne, and anyone else we knew. We never used to drink anything, when we could afford to drink, unless we could get properly drunk on it. It made us merry and helped us to forget. The majority of young soldiers that joined us from this time on soon followed our example.

Each division had its Concert Party, the artists generally staying at Divisional Headquarters when the Division was in action, and entertaining the troops when they were out. We had some first-class artists in our Divisional Concert Troupe and I used to enjoy myself very much when I attended their shows. The Battalion had a drum-and-fife band, formed the latter end of 1915, who sometimes played selections when we were out of action and also when we were on the line of march. They stayed with the transport when we were in the line.

Permanent Battalion runners were now formed who stayed with Battalion Headquarters in the line and out. We signallers, the runners and the regimental police formed a platoon of our own when on the march. One day when we were route-marching a newly-joined officer was put in charge of us. After every fifty minutes' marching there was a ten minutes' rest and the command

was given, "Halt! Fall out on the side of the road!"
But we had no ten-minute rest with our new officer,
who gave the command, "Halt! Order arms!" Then,
considering that we had ordered arms very slovenly, he
gave the command, "Slope arms!" This also was not
very satisfactory, so we were soon doing a little arms
drill. By the time he had given the command, "Fall
out!" it was time to fall in again. This happened on
several occasions until the Adjutant spotted him and
called him aside and I expect gave him a good talking
to, as the next halt we had there was no drilling. Many
impromptu prayers went up for him, but an old hand
called Snooky said he would offer up a pukka one for
him when he arrived back in billets. Snooky, who had
served in India with us had a mania for praying: once in
India he had had a touch of the sun, which we old
soldiers called the "Deolalic Tap". The following day
I found him with his two hands clasped in front of him
and down on his knees praying beautifully. He prayed
that the next time we were in the line every German
shell on our part of the Front would be directed by
heavenly guidance right on top of the new officer's
pound and blow him into a million little pieces for the
misery he had caused the humble, God-fearing troops
the day before.

Just before we moved back towards the line I came
across the new officer twirling a club with spikes on. He
said, "These are very handy weapons in a trench." I
replied that they were, at close quarters, but that if we
went back to the same part of the Front as we had last
left he would be very lucky if he ever used one, as he had
every chance of being killed a few miles before he ar-

rived there. He said that he had heard that yarn before and that we old soldiers were all the same, we thought we knew everything, and that every old soldier he had met had given him the jerks. I then told him he might have a good jerk before he was many days older. He then threatened to put me on the peg for speaking to an officer in such a manner. Every young officer that I can remember with the exception of two who had joined us since we had been in France had proved themselves real good men, but this man was the limit.

We moved up by easy stages and stayed a few days near Albert. The statue of the Virgin on top of the church was hanging head downwards and the French people believed that when it fell the War would come to an end. We moved up to Fricourt Wood. Just inside the Wood were some decent shacks, made out of tree branches, which a few of us got into. During the afternoon some of the signallers were sent to their companies, leaving an old signaller, Private Salisbury, whom we called "Sol", in one shack and I in another about five yards apart. The shack I was in was really a shell hole with tree branches tied together over it. Sol, who had been a signaller in India, had did his first twelve months in France as a rifle-and-bayonet man and had won the D.C.M. and Russian Order of St. George, which always went with the D.C.M. in the first part of the War. He had been invalided home with shingles when we were in Bois Grenier and had rejoined the Battalion early in 1916. The two of us had been detailed off to proceed to Divisional Headquarters the following morning for a forty-eight hours' course of instruction in a new trench telephone, called the Fullerphone. Sol and

I were smoking and yarning about the times we had together abroad. Just before I left he said, "Why not shift your equipment into my shack? It's better than the one you are in. You can spend the night with me." I replied that it wasn't worth the trouble, being as we were going to Division early in the morning. We wished one another good night and I entered my shack and was soon fast asleep. During the night I was woke up by the explosions of shells. The enemy were bombarding us with heavy stuff and bursting shells in a wood were a lot more nerve-racking than when out in the open. My shack was blown in on top of me and I had a job to work my way out of the tree branches. Men were bolting out of the wood and some of the youngsters were yelling. Sol's shack was blown down too and I could hear groans. I began to clear the branches and other stuff off him and called his name, but he did not answer me. The enemy were still shelling and the majority of shells were falling just inside the fringe of the wood. I had cleared the debris off him but without a torch I could not tell where he was hit. I went to the Aid Post cart which was just outside the wood and found the Aid Post Corporal who willingly came with me in the wood. By the aid of his torch we could see that Sol was beyond our help: he had been badly hit in three places. He never recovered consciousness and died about half an hour later. All the good ones seemed to be going West. If it had not been that my shack had been built over a shell hole and I had been laying in it, I would have been finished too.

Paddy went back with me to Division. Our bacon ration in the Battalion was never very much: there was always a bit of sharking done with it, the same as with the rum, but we found that things were even worse in the Division: the following morning we had to file by the cooks for our tea and bacon and were told that we could either have a bit of bacon (about half the size of a Woodbine packet) or a dip in the fat. I chose a dip in the fat and considered I had backed a winner. Paddy was lucky that he was not put in clink for airing his views on the subject. We were glad that we were rejoining the Battalion that evening.

About the middle of August and early in the morning we took over the trenches in High Wood. Communication trenches had been dug and troops could now enter the wood by day. Since July two separate attacks had been made to drive out the enemy from the portion they were holding but both had failed with heavy losses. I was posted to my own Company with a young signaller who had been in France about nine months, the first five months as a rifle-and-bayonet man. He was a very decent chap but had been through one experience which he had never recovered from. He had only been a month in France when he took part in the attack on the R.W.F. Crater: in the rush across no-man's-land a bullet went through his steel helmet and parted his hair on the top of his head, knocking him unconscious. When he came to his self the enemy were putting up their barrage and shells were exploding around him. He ran back to the front line screaming and more frightened than hurt. He was only away about a month and since then it was a pity to see him when we were under intense shellfire.

Our trench ran from just inside the wood to the centre

of it and we dumped our telephone on the fire-step in a bay by ourselves. Anyone leaving the centre of the wood would have to pass us to make their way to the communication trenches. Some parts of the parapet had been built up with dead men, and here and there arms and legs were protruding. In one bay only the heads of two men could be seen; their teeth were showing so that they seemed to be grinning horribly down on us. Some of our chaps that had survived the attack on the 20th July told me that when they were digging themselves in, the ground being hardened by the sun and difficult to dig away quickly, if a man was killed near them he was used as head cover and earth was thrown over him. No doubt in many cases this saved the lives of the men that were digging themselves in. The troops who relieved them would immediately begin to deepen the trench and since that time the rain and shells had exposed the bodies in their different ways.

About 8 a.m. the enemy started shelling us very heavily. It was big stuff they were sending over and by 10 a.m. we had sixty casualties in the Company. Great trees were uprooted and split like matchwood, some falling over the trench. We were throwing our dead on the back of the parapet, from where in some cases they were blown up again and thrown further afield. All communication had gone West and the young signaller was huddled up in a heap on the fire-step and shaking like a madman. I told him to buck up and that it would be better if he moved about. I asked him to go halfway along the lines to Battalion Headquarters and repair any breaks, pointing out to him that we were just as liable to be blown to bits where we were as in any part of the trench, but he wouldn't move. I then told him to stick on the telephone and that I would go along the lines and also run any messages that we received. For thirty-six hours he hardly moved off that fire-step to do anything. He took no food but was constantly drinking out of his water bottle until it was empty. The lines had been repaired between us and Battalion Headquarters by one of their signallers, so I made my way along the other lines to C Company. When I was about halfway there I was told that a large shell had burst right on top of the dug-out C Company signallers were in, killing and burying them at the same time.

In the afternoon the shelling ceased and about an hour later I heard the sharp explosions of bombs somewhere on the left of us. A few minutes later about half a dozen newly-joined men came running down the trench towards us. They had no rifles and looked properly scared. I barred their way and asked what was the matter, but they couldn't get a word out. A young Platoon-Sergeant who had been with us a decent time now, came running down the trench in rear of the men. He shouted, "Don't let any of them pass you, Dick. They're running away." He told me that some German bombers, dodging from tree to tree, had crept close up and hurled their bombs in the trench and these men had dropped their rifles and ran away. He now drove them back to their part of the trench, but never reported them. They would have been all court-martialled and probably shot if he had. If a proper look-out had been kept those German bombers should have been shot down before ever they came in bombing range. Then the shelling started again and kept on more or less until we were relieved.

TRENCHES IN HIGH WOOD

Late in the afternoon a shell burst near a group of ten men. There were nine mangled bodies but no trace of the other man: we thought he had been blown to pieces. But we were mistaken; six weeks later when we were out of action he was brought back to the Battalion under escort. While he was waiting for his court-martial for deserting in face of the enemy he told a few of us what had happened. He had been blown clean out of the trench and landed in a shell hole on the back of the parapet. When he recovered consciousness it was dark and he could see the stars twinkling overhead. For a few minutes he didn't know where he was or what had happened to him. The enemy were still shelling and he was dazed and terror stricken. He got up and ran for all he was worth until he got out of the shelling, and had been scrounging around Back Areas until he was arrested. He was sentenced to death, but owing to his extreme youth the sentence was commuted to a term of imprisonment; but he still stayed with the Battalion. I believe our Colonel, who was given the full facts of the case, was instrumental in getting the young chap away with it. In 1917 he was either killed or taken prisoner on the Arras front.

The new officer who said that we old soldiers gave him the jerks was blown to pieces by this same barrage, and Snooky, who I met a little later, said it was wonderful how his prayer had been answered so quickly, and that little prayers sometimes did a great deal of good. The first evening at High Wood the whole of the ration party, mail and all, were blown to bits. I was expecting a parcel with a pint-and-half tin-jack of whisky in it, which was to be labelled "Sauce", and was wondering if it had gone West. The following evening rations and mail arrived safe, and also my parcel, which I found at Battalion Headquarters. I left half of the whisky with the signallers there and took the other half back with me, giving some stiff doses to the young signaller, but which had no effect on him: it was good stuff wasted. One of the newly-joined men called Sealyham, who was about forty years of age, had been appointed a Battalion runner and although it was his first time in action he conducted himself like a veteran. He had a business in the Midlands and had joined the Army because he was patriotic. He was one of the best amateur elocutionists I ever heard.

CHAPTER XVI

LES BOEUFS AND TRONES WOOD

We were relieved at last, and a fortnight later the whole Division was marching away from the Somme. We marched by easy stages, picking up drafts of reinforcements on the way. We had a song at this time, the words being sung sadly to the tune of "The Church's One Foundation":

> We are in Kitchener's Army
> The ragtime A.S.C. :
> We cannot fight, we cannot shoot,
> What bloody use are we?
> But when we get to *Ber*lin
> We'll hear the Kaiser say,
> 'Hoch, Hoch! Mein Gott, what a bloody fine lot,
> To draw six bob a day!"

This song was sung out of no disrespect to Kitchener's Army, but was a kick against the motor lorry drivers of the A.S.C., who were receiving between four and six shillings a day.

During this time an old regular officer joined us who had been in West Africa when the War commenced and had taken part in the operations there. This was his first appearance in France and he was put in charge of

the signallers: we called him "The Peer". Discipline
was still good in the Battalion, but not so severe as it had
been, and gone were the days when a man would be
brought up and punished for having the lace of his rifle-
sling not properly tied. There was also a better spirit of
comradeship between officers and men than what there
had been. But we soon found out that The Peer had not
lost his pre-War ways. On the very first morning that he
inspected us before moving off, Paddy and I, who had
been drinking some rotten ving blong the night before,
had made some rapid journeys to the latrine which was
situated at the bottom of a wet and muddy orchard, and
when we fell in there was mud around the soles of our
boots. The Peer passed along the ranks and when he
came to me he noticed my boots. He exclaimed to the
sergeant who was following behind him: "Good heav-
ens, Sergeant! This man is absolutely filthy!" I said:
"I beg your pardon sir . . ." (I was going to explain to
him how it was that my boots were dirty) but I got no
further with my sentence. He roared at me: "Damn
you, who are you? I'll run you in. How dare you speak
to an officer before he addresses you?" Paddy was also
checked, and The Peer instructed the sergeant to warn
the both of us to parade in full marching order and
properly cleaned two hours after we had completed the
day's march; which was a very stiff one that day. Two
days later he gave orders that the whole of the signallers
would parade in the same way, two hours after each
day's march was completed. Snooky, who was now the
signallers' cook, was severely reprimanded by him for
some other trivial thing. We all offered up the usual
soldiers' prayers, and when Snooky was not cooking he

was praying. But all his prayers were in vain. The Peer survived the War.

We took over some trenches on the Arras front and they were proper convalescent homes compared to some we had been in. We had very few casualties during the time we were there, and The Peer became worse than ever. He must have thought that all parts of the Front were the same. We were in a village about six miles from Doullens and the Battalion were in strict training for an attack on Gommecourt Wood; the attack that had been made on it on the 1st July had been a failure. I didn't do any of that training, having a knee which had swelled very badly. Dr. Dunn detained me in the Aid Post for four days and then lanced it. Afterwards I was attending hospital and excused all duties during the time we were there.

One morning in the Aid Post I noticed a man who had a very bad boil high up on his back. The doctor lanced it and removed a large core, which left a decent hole. The Aid Post sergeant put a little dressing on, with some strips of sticking plaster over it. The following morning the man informed the doctor that he had spent a very restless night, and that if he could have reached the spot where the dressing was he would have ripped it off. When the plaster and dressing were removed, inside the hole were three lice. No wonder the man had spent a restless night, and yet only forty-eight hours previously the man had had a bath and a supposed clean shirt.

At the last moment the attack on Gommecourt Wood was cancelled and we departed by buses and arrived back on the Somme. The portion of High Wood had now been captured and Guillemont, Ginchy and Les Boeufs had also been taken. It was impossible to tell whether a house had ever existed in these villages, so heavy had been the shelling on both sides. We were in shell holes around Ginchy, and on the way there we saw a few tanks, which were first in action on September 13th.

In October we took over the trenches in front of Les Boeufs. The enemy trenches were in front of Le Transloy, which was directly facing us. Our trenches were shell holes linked up, with gaps here and there; on our right were the French. There was also a gap between us and them. About sixty yards behind the front line was a small trench which was used as an advanced signal station. Messages were brought by runners who made use of an old German communication trench to this station: they were then transmitted back to Battalion Headquarters which was in a sunken road about five hundred yards behind. I and three young signallers were posted to the advanced signal-station and we decided to go along the line in turns to repair any breaks, and also made arrangements with Battalion Headquarters for they to keep one half of the line in repair, and we would keep the other half. In standing trenches Battalion Headquarters always appointed linesmen to look after the lines running to the front line, company signallers repairing their own between companies, but in a case like this every N.C.O. and man, with the exception of the signalling-sergeant, took their turns along the lines to repair the breaks.

It had been raining for days, and the ground was nothing but a sea of mud. On the second night the enemy, who had been sending over an occasional shell, began a heavy bombardment and we were continually repairing the lines. One of our young signallers had taken his turn and as he was a long time coming back, and we were still out of communication, I went along the line to look for him; about fifty yards from the trench I came across his body: he had been killed in the act of repairing a break. I repaired the break myself and walked back further along the line and found another break about halfway. I saw a man approaching me, who turned out to be an old signaller from Battalion Headquarters out on the line. I told him about the young signaller being killed, and he said he was sorry to hear it, as he was a damned good kid. He then began to swear, and when he cooled down a bit said: "It's rotten, Dick, how the good ones are popped over so quick and the rotten ones simply get nice blighty wounds. There's a bloody bun-punching swine back there who has just gone back with a beautiful blighty one in the arm. When it came his turn to go along the line he refused. He said it was not the place for a full corporal to go out on the lines. The sergeant warned him if he didn't go out on the lines he would report him to the Adjutant. I was hoping he would refuse, so that I would have the pleasure of reading that he had been shot at dawn for cowardice in face of the enemy, but he didn't. He left the dug-out and I followed him out and drove him up over the bank of the sunken road as the sergeant had warned me to do. He hadn't walked ten yards along the line when a shell burst some distance from him and a bit of shrapnel hit him in the arm. He howled like a stuck pig and ran back to me. As I was dressing his

wound I told him that if he had his due he would have
had his bloody head knocked off. That's the third we
have had hit to-night on the blasted line; but the other
two were good kids." This corporal had joined us about
four weeks previously; he had been sent out to France as
a signalling corporal and was a pukka bun-puncher.
When we were near Doullens I had often seen him buying tins of condensed milk and sucking them like a kid.

A few hours before we were relieved, the following
night, The Peer who was back at Battalion Headquarters paid us a visit. It was pretty quiet at the time,
only an occasional shell coming over. Just after he
arrived the enemy opened out again and put up a barrage from our front line to about fifty yards in the rear
of us. There were about a dozen men in the little trench
and they tried to get into the signallers' dug-out, but
there wasn't room for them. I was speaking to The Peer
when the barrage started, and was wondering whether
Old Jerrie was about to make an attack when the shelling finished. We were in the trench at the time, and The
Peer made no effort to get into the dug-out. He showed
he had guts and went up twenty holes in my estimation.
If a large shell burst on the dug-out the men in it would
be finished with, and if one pitched anywhere on our
part of the trench we would be the same. It was heavy
stuff they were sending over, with an occasional salvo of
whizzbangs. I expect The Peer did more ducking that
night than ever he had during the whole of his life before. The barrage lasted about an hour and then suddenly stopped. He asked me if I had ever been under a
worse barrage and when I told him it was a popcorn
barrage compared to some I had been under, he thought

I was romancing. I then told him that the enemy might make an attack and some of them rush through the gaps in our front line, and be on us in no time. He lined every man in the trench, and looking over the parapet we saw a party of men crossing our front. We challenged them sharply, but they turned out to be some French troops who had been relieved and making their way back had hopelessly lost themselves. They had been wandering about for some time. The Peer gave the officer along with them his bearings and they went on their way. It was a very dark night and raining very heavily. The enemy made no attack, but just before we were relieved began shelling again.

Making my way back I came across Captain Radford whose company had been relieved, trying to rally his men together. The majority were newly joined and the rain and mud had completely beat them. As I passed him he said: "Hullo, Richards! What would the old hands say about this crowd?" I replied that no doubt they would curse a bit. Captain Radford had joined my company after the Loos battle, having been an officer in the Loyal North Lancashire Regiment, but now transferred to us. He was highly respected and very popular with the old hands. He was commanding C Company. My young Company Commander, Captain Higginson, had been sent home three weeks previously with a nervous breakdown. My present Company Commander, Lieutenant Greaves or Grieves, I did not know. He was a tall slight chap with a stutter, and a very decent officer. There were only about half a dozen men I knew in the whole of the Company. The little experience that The Peer had just gone through had did him and us a lot of good; he dropped his pre-War ways and started to act like a sensible human being.

We went back to a sunken road on the edge of Trones Wood. Signallers and some of the runners stayed in an elephant hut. Early the following morning Hammer Lane, who was now the Colonel's orderly, and I went out on the scrounge for wood. The first thing we saw as we stepped out of the hut was a dead German hung up on the branch of a tree, and he seemed to be carefully watching over the hut. No doubt he had been blown up by a large shell, and in falling the sharp end of a branch pointing upwards had pierced his jacket and held him. He looked like a man who had been hung up on a hook and left there, yet there seemed to be no mark on him.

On November 4th, 1916, we went back in the line, Paddy taking his turn with B Echelon, which consisted of the transport and a small number of officers and men who were left out of the line when the Battalion went in. Some time later Minimum Reserve was introduced and a certain number of officers and men of each battalion were left out, so in case of a battalion being wiped out there was something left to make a new one with. We were only going in for forty-eight hours, and it was decided not to send the mail up for that period. I instructed Paddy that if anything happened to me he was to do what he liked with a parcel I was expecting, and to give the tobacco away to a pipe smoker. About an hour before we moved off, one of our planes brought a German plane crashing to the ground about half a mile in front of us and on the edge of a sunken road which we knew we would have to pass. I had seen it happen once or twice that when a German plane had been shot down just behind our front line some time later the enemy would do their level best to blow it to pieces. This plane was about a mile behind our front. I had been posted to Battalion Headquarters and it was dark when we were passing the plane, which was now being shelled. We had a few casualties and one of the killed was the Regimental Sergeant-Major's batman, who was carrying a lovely bag of rations. One of our old signallers picked it up. During the following day each one of us put on a little weight and the R.S.M. lost a little. There were more rations in that bag than what the whole of the signallers had, put together.

We stayed in an old German dug-out. Two steps below us in another dug-out stayed the Colonel and Adjutant. All communication with our front line was by runners. We had lines running back to Brigade, which were very weak and we had difficulty in receiving Morse or speaking to them. The following morning the Colonel's servant came into the dug-out and reported that the Colonel's raincoat, which was a new one, was missing. The servant had put it on the bank of the sunken road by the dug-out, along with other stuff, and no doubt someone of the troops we relieved had walked off with it. The servant seemed more cut up over the loss than what the Colonel did, who took it as the fortune of war. Sealyham now went out of the dug-out saying that he had dumped his haversack on the bank, which had two fine razors and other valuables in it; at the same moment the Adjutant got on the phone to speak to the Brigade-Major and the line being so weak he was continually asking "What's that?" Sealyham came to the mouth of the dug-out and shouted down: "The swine have pinched my haversack too." "What's that?" asked the Adjutant. "The bloody pigs have pinched my haversack with the two best razors in France in it." "What's that?" shouted the Adjutant, but this was too much for Sealyham who, being under the impression that one of us was answering him and pulling his leg, launched out with a flow of language which would have done credit to the Old Soldier. The Adjutant put the phone down and burst out laughing and told me to go outside to tell him to shut up until he had finished speaking on the phone. He had been our Adjutant for over twelve months, and was an excellent officer in every way: his name was Mr. Mann. Sealyham found his haversack a few yards away, but it was empty. Haversacks were easy to get, but razors were scarce.

We and the Public Schools Battalion on our left, with the French on our right, now had to advance and capture a position in front of us. On this part of the Front the enemy were scattered here and there in shell holes and it was quite possible that the first wave of attacking troops would miss some of the enemy, who would then be popping up and firing on them from behind. So a mopping-up party was detailed off to follow in the rear of the first wave and mop up everything they had left. I was with Headquarters so I saw none of the actual fighting. Our companies and the French reached their objectives and began consolidating the position—which meant to turn the firing positions the other way about, block communication trenches and put out a bit of barbed wire. But the troops on our left never advanced a yard. The captain of the Public Schools company on our left reported to our Colonel that they had been held up by heavy machine-gun fire—which was all bunkum: they had never made any effort to advance, and our Colonel told him so. I had never seen the Colonel in such a rage as he was that day, and he told the captain that he and his rotten men were no good as they had endangered the lives of decent soldiers. Our left flank was now up in the air, and anything might happen.

Some of the mopping-up party discovered a concealed dug-out in a large shell hole. They were just about to throw bombs into it when they heard an English voice cry out: "Don't throw bombs in here." Inside the dug-out were six Germans, and one of our own men who was badly wounded in the legs. He told them he had been part of a strong patrol that had been sent out to reconnoitre the night before. A German shell had fallen short and caused several casualties. He had been knocked unconscious and left for dead in the confusion. When he came to his self he tried to crawl back to our lines. He had crawled some way but could not get any further. His groans had attracted these Germans, who had carried him in and dressed his wounds and attended him as if he had been one of their own men. He had heard the first wave go by and was wondering if any of the mopping-up party would discover the dug-out, and had shouted out as soon as he heard their voices.

We were relieved that evening, and the following morning I met Paddy, who was thunderstruck to see me. "Hell!" he exclaimed, "I thought you was on the way to Blighty." I enquired what was the matter, and he replied: "I am glad to see you quite safe, but I have devoured your parcel and given the tobacco away, the same as you told me." He then explained that the night we went in the line there were all manner of yarns flying around the transport about the casualties in Battalion Headquarters. The first yarn was that every one had been killed and wounded and that I had received a lovely one in the muscle of the arm. Another yarn then came that I had one arm blown clean off and also a leg. Another yarn came that I was seen walking back with my arm in a sling and smoking my pipe. My parcel had arrived the next day and he had opened it, and gave the tobacco away as I had told him to. Paddy brought up so many different yarns that he said he had heard that I almost smelled a rat. I was hard up for tobacco at the time and I thought my luck was dead out.

CHAPTER XVII

SOMME: WINTER 1916-1917

We were back in a village, about twenty miles from Abbeville, on rest. The villagers were not very sociable: they wanted our money but not us. In this place it was very difficult to get wood, and a fire was everything: Sealyham, Lane, Paddy, an old signaller called Ricco and I were staying in a little place on our own and with bottles of wine and a pint-and-half of rum decided to make a night of it. But we were short of a fire. There was a house near us, which was also a bit of a farm, with a cesspool in front. The lady of the house sold eggs and chips, and drink that was highly watered, and she was a proper shark. Ricco and I pinched two massive tubs belonging to her, knocked them up and threw the hoops in the cesspool. During the night we had a good drink, a good fire, and swopped yarns and sung in turns. Sealyham was the star performer and excelled himself in his impersonation of characters from Dickens. He proved himself as excellent out of the line as in. The lady made more row over the loss of her tubs than what she would have done if she had lost her whole kith and kin in the War. There were a lot more tubs disappeared in that village during the next few days and we were never without a fire.

We were now in the South African Corps and I was sent back to the Corps for a special course of signalling which I never completed, the Division being ordered back up the line after I had been there a week. I found the South Africans very good chaps; also the food was excellent and plenty of it. During a lecture by the Chief Intelligence Officer, he mentioned that during the whole of the Somme operations only one important message had been picked up from the enemy and before it could be made any use of it was too late.

We took over the line the other side of Combles. During this winter the British Army was gradually taking over a big part of the line from the French. We spent Christmas Day in some huts and in January were back for a three weeks' rest in a village a mile or two from Abbeville. We relieved a French battalion in the line in front of Clery and the longest communication trench I ever saw was in this sector. I was posted to the Company again. When we relieved the French signallers, instead of decently showing us which way our lines ran, they unhitched the wires off their instrument, packed it up and were out of the dug-out like greased lightning. It was the same with the rest of their men: as soon as they saw our chaps arriving they were out of the trench and making their way back over the top as if the whole of the German Army were at their heels.

It was hard, frosty weather and on two days it snowed very heavily. We used the snow for making tea but it took a mountain of snow to make a quart of water. Our trenches ran into the River Somme, which was soon frozen over a foot thick, except for a small stream in the middle. The whole of this sector was nothing but bleak hills and valleys and the only life around were the wild ducks and moorhens. It was one of the most desolate places that I had been in in France. There was hardly a fire-bucket in the trenches and fire-wood was equally scarce; also our charcoal and coke rations were very small. We took the wooden crosses from lonely graves that we found here and there. They were no good to the dead but they provided warmth for the living. Our Division was the worst in the whole of France for rum issues: if we got any at all we were issued with half a ration instead of a whole one. In lieu of the half ration of rum the Divisional General, Major-General Pinney, erected places a couple of miles behind the front line where men returning from the line could have a cup of hot tea and one small biscuit. In his comfortable quarters many miles behind the Front I expect he couldn't see what benefit rum was to any man. Because of this there were more prayers offered up for him than for any general in France. He was called a bun-punching crank and more fitted to be in command of a Church Mission hut at the Base than a division of troops.

One beautiful frosty morning I went back to Battalion Headquarters for some candles. The ground dipped from the front line to Battalion Headquarters which were in the valley. Just as I arrived there a fight started overhead between a French plane and a German scout which had been hovering over our lines during the morning. Suddenly smoke appeared coming out of the tail of the German plane which began to make its way to its own lines. It hadn't gone very far before it turned around and came back over our lines, a mass of flames.

A bundle fell out of it, which struck the hard ground about one hundred and fifty yards from where a few of us were standing, the plane crashing on a hill behind us. Hammer Lane and I rushed to the bundle, which turned out to be one of the German airmen, who had either fallen out or deliberately thrown himself out. Every bone in his dead body was broken. As we started to search him one of our new officers appeared on the scene and told us that anything we found on the German he would take back to the Colonel. We found a few valuables and some papers, which we handed to him. We found out later that he handed over the papers to the Colonel but retained the valuables for his self. He must have been a distant relation to A Company's old sanitary men, who had now both gone home wounded. The plane was burning merrily on the hill and against my better judgment I accompanied Lane towards it. When we were about fifty yards from it we could see the other German still sitting strapped in his seat with his head and arms hanging limply down and the flames licking his body. We were now in full view of the enemy but too far away from them to be popped over by bullets, but they soon opened out with whizz-bangs and we were very lucky to get back in the valley.

During one spell in the line we lost Colonel Crawshay who went away badly wounded. When snow was upon the ground all patrols went out with white smocks on. Two nights running a German patrol had been spotted moving about no-man's-land and the Colonel, Dr. Dunn and Lane went out the following night with the intention of capturing this patrol. They went out from the extreme right of the Battalion's front. After they had been out some time the left-hand sentry of the Public Schools Battalion on our right, who happened to be a Lewis gunner, was relieved. He forgot to warn his relief about the patrol. Shortly after, the new sentry saw some white forms moving about not far off and opened fire with his Lewis gun, the Colonel being badly hit, but the other two not touched. The whole of the Battalion was very cut up over the loss of Colonel Crawshay: we knew we would be very lucky if we got another who would be as good in every way as what he was. I have heard since the War that he recovered but still suffers from his wounds and is often in nursing homes. The officer we called Jimmie, who was with us again, became Acting-Colonel.

We were relieved the first week in March and two days before we were relieved the thaw set in. We lost nearly a hundred men through trench feet, the trenches being knee-deep in mud when we left them, and from having our rum ration taken from us. We went back to Suzanne and from there to some huts which were erected in a hollow and miles from anywhere. There was nearly as much mud around the huts as in the trenches we had just left. I was down with a touch of fever for the first four days but with the help of some quinine pills which I got from the Aid Post N.C.O. I recovered. The Battalion received drafts of officers and men: we had now on the signallers a schoolmaster, two school teachers, two bank clerks and a young architect.

A few days after the Battalion was relieved, the relieving battalion sent out a patrol which entered the German trenches and found them empty. The German Army had begun their retirement back to the Hindenburg line. When we received the news that the enemy had retired to within four miles of St. Quentin, Paddy wanted to bet two to one that the German front line would still be four miles this side of St. Quentin in twelve months' time. If anyone had accepted the bet Paddy would have been an easy winner. Yet one famous war correspondent had written that it was only a question of hours before our victorious troops would occupy that place.

We had one old soldier called Bob who had been a Battalion scout, but for the last twelve months had been a signaller. He was a very humorous sketcher and one of the first humorous sketches of the troops in the trenches which appeared in *Punch* he sketched an addition to it and sent it to the Editor of *Punch*; who sent him an autographed letter in reply, complimenting him on his skill, which Bob prized more highly than anything he possessed. He was also a born pessimist and had a great admiration for the German General von Mackensen whom he called "The Ramrod" and who was commanding the German forces on the Eastern Front against the Russians. He often used to say that, with the exception of The Ramrod, there wasn't a general on any side that had the brains of a gander. Paddy came in the hut one day and, winking at me, said: "What do you think, boys? Von Mackensen is coming to the Western Front to take command of the German Army." Bob was lying down but he sprung to his feet and exclaimed, "Thank God for that news! The bloody War will now soon be over. The Ramrod will roll up the British and French Armies like a man rolling a blanket up. As sure as God made me, in the next stunt

I am in, if I'm not popped over, I'm going to surrender to the Germans and volunteer to do batman to The Ramrod. It will be a pleasure to black his boots."

The following month in a stunt in the Hindenburg Tunnel when it was every man for his self, Bob received a flesh wound in the arm. He went stone-mad for a while, bayoneted two Germans and fought like a tiger until his arm gave out. He was lucky enough to get out of it and was sent to England. I corresponded with him for a time and in every letter I received there was a newspaper cutting about Mackensen on the Eastern Front.

We had a new Colonel, Garnett by name. I had soldiered with him abroad; he was a decent old stick but not to be compared with the colonel we had just lost. Two new officers that had just arrived seemed of a far better stamp than some that we had had during the last few months, and one named Mr. Sassoon, who was wearing the ribbon of the Military Cross was soon very popular with the men of the Company he was posted to. He had been with the First Battalion before he came to us. The Battalion was doing the ordinary training but I did no parades. From this time on when we were out of action I cleaned the signallers' billet up. I much preferred doing this than the monotonous parades that we were put on when out of action. I had refused promotion many times. If I went as a sergeant to the Company I should have been on parade day and night. If I had been a N.C.O. on the signallers the same thing would have happened. But, as it was, every morning the officer would inspect the billet and then I was free to go scrounging around. Lane, who also did no parades, and I had some glorious days in the villages some miles from the huts. We at least were getting all the enjoyment we could before going back to the blood-tub where we never knew what might happen to us.

We had seven signallers killed and six wounded between July and August and had lost six around Les Boeufs. Signallers who went into attacks with their companies had to muck in with the scrapping until the objective was taken and then if they were still on their feet were generally converted into runners. A runner's job was very dangerous: he might have to travel over ground from where the enemy had just been driven and which now was being heavily shelled. In shell holes here and there might be some of the enemy who had been missed by the mopping-up party or who had been shamming dead; they would pop up and commence sniping at him. I remember one show we were in later on, where extra runners had been detailed off for the day, losing fifteen out of twenty. Each battalion was now supposed to have thirty-two signallers, and a new signalling lamp called the Lucas Lamp was introduced which could be used by day or night. Only once during the whole of 1917 did I see this lamp worked in attacks, and then it was only from Battalion Headquarters back to Brigade, and then not very successfully. But during the last few months of the War, when the shelling was not a flea-bite to what it had been, it was used very frequently.

We also had an aeroplane signalling-sheet which was pegged down to the ground to send messages to an aeroplane circling overhead, which had a kind of horn attached to it which conked back answers in Morse. This sheet was all right in Back Areas where there were no ironfoundries exploding around one, but useless in attacks. In one stunt we were in on the Arras front a wireless instrument was introduced which sent messages but could not receive them. With the attacking troops one signaller carried the instrument and the other man with him the cells in a bag on his back. The one was no good without the other; only once was this experimented with and it was a rotten failure. We never saw no more of those instruments after that.

There was also a wireless instrument called "the amplifier", which picked up any message within so many miles of the amplifying station, which was generally near Battalion Headquarters, being manned by Brigade signallers. When first introduced the amplifier could only pick up messages but not send them. If ever they picked up a German message, which was once in a blue moon, the message was brought to Battalion Headquarters to be transmitted back to Brigade. Later in the War these stations had sending and receiving sets. I spent many an hour in the stations and found it very amusing. I was listening one day to a conversation over the line between two of our front-line signallers. One was speaking very thickly and the other lost his temper and told him to pull the bloody frog out of his throat, for he couldn't understand a bloody word he was speaking. There was some delightful language over the line after that.

CHAPTER XVIII

ARRAS: HINDENBURG LINE I

We left the huts on April 1st and although we were not told where we were off to we had a good idea that we were going to the Arras front. The second day's march it was raining and snowing and under a tree on the side of the road was the General of the Corps we were joining with a few of his staff, who inspected the Battalion as it marched by him. Wet snow was falling at the time and we old hands couldn't make out how he had ventured out on such a miserable day. Bob said, "I expect the old B—— will receive a big decoration for this day's work." I was told later that he had played up holy hell with the Colonel because the cookers were carrying brooms stuck up on the carts.

We arrived some days later at a place named Basseux and passed some cavalry lined up on a road. The young soldiers who had never been in action were very optimistic and one of them said, "I expect they are getting ready for a break through." We old hands laughed like anything and Paddy said, "They couldn't break through my granny's apron-strings! And they might as well be mounted on bloody rocking-horses for all the good they are going to do." Since the first four months of the War the cavalry had been mostly converted into infantry, even including a battalion of Household Cavalry who relieved us at Clery and whom we had to relieve again forty-eight hours later because fifty per cent of them were down with trench feet. I did see one lot of Bengal Lancers in July on the Somme riding forward into action, but was told that they were very nearly wiped out. One good German machine-gunner who kept his nerve could easily mow down a squadron of cavalry.

On Easter Sunday we were in Basseux. The old trenches which the Germans had retired from were not far from this place and although many a man on both sides had endured great hardships in their trenches it must have been a quiet part of the Front, otherwise Basseux would have been blown to bits. The people were still living there. We could get a drink in cafés and the whole of the village, including the church, had hardly been touched by shellfire. The Battle of Arras had started and we listened to our artillery bombardment which some of us were now so familiar with. One afternoon we left Basseux. We were in fighting order, leaving our top coats and packs in the village, though it was snowing heavily. We marched over ground the enemy had retired from. They had carried out their retirement in a very efficient manner. Villages had been levelled and everything that could have been of any use to us had been destroyed. From Basseux to the Hindenburg Line, which was about eight miles away, it was now a desert. A few days later we were in the Hindenburg Line which was now our front-line trench and which had only lately been captured. On the way there we saw a tank which had got stuck fast passing over a wide trench. In the autumn fighting I saw many in the same plight, especially when it was muddy. A very wide trench or large shell hole was the cause of many being put out of action. Passing one place we saw the corpses of between three and four hundred British soldiers which had been collected and laid out in rows for burial. I told some of the newly joined, who turned a bit queer at the sight, that if they were alive in a month's time they would take no more notice of a dead man than they would of a dead crow.

The Hindenburg Trench and Tunnel combined was a marvellous piece of work. In parts of the trench were entrances with very wide steps and handrails on the side leading down into the tunnel which was about sixty feet below the earth. The tunnel had a concrete floor with boarded sides and roof. There were recesses in parts and tiers of wire-netting beds on one side. Between the beds and the other side was sufficient room to carry a man on a stretcher. If all the artillery in France had been bombarding, though they would have levelled the trench all right, they would have made no impression on the tunnel. It had its advantages but also its disadvantages. If troops holding the trench were sheltering in it from a fierce bombardment before an attack, it was quite possible for the attacking troops to be in the trench before they could climb out of the entrances, which were very steep, and men could not come up them very well without the assistance of the handrail. Once the trench was captured they in the tunnel would be bombed from front, rear and side entrances.

The tunnel ran into a little river on our left. On our right there was a block-end in both trench and tunnel.

The other side of the block-end the trench and tunnel continued, which was still held by the enemy. There were enemy dead still laying about in some parts of the tunnel which was littered with weapons of all descriptions. With the aid of a candle one of the newly-joined men was about to drag some things from underneath a bed. I pulled him sharply away; he might have blown us all to bits. Underneath some of the beds were German stick-bombs which exploded in five seconds after the string was pulled, and he could have easily pulled one of the strings of them by mistake. I gave him and a couple more instructions what to do and what not to do.

The following morning one hundred bombers of the Battalion under the command of Mr. Sassoon were sent to the Cameronians to assist in a bombing attack on the Hindenburg Trench on our right. A considerable part of it was captured but was lost again during the day when the enemy made a counter attack. During the operations Mr. Sassoon was shot through the top of the shoulder. Late in the day I was conversing with an old soldier and one of the few survivors of old B Company who had taken part in the bombing raid. He said, "God strike me pink, Dick, it would have done your eyes good to have seen young Sassoon in that bombing stunt. He put me in mind of Mr. Fletcher. It was a bloody treat to see the way he took the lead. He was the best officer I have seen in the line or out since Mr. Fletcher, and it's wicked how the good officers get killed or wounded and the rotten ones are still left crawling about. If he don't get the Victoria Cross for this stunt I'm a bloody Dutchman; he thoroughly earned it this morning." This was the universal opinion of everyone who had taken part in the stunt, but the only decoration Mr. Sassoon received was a decorated shoulder where the bullet went through. He hadn't been long with the Battalion, but long enough to win the respect of every man that knew him.

At night we used to pop over the parapet of the trench and into any shell hole when we wanted to go to the latrine. We also got our drinking water from the shell holes. On the third night we discovered that the water we had been drinking and making tea with had been brought from a shell hole which a couple of us had used for another purpose. I asked the man who had brought the jars of water the night before to come and show me which shell hole he had brought it from, as it seemed better water than the stuff we had the day before. He replied, "You come with me and I'll show you the best shell-hole water in France." We hopped over the top and he took me to a shell hole which I knew very well. When I told him so he exclaimed, "Hell, how was I to know? I also took a jar of water from this hole for the officer's cook, who gave me a packet of
· Woodbines and a piece of bread for it. He told me during the day that the officers had complimented him on the excellent tea he had made with it." I didn't fill my jar out of that hole but went to another, and the same thing may have happened there for all I knew.

We were relieved and went back a few miles. Paddy and I visited a German cemetery which had been beautifully kept. There were a number of British soldiers buried in it and their graves had been equally as well cared for as their own men's and each man had a cross with his number, rank, name and regiment on, which they took from the identity discs which the men had on them. The finest grave in the cemetery belonged to a British airman which in addition to the cross also had two propellers at the head of the grave.

Five days later we went up the line to do an attack. Two companies were to attack a part of the Hindenburg Trench, the other two were to attack a position to the left front of that trench. I was with one of the latter companies. The two companies who were attacking the trench under cover of our barrage got as near as they possibly could to it, and as soon as the barrage lifted they made a dash for the trench and were in it before the majority of the enemy could come up the entrances. A part of the trench and tunnel was captured and droves of prisoners were filing by us as we moved forward to take up our position.

We took up our position in a trench which was about two hundred and fifty yards in front and to the left of the Hindenburg Trench which had just been taken. Our objectives were now some trenches and a strong point a little over an hundred yards in front of us. Two attacks had been made on it during the last four days by troops of our Division, but the enemy had repulsed both. From our parapet across to the objective our dead were laying thick, and for the first fifty yards it would have been impossible for a man to have walked three paces unless he stepped on a dead man. In the afternoon we attacked but were held up by machine-gun and rifle-fire the same as the previous battalions: not a man got further than halfway. The fortunate ones got back to their own trench, but the majority were laying where they fell. We company signallers were in communication with no one and Battalion Headquarters who were in the same trench were also in the same plight.

Late in the afternoon a runner arrived from the Hindenburg Trench with the news that the enemy had made a counter attack and had recovered part of it. We received no further news and at dusk the Adjutant sent Lane and another man to find out whether the Hindenburg Trench on our right was still held by our chaps. It was quite possible that the enemy had recovered the trench they had lost in the morning and also recaptured a part that we had been holding for some time. The two returned from their dangerous job and reported that the trench on our right was still occupied by our chaps but that the enemy were back again in the other. Lane told me that there had been some fierce scrapping with bomb and bayonet. Barricades had been erected in trench and tunnel when the enemy counter attacked, the two companies having heavy casualties. We brought our wounded in during the night, the enemy not firing a shot.

The following day we were without food and water and during the night some of us were out searching the dead to see if they had been carrying any with them. I was lucky enough to discover a half-loaf of bread, some biscuits and two bottles of water, which I would not have sold for a thousand pounds. The majority of shell holes were quite dry around this place.

Early next morning we had a surprise. A man of the Argyles who had taken part in one of the attacks some days before came limping over from the German position and informed us that the enemy had retired from their position during the night. He had been shot through the leg quite close to the German trench and for the last few days had been laying in a deep shell hole. He had heard a lot of noise during the night and hearing no sounds for the last few hours had decided to chance it and have a look around. He crawled to the German trenches and found they had retired from it during the night. Our objective which we had failed to take we now occupied without having a shot fired at us. We were relieved and went back to a village about ten miles behind the Front, where we received drafts of officers and men. We had lost heavily in that last show.

CHAPTER XIX

ARRAS: HINDENBURG LINE II

One lady in the village received a letter from her husband, who was a French soldier, informing her that he was coming on leave and would probably arrive home on the evening of a certain date. A few hours before her husband was due she went for a walk, and just after he arrived she returned with dishevelled hair and crying bitterly. She complained to him that when she was returning from her walk some British soldiers had assaulted and outraged her. There was a rumour that there was going to be an identification parade so that the lady could pick out the guilty ones; but nothing came of it. If the parade had taken place, although we had only been in the village a week, she could have identified at least forty men who had outraged her—at so much the crime. The lady was a star turn, but her husband thought he had one of the most virtuous wives in France. British soldiers often got blamed for things which they were entirely innocent of.

A message was read out from the Commander-in-Chief, Sir Douglas Haig, which ran something like this: "On the 1st of May a division made an attack which was very successful. After capturing lines of trenches they were soon in open country and advanced a considerable way. During the afternoon the enemy counterattacked and instead of making use of the rifle to beat back the attack they depended on the bomb. Late in the evening they were back in the trenches which they had left in the morning. Officers commanding units must see that their men are thoroughly instructed in the use of the rifle and also inform them how the original divisions kept the enemy at bay at Le Cateau and the First Battle of Ypres solely by rifle-fire." The Commander-in-Chief was right. Everybody at this time seemed to be bomb mad. The Mills bombs were wonderful for throwing into shell holes, trenches and dugouts, but were absolutely useless for holding up attacks. The distance one could be thrown was only between twenty and thirty yards; some men could throw them a bit further but many not so far. The young soldiers that were now arriving had been taught more about the bomb than about the rifle, which some of them hardly knew the way to load.

We had lost several of our young signallers in the last show, including one of the school teachers, and I very nearly sent the schoolmaster home in our next turn in the line. He brought me a captured German sniping rifle. I detached the magazine and pointing the rifle downwards I pulled the trigger. I had forgot there might have been a round in the breech, which there was in this case, and the bullet struck the ground between his feet. We were in the tunnel at the time. The candle got blown out and I didn't know whether I had shot him or not until someone hurriedly lit it again. I had witnessed so many accidents since the War began that I had got into the habit, when unloading a rifle, to point the muzzle downwards. A man on the Marne who was going to clean his rifle dropped his magazine out, and forgetting about the round in the breech, pulled the trigger: the bullet went clean through two men in front of him who were standing behind one another, killing the both of them. I knew many cases fatal or otherwise which had occurred through the same mistake.

During the course of the War there were many cases of self-inflicted wounds and a few suicides in the Battalion. Some men would deliberately wound themselves to get out of it. What punishment they received after they recovered I never heard. There were also cases where men had wounded one another. In one part of the line, when we were in standing trenches, three men who were out at a listening-post decided one night to shoot one another through the forearm, and choose the moment for it when the enemy in front of them had opened out with heavy rifle-fire. They wrapped a part of their overcoats around their forearms so that the flesh would not be scorched by firing with the rifle so close to the arm. Two of them returned to their trench wounded, leaving the other man on his own, neither of them being able to raise their rifles to do the same for him. He considered his luck was dead out. In one little stunt we were in two men dropped in a shell hole. They were supposed to have been hit. They *were* hit all right when they limped out of the shell hole. Wrapping some sand-bags which they were carrying around their legs, they had shot one another just above the ankle. In both cases the men left the Battalion honourably wounded;

they were wise birds and evidently didn't believe in getting punished after they were shot.

We were back out of action in a desolate place where we could not spend our money, and the Friday before Whit-Sunday Lane and I and the Regimental Officers' Mess-Sergeant named Owens paid a visit to our First Battalion who were out of action some miles away from us. The officers of the Battalion had been invited over by the officers of the First, and late in the afternoon a tug-of-war was arranged between them, twelve aside. Only ten of our officers were present, so Owens and I made up the number. After a long pull we were the victors. We spent a very pleasant evening, the First Battalion having a wet canteen, and when we started back we were three sheets in the wind. About halfway back we had a rest in a cornfield, and Owens said: "We may as well drink this bottle of whisky," which he was carrying. We both agreed. Having no corkscrew to pull the cork with, we knocked the neck off and poured the stuff in one of our caps. I expect we drunk about one half and wasted the other. We now decided to have a couple of hours sleep and got down to it. I was woke up some time during the night by what I thought was heavy rain falling. I was still half drunk and muddled and for a moment did not know where I was. Owens sprung to his feet, cursing, and I did the same. Lane in his half-drunken condition had got up and had been mistaking the both of us for a shell hole. But Lane had unwittingly done us a good turn, saving us from a court-martial for desertion. We arrived back just in time to move off with the Battalion who were marching towards the line to make an attack on the following morning, which was

Whit-Sunday. Another half hour's sleep and we should have been posted absent.

There was a part of the Hindenburg Trench which the enemy were still holding, and all efforts so far had failed to dislodge them. It was this part that was going to be attacked. I was posted to Battalion Headquarters and the two other battalions who were taking part in the attack, the 1st Cameronians and the 5th Scottish Rifles, had their headquarters close to ours. We took over our trenches during the night, and the attack started at 6 a.m. the following morning.

Whitsun of 1917 was a fine day from the weather point of view, but a damned rotten dirty day from our point of view. We lost half the Battalion in the rush across to the enemy's trench. The Cameronians on our left were held up by machine-gun and rifle-fire and suffered heavy losses. The enemy put up a tremendous barrage on our trenches, which extended to three hundred yards behind us. In addition to heavy stuff they were sending over a lot of high shrapnel which exploding in the air made more noise than the heavy shells. Our lines running back to Brigade soon went West and we did our best to keep up communication with the Lucas Lamp but found it very difficult owing to the smoke and dust that was being blow up. It was only a matter of luck whether we would make a rapid exit into the next world or not. Some men were perfect philosophers under heavy shellfire, whilst others used to go through severe torture and would cower down, holding their heads in their hands, moaning and trembling. For myself I wasn't worrying so much if a shell pitched clean amongst us: we would never know anything about it.

It was the large flying pieces of a shell bursting a few yards off that I didn't like: they could take arms or legs off or, worst still, rip our bellies open and still leave us living; we would know something about *them* all right.

During this day when the barrage was at its worst two runners and a signaller were in a shell hole by a sandbagged shack playing pontoon. Any moment they might have been blown to smithereens yet they were carrying on with their game as if they were in a barrack-room at home. The game was only broken up when the runners were called upon to take messages back to Brigade. Both carried identical messages: in case one was knocked out the other might get there. The signaller was doing a good old-soldier's grouse saying that as soon as his luck began to turn the bloody game was broken up. Five minutes later the sandbagged shack was blown to bits, and also the men inside it. Undoubtedly the card party would also have been killed if they had still been playing in the shell hole.

We found it impossible to send or receive messages with the lamp, and runners were now employed. The 5th Scottish Rifles on our right had lost heavily in signallers and runners, and on one occasion there was no one left around their headquarters to take a message, so the Adjutant ran with it. He hadn't gone very far when he was knocked over, shot through the thigh. We had received no news of our attacking troops since they had entered the enemy's trench, but during the afternoon one of our signallers arrived back with a verbal message that a part of the trench had been captured, but the enemy were making a counter-attack when he was sent back with this message. That was the last news we received until later in the day when some of the survivors arrived back with the news that the enemy had recaptured their trench. Only one officer returned who had went over with the attacking troops. It was Captain Radford. Meeting me later in the evening, he said: "Well, Richards, only you, Sergeant Owens and I are left out of that tug-of-war team of the day before yesterday."

Dr. Dunn had been wandering about no-man's-land attending to the wounded and doing what he could for them. How he didn't get riddled was a mystery. Some of the men who did not know him so well as the rest of us were saying that he was fed up with life and was doing his level best to get killed. It was a disastrous day for all concerned. The attack had been a complete failure all along the line.

We were relieved the following evening, and after knocking around this Area for a little while the whole Division marched many miles away behind this front. We were billeted in houses in a fair sized town where we had large drafts of officers and men. One old regular officer whom I had known in my pre-War soldiering came with one of the drafts. Since I had gone on the Reserve he had been seconded to the Egyptian Army. He was Mr., now Major, Kearsley, and had been severely wounded with the First Battalion in 1915. Although his one arm was practically useless he had volunteered to come out to the Front again. He was soon much respected. He was a neat precise little man with fair hair and not a very strong word of command, but a first-class soldier.

A dozen new signallers joined us. One was the owner

of a large business and the others were pretty well off with this world's goods. One of them was a bit religious and told me that he had been studying for the ministry but had joined up at his country's call. I told him that if he was lucky enough to be still alive and with the Battalion in four months time his language would be the same as mine. He wouldn't believe me, but said that every old soldier he had met at home had told him the same thing. In three months he was the only one left out of the twelve, and by that time, which was a month less than I had said, nobody would have thought who came in contact with him that he had ever studied for the ministry. His bad language won universal approval and he also became highly proficient in drinking a bottle of ving blong, and proved himself a very brave and good soldier as well. He was killed in December on Passchendaele Ridge.

Paddy, Ricco and Tich were still kicking. Also the bank clerk and architect had survived the Arras stunts. The schoolmaster who was still with us was a very decent chap. He took a commission some months later in the Garrison Artillery. From now on it was very easy for a man to get a commission in the infantry, and many that I knew put in for one simply to get sent home to a Cadet School, so as they could get out of the War for a spell, hoping that the War would end before they had completed their cadet training. An old regular soldier who had been a non-commissioned officer for any length of time was generally granted a commission in the field, and it was very rare that they were sent to the cadet schools at home. Hammer Lane and Sealyham were still alive and Lane, who had been a former featherweight champion of India, won a boxing contest against the light-weight champion of the Cameronians, whose name was Newman, a cockney and a very decent chap. Hammer won by a knock-out. We had sports, and a newly joined officer whom we called "the Athlete" easily won the chief running events.

About this time the Germans first used their mustard-gas, and all manners of yarns were going around regarding it. One of the transport men, who were noted for their tall stories, solemnly informed me that the Germans had used it on a twenty mile front and had killed everyone in the front line and Back Areas for a distance of five miles. I did a good grin over that one, The worst yarn of all was that, even if a man did not inhale it, it would penetrate his clothes and burn certain parts of the body and leave him in the same state as a man in the last stages of venereal. The majority believed this yarn and several lectures were given to reassure the men that it was all bunkum. Later we were to find out for ourselves that mustard-gas was the most deadly sort that was used during the course of the War.

Our new box-respirators, however, were proof against it. I have seen cases where it had burned through the gas mask and a few days later the men were temporarily blind, but in each case they were breathing their oxygen and did not inhale it. It would burn through the clothes and nasty blisters would break out over certain parts of the body. If an area had been shelled with these gas-shells it was never safe to use a shell hole as a latrine: the gas being heavier than air would hang around the shell holes for a day or two and many a man had become a gas casualty in this way. I received several letters from gas cases who had been sent to England, and in each case they had recovered with no after-effects. Of course these cases were the temporary blinded and blister ones. But the men who slightly inhaled and are still living must still be suffering terrible agonies. During the last fifteen months of the War I don't believe the Battalion had fifty gas cases, and very few of them were fatal.

CHAPTER XX

THIRD BATTLE OF YPRES:
POLYGON WOOD

The third Battle of Ypres commenced on July 31st and our Division were sent to the Belgian coast. We travelled by train and barge and arrived at Dunkirk. A little higher up the coast was a place named Bray Dunes, where we stayed about a week, and the architect and I went for many a long swim in the sea. We moved closer to the line along the coast and arrived at a place which the majority of inhabitants had only just evacuated. In July a British division had relieved the Belgian troops around this part. Ever since November 1914 the people had been living in peace and security in the towns and villages in this area, but as soon as the British troops took over the enemy began shelling these places and the people cleared out. In one place we were in the people were in the act of leaving and complaining very bitterly because the arrival of British troops had caused a lot of shelling and forced them to leave their homes. In one pretty village by the sea there hadn't been enough of shells exploded in it to have frightened a poll parrot away, yet there wasn't a soul left there now. They were evidently not such good stickers as the French people who worried less about their lives than about their property and hung on to the last possible minute.

At Bray Dunes I got in conversation with a Canadian officer who was in charge of some men building a light railway. He said it was a good job that the States came in the War as the French were ready to throw the sponge up. A few days later two of our signallers overheard a full colonel of the Staff telling our Colonel that he did not know what would have happened if the United States had not come in when they did. It was common knowledge among the Staff that the whole of the French Army were more or less demoralized, and the States coming in had to a great extent been the means of restoring their morale. We got wind that our Division and another had been sent up the coast to try and break through the German Front and capture Ostend. This was freely discussed by the officers, but no break through was attempted owing to so little progress being made on the Ypres front.

One of the largest concentration prison camps I ever saw was erected in this area. It was estimated to hold between ten and fifteen thousand prisoners, but all I saw in it were two solitary prisoners who must have been very lonely in so large a place.

On the night the Battalion went in the line I went on leave. It was eighteen months since I had the last one and as usual I made the most of it. I didn't spend the whole of it in pubs: I spent two days going for long tramps in the mountains, which I thoroughly enjoyed after being so long in a flat country. I was presented with a gold watch, in recognition of winning the D.C.M., which I still have, but it has been touch-and-go with it several times since the War. Probably if there hadn't been an inscription on it I should have parted with it. This time every man of military age that I met wanted to shake hands with me and also ask my advice on how to evade military service, or, if they were forced to go, which would be the best corps to join that would keep them away from the firing line. They were wonderfully patriotic at smoking concerts given in honour of soldiers returning from the Front, but their patriotism never extended beyond that.

When I landed back at Boulogne I came across the man who had been shot through his cheeks at Bois Grenier in April 1915. If anything, that bullet had improved his appearance. He now had a nice little dimple on each side of his face. We had a chat. I asked what he was doing now and he said that he had a Staff job, as a military policeman around the Docks. He told me very seriously that if it was possible, and he had the name and address of the German that shot him, he would send him the largest parcel he could pack and a hundred-franc note as well. He was having the time of his life on his present job and had one of the smartest fillies in Boulogne, who was the goods in every way. As I left him I could not help thinking how lucky some men were and how unlucky were others.

When I arrived back I found that the Division had left the coastal area on short notice. All returning leave men of the Division were in a little camp outside Dunkirk. One night some German planes came over bombing and one of our searchlights kept a plane in its rays for some time. Anti-aircraft guns, machine-guns and Lewis guns, and we with our rifles were all banging at him, but he got away with it. Whilst everyone was busy firing at that one, his friends were busy dropping their bombs on Dunkirk. It was very rare that a plane flying at any height was brought down by anti-aircraft guns or rifle-fire but we lost a lot of planes on the Somme by rifle-fire when they came down very low, machine-gunning the enemy before our troops attacked. German planes used to do the same thing and seldom got away with it either.

I rejoined the Battalion in a village near Ypres and guessed that we would soon be in the blood tub. Ricco and Paddy had been made full corporals but Paddy had taken a lot of persuading before he consented to be made an N.C.O. He was sent back to Division Headquarters for a special course of signalling and was lucky enough to miss the next show we were in. Our Colonel went on leave and missed the show too. The name of our Acting-Colonel was Major Poore. He was not an old regimental officer but had been posted to us some six months before from the Yeomanry, I believe. He was a very big man, about fifty years of age, slightly deaf, and his favourite expression was "What, what!" He was a very decent officer. A tall, slender young lieutenant who had just returned from leave was made Assistant-Adjutant for the show. I believe he was given that job because he was an excellent map-reader. As we were marching along the road, Sealyham asked him if he had come across Mr. Sassoon during his leave. He replied that he hadn't and that he had spent a good part of his leave trying to find out where he was but had failed to get any news at all. This young officer had joined the Battalion about the same time as Mr. Sassoon and we old hands thought he was a man and a half to spend his leave looking for a pal. His name was Casson. I wrote it down first here as Carson, but an old soldiering pal tells me that I had it wrong. Mr. Casson was said to be a first-class pianist, but trench warfare did not give him much opportunity to show his skill at that. If he was as good a pianist as he was a cool soldier he must have been a treat to hear.

During the night we passed through a wood where a Very-light dump had been exploded by a German shell. It was like witnessing a fireworks display at home. We stayed in the wood for the night. Our Brigade were in reserve and ready to be called upon at any moment. Orders were given that no fires were to be lit. September 26th, 1917, was a glorious day from the weather point of view and when dawn was breaking Ricco and I who were crack hands at making smokeless fires had found a dump of pick-handles which when cut up in thin strips answered very well. We soon cooked our bacon and made tea for ourselves and the bank clerk and architect, and made no more smoke than a man would have done smoking a cigarette. We had at least made sure of our breakfast which might be the last we would ever have.

At 8 a.m. orders arrived that the Battalion would move off to the assistance of the Australians who had made an attack early in the morning on Polygon Wood. Although the attack was successful they had received heavy casualties and were now hard pressed themselves. Young Mr. Casson led the way, as cool as a cucumber. One part of the ground we travelled over was nothing but lakes and boggy ground and the whole of the Battalion were strung out in Indian file walking along a track about eighteen inches wide. We had just got out of this bad ground but were still travelling in file when the enemy opened out with a fierce bombardment. Just in front of me half a dozen men fell on the side of the track: it was like as if a Giant Hand had suddenly swept them one side. The Battalion had close on a hundred casualties before they were out of that valley. If a man's best pal was wounded he could not stop to dress his wounds for him.

We arrived on some rising ground and joined forces with the Australians. I expected to find a wood but it was undulating land with a tree dotted here and there and little banks running in different directions. About half a mile in front of us was a ridge of trees, and a few concrete pillboxes of different sizes. The ground that we were now on and some of the pillboxes had only been taken some hours previously. I entered one pillbox during the day and found eighteen dead Germans inside. There was not a mark on one of them; one of our heavy shells had made a direct hit on the top of it and they were killed by concussion, but very little damage had been done to the pillbox. They were all constructed with reinforced concrete and shells could explode all round them but the flying pieces would never penetrate the concrete. There were small windows in the sides and by jumping in and out of shell holes attacking troops could get in bombing range: if a bomb was thrown through one of the windows the pillbox was as good as captured.

There was a strong point called Black Watch Corner which was a trench facing north, south, east and west. A few yards outside the trench was a pillbox which was

Battalion Headquarters. The bank clerk, architect and I got in the trench facing our front, and I was soon on friendly terms with an Australian officer, whom his men called Mr. Diamond. He was wearing the ribbon of the D.C.M., which he told me he had won in Gallipoli while serving in the ranks and had been granted a commission some time later. About a hundred yards in front of us was a bank which extended for hundreds of yards across the ground behind which the Australians were. Our chaps charged through them to take a position in front and Captain Mann, our Adjutant, who was following close behind, fell with a bullet through his head. The enemy now began to heavily bombard our position and Major Poore and Mr. Casson left the pillbox and got in a large shell hole which had a deep narrow trench dug in the bottom of it. They were safer there than in the pillbox, yet in less than fifteen minutes an howitzer shell had pitched clean in it, killing the both of them.

During the day shells fell all around the pillbox but not one made a direct hit on it. The ground rocked and heaved with the bursting shells. The enemy were doing their best to obliterate the strong point that they had lost. Mr. Diamond and I were mucking-in with a tin of Maconochies when a dud shell landed clean in the trench, killing the man behind me, and burying itself in the side of the trench by me. Our Maconochie was spoilt but I opened another one and we had the luck to eat that one without a clod of earth being thrown over it. If that shell had not been a dud we should have needed no more Maconochies in this world. I had found eight of them in a sandbag before I left the wood and brought them along with me. I passed the other six along our trench, but no one seemed to want them with the exception of the bank clerk and architect who had got into my way of thinking that it was better to enter the next world with a full belly than an empty one.

The bombardment lasted until the afternoon and then ceased. Not one of us had hardly moved a yard for some hours but we had been lucky in our part of the trench, having only two casualties. In two other parts of the strong point every man had been killed or wounded. The shells had been bursting right on the parapets and in the trenches, blowing them to pieces. One part of the trench was completely obliterated. The fourth part of the strong point had also been lucky, having only three casualties. Mr. Diamond said that we could expect a counter attack at any minute. He lined us up on the parapet in extended order outside the trench and told us to lie down. Suddenly a German plane swooped very low, machine-gunning us. We brought him down but not before he had done some damage, several being killed including our Aid Post Sergeant.

A few minutes later Dr. Dunn temporarily resigned from the Royal Army Medical Corps. He told me to get him a rifle and bayonet and a bandolier of ammunition. I told him that he had better have a revolver but he insisted on having what he had asked me to get. I found them for him and slinging the rifle over his shoulder he commenced to make his way over to the troops behind the bank. I accompanied him. Just before we reached there our chaps who were hanging on to a position in front of it started to retire back. The doctor barked at them to line up with the others. Only

Captain Radford and four platoon officers were left in the Battalion and the Doctor unofficially took command.

We and the Australians were all mixed up in extended order. Everyone had now left the strong point and were lined up behind the bank, which was about three feet high. We had lent a Lewis-gun team to the 5th Scottish Rifles on our right, and when it began to get dark the Doctor sent me with a verbal message to bring them back with me, if they were still in the land of the living. When I arrived at the extreme right of our line I asked the right-hand man if he was in touch with the 5th Scottish. He replied that he had no more idea than a crow where they were, but guessed that they were somewhere in front and to the right of him. I now made my way very carefully over the ground. After I had walked some way I began to crawl. I was liable any moment to come in contact with a German post or trench. I thought I saw someone moving in front of me, so I slid into a shell hole and landed on a dead German. I waited in that shell hole for a while trying to pierce the darkness in front. I resumed my journey and, skirting one shell hole, a wounded German was shrieking aloud in agony: he must have been hit low down but I could not stop for no wounded man. I saw the forms of two men in a shallow trench and did not know whether they were the 5th Scottish or the Germans until I was sharply challenged in good Glasgow English. When I got in their trench they told me that they had only just spotted me when they challenged. The Lewis-gun team were still kicking and my journey back with them was a lot easier than the outgoing one.

I reported to the Doctor that there was a gap of about

one hundred yards between the 5th Scottish Rifles and we; and he went himself to remedy it. The whole of the British Front that night seemed to be in a semi-circle. We had sent up some S O S rockets and no matter where we looked we could see our S O S rockets going up in the air: they were only used when the situation was deemed critical and everybody seemed to be in the same plight as ourselves. The bank clerk and I got into a shell hole to snatch a couple of hours rest, and although there were two dead Germans in it we were soon fast asleep. I was woke up to guide a ration party to us who were on their way. Dawn was now breaking and I made my way back about six hundred yards, where I met them. We landed safely with the rations.

Major Kearsley had just arrived from B Echelon to take command of the Battalion. The Brigadier-General of the Australians had also arrived and was sorting his men out. It was the only time during the whole of the War that I saw a brigadier with the first line of attacking troops. Some brigadiers that I knew never moved from Brigade Headquarters. It was also the first time I had been in action with the Australians and I found them very brave men. There was also an excellent spirit of comradeship between officers and men.

We were moving about quite freely in the open but we did not know that a large pillbox a little over an hundred yards in front of us was still held by the enemy. They must have all been having a snooze, otherwise some of us would have been riddled. Major Kearsley, the Doctor and I went out reconnoitring. We were jumping in and out of shell holes when a machine-gun opened out from somewhere in front, the bullets knocking up the dust around the shell holes we had just jumped into. They both agreed that the machine-gun had been fired from the pillbox about a hundred yards in front of us. We did some wonderful jumping and hopping, making our way back to the bank. The enemy's artillery had also opened out and an hour later shells were bursting all over our front and in the rear of us.

A sapping platoon of one sergeant and twenty men under the command of The Athlete were on the extreme left of the bank, and the Major and I made our way towards them. We found the men but not the officer and sergeant, and when the Major inquired where they were they replied that they were both down the dug-out. There was a concrete dug-out at this spot which had been taken the day before. I shouted down for them to come up, and the Major gave the young officer a severe reprimand for being in the dug-out, especially as he knew our men had just started another attack. Our chaps and the 5th Scottish Rifles had attacked on our right about fifteen minutes previously. The Major gave The Athlete orders that if the pillbox in front was not taken in fifteen minutes he was to take his platoon and capture it and then dig a trench around it. If the pillbox was captured during that time he was still to take his platoon and sap around it. I felt very sorry for The Athlete. This was the first real action he had been in and he had the most windy sergeant in the Battalion with him. Although The Athlete did not know it, this sergeant had been extremely lucky after one of the Arras stunts that he had not been court-martialled and tried on the charge of cowardice in face of the enemy.

We arrived back at our position behind the bank. We and the Australians were in telephone communication with no one; all messages went by runners. Ricco, the bank clerk and the architect were running messages, the majority of our Battalion runners being casualties. Sealyham was still kicking and Lane was back in B Echelon; it was the first time for over two years he had been left out of the line. The Sapping-Sergeant came running along the track by the bank and informed the Major that The Athlete had sent him for further instructions as he was not quite certain what he had to do. The Major very nearly lost his temper and told me to go back with the Sergeant and tell him what he had to do. Just as we arrived at the sapping-platoon we saw some of our chaps rushing towards the pillbox, which surrendered, one officer and twenty men being inside it.

C and D Companies were now merged into one company. They advanced and took up a position behind a little bank about a hundred yards in front of the pillbox. I informed The Athlete that he had to take his platoon and sap around the pillbox, and that this was a verbal message which Major Kearsley had given me for him. I left him and the Sergeant conferring together and made my way back by a different route.

The enemy were now shelling very heavily and occasionally the track was being sprayed by machine-gun bullets. I met a man of one of our companies with six German prisoners whom he told me he had to take back to a place called Clapham Junction, where he would hand them over. He then had to return and rejoin his company. The shelling was worse behind us than where we were and it happened more than once that escort and prisoners had been killed making their way back. I had known this man about eighteen months and he said, "Look here, Dick. About an hour ago I lost the best pal I ever had, and he was worth all these six Jerries put together. I'm not going to take them far before I put them out of mess." Just after they passed me I saw the six dive in one large shell hole and he had a job to drive them out. I expect being under their own shelling would make them more nervous than under ours. Some little time later I saw him coming back and I knew it was impossible for him to have reached Clapham Junction and returned in the time, especially by the way his prisoners had been ducking and jumping into shell holes. As he passed me again he said: "I done them in as I said, about two hundred yards back. Two bombs did the trick." He had not walked twenty yards beyond me when he fell himself: a shell-splinter had gone clean through him. I had often heard some of our chaps say that they had done their prisoners in whilst taking them back but this was the only case I could vouch for, and no doubt the loss of his pal had upset him very much.

During the afternoon the Major handed me a message to take to A Company, which consisted of the survivors of two companies now merged into one under the command of a young platoon officer. They had to advance and take up a position about two hundred yards in front of them. The ground over which I had to travel had been occupied by the enemy a little while before and the Company were behind a little bank which was being heavily shelled. I slung my rifle, and after I had proceeded some way I pulled my revolver out for safety.

Shells were falling here and there and I was jumping in and out of shell holes. When I was about fifty yards from the Company, in getting out of a large shell hole I saw a German pop up from another shell hole in front of me and rest his rifle on the lip of the shell hole. He was about to fire at our chaps in front who had passed him by without noticing him. He could never have heard me amidst all the din around: I expect it was some instinct made him turn around with the rifle at his shoulder. I fired first and as the rifle fell out of his hands I fired again. I made sure he was dead before I left him. If he hadn't popped his head up when he did no doubt I would have passed the shell hole he was in. I expect he had been shamming death and every now and then popping up and sniping at our chaps in front. If I hadn't spotted him he would have soon put my lights out after I had passed him and if any of his bullets had found their mark it would not have been noticed among the Company, who were getting men knocked out now and then by the shells that were bursting around them. This little affair was nothing out of the ordinary in a runner's work when in attacks.

The shelling was very severe around here and when I arrived I shouted for the officer. A man pointed along the bank. When I found him and delivered the message he shouted above the noise that he had not been given much time; I had delivered the message only three minutes before they were timed to advance. During the short time they had been behind the bank one-third of the Company had become casualties. When I arrived back I could only see the Major. All the signallers had gone somewhere on messages and the Doctor was some distance away attending wounded men whom he came across. He seemed to be temporarily back in the R.A.M.C.

The Major asked me how my leg was. I replied that it was all right when I was moving about, but it became very stiff after I had been resting. During the two days many pieces and flying splinters of shells and bullets must have missed me by inches. But when a small piece of spent shrapnel had hit me on the calf of the leg I knew all about it. I thought at the time that someone had hit me with a coal hammer. I had the bottom of my trousers doubled inside the sock on the calf and also my puttee doubled in the same place which, no doubt, had helped to minimize the blow. If it had not been a spent piece it would have gone clean through the calf and given me a beautiful blighty wound, which I don't mind admitting I was still hoping for.

Ricco in returning from running a message to Brigade had come across the ration party of another battalion who had all been killed, and he had brought back with him a lovely sandbag full of officers' rations. There were several kinds of tinned stuffs and three loaves of bread. The bank clerk, architect and Sealyham had also arrived back and we all had a muck in. The way the bank clerk and architect got a tin of cooked sausages across their chests made me wonder whether their forefathers had not been pure-bred Germans. The officers who the bag of rations were intended for could never have enjoyed them better than we did.

Just as we finished our feed Major Kearsley called me and told me to follow him. I could see we were making our way towards where we had visited the sapping-platoon, but I could not see any men sapping around the pillbox and was wondering if they had been knocked out. When we arrived at the concrete dug-out some of the sapping-platoon were still outside it and some had become casualties, but The Athlete and the Sergeant were still down in the dug-out. I shouted down and told them to come up and the Major asked The Athlete the reason why he had not carried out his orders. He replied that the shelling had been so intense around the pillbox after it was taken that he decided to stop where he was until it slackened. Then he had seen our troops advance again and he was under the impression that the trench would not be needed. The Major again gave him a severe reprimand and told him to take what men he had left and sap around the pillbox as he had been ordered at first.

Shortly after, the Major said he was going to visit the positions our companies had lately taken. We set off on our journey and when we passed through the Australians they started shouting, "Come back, you bloody fools! They've got everything in line with machine-gun fire." We took no notice and by jumping in shell holes now and again we reached halfway there. We had only advanced a few yards further when in jumping into a large shell hole an enemy machine-gun opened out and the ground around us was sprayed with bullets. The Major was shot clean through the leg just above the ankle. As I dressed his wound we discussed the possibility of returning to the bank. I said that it would be dusk in two hours' time and that we had better wait until then. He replied that he could not do that as he would have to hand over the command of the Battalion, and also wanted to discuss matters with the Commanding Officer of the 5th Scottish Rifles, and that we would make our way back at once. He clambered out of the shell hole and I followed. He hopped back to the bank, taking a zig-zag course and I the same. How we were not riddled was a mystery: the machine-gun had been playing a pretty tune behind us.

We met the Doctor and Captain Radford, who had been sent for some time before, advancing along the bank. They had decided to shift Battalion Headquarters more on the left of the bank and they had just shifted in time. The spot where Battalion Headquarters had been was now being blown to pieces. Shells were bursting right along the bank and for a considerable way back and men were being blowed yards in the air. The Major said that the Battalion would be relieved at dusk and he would try to stick it until then; but the Doctor warned him, if he did, that it might be the cause of him losing his leg.

He then handed over the command to Captain Radford, who said that he would much prefer the Doctor taking command, as he seemed to have a better grip of the situation than what he had. But the Major said he could not do that as the Doctor was a non-combatant, but that they could make any arrangements they liked when he had left. We made our way to the 5th Scottish Rifles and met their colonel outside a little dug-out. He mentioned that only three young platoon-officers were left in his battalion. They went in the dug-out to discuss matters and when we left the Major had a difficult job to walk. The Casualty Clearing Station was at Clapham Junction and all along the track leading down to it lay stretcher-bearers and bandaged men who had been killed making their way back. Many men who had received what they thought were nice blighty wounds had been killed along this track. The previous day the track, in addition to being heavily shelled had also been under machine-gun fire. As we were moving along I counted over twenty of our tanks which had been put out of action. Mr. Diamond, whom I had not seen since the previous day, passed us with his arm in a sling and said, "Hello. I'm glad to see you alive." He had been hit through the muscle of his arm. Shells were bursting here and there and we could sniff gas. We put our gas helmets on for a little while and it was twilight when we reached Clapham Junction.

The Major told me that the Battalion was going back to Dickiebusch after it was relieved and that I had no need to return. He wrote me out a note to take back to the transport. He then said that he would have liked to have remained with the Battalion until they were relieved but he thought it best to follow the Doctor's advice, especially when he said that he might lose his leg. I told him not to take too much notice of the Doctor, who would have made a better general than a doctor, and that I had seen worse bullet-wounds than what he had which had healed up in a fortnight's time. I hoped he would be back with the Battalion inside a couple of months. We shook hands and wished one another the best of luck and I made my way back to the transport.

The enemy bombed Dickiebusch that night but it was such a common occurence around this area and I was so dead-beat that I took no notice of it. The following morning I rejoined the remnants of the Battalion and found that Ricco, the bank clerk, the architect and Sealyham were still kicking. They thought I had gone West and were as delighted to see me as I was them. We had lost heavily in signallers, but Tich was still hale and hearty.

CHAPTER XXI

FIVE WEEKS AT ROUEN BASE CAMP

We were back in a village many miles from the Front, and one dark evening when I was standing outside my billet The Athlete came up to me and asked me if I would mind going for a walk with him. I thought it was a strange request for an officer to make to a private, especially when out of action, but I accompanied him. If he had been seen by a senior officer he might easily have been brought up for a breach of discipline. The Peer who had been back with Minimum Reserve had rejoined us, and also the Colonel from leave. When we were out of the village he said: "Richards, I'm in a fix, and what I am going to tell you is in confidence." He then told me that the previous day he had been sent for to appear in front of the Colonel, who informed him that he had received a very bad report on the way he had conducted himself in action on September 26th and 27th, and then read out the charges that had been made against him. He was then asked what explanation he could give in answer to the charges. He had explained to the best of his ability, and the Colonel had then dismissed him. He did not know whether he would be court-martialled or not. In case he was, he thought about calling upon me as a witness. I told him I was very sorry, but if he called upon me as a witness I was afraid I would do him more harm than good. I said that the sergeant he had with him was the most windy man in France and didn't care a damn who else got in the soup as long as he didn't, and that he should never have listened to his advice. The Athlete said that a young officer who had been left out in Minimum Reserve had since told him the same, and he wished he had realized it before. We then parted. When I arrived back at my billet the boys wanted to know where I had been, and when I told them I had picked up with a fair young maid they called me a scrounging old hound.

Two days later I called at the transport lines and an old soldier asked me if I thought The Athlete would be stuck against the wall and shot. I inquired what for. He then gave me full details of the case and said it was now stale news on the transport and was surprised I knew nothing about it. Our transport men were marvels: they knew everything that was happening on the Western Front. The Old Soldier when he was with the Battalion often used to say that they had a private telephone line to the Commander-in-Chief's bedroom.

The Athlete was not court-martialled, however, and later proved himself a very brave and capable officer, winning the Military Cross. In July 1918 he was wounded in a night raid on Beaumont-Hamel. I don't remember what became of the windy sergeant in the end; if he had had his just deserts he should have been given a couple of severe reprimands and then put against the wall and shot. All I know is that he later was with one of our new service battalions as a company-sergeant-major. It was only natural that a young in-experienced lieutenant would look for guidance from an experienced sergeant, but in this case it very nearly proved the undoing of what turned out to be a brave and capable officer.

The calf of my leg was badly bruised, but in a few days the stiffness had wore off. We did two days heavy marching and arrived at Neuve Eglise. I was suffering very badly with hæmorrhoids and was forced to go sick. After the doctor examined me he told me that he would send me away for a three weeks' rest. At this time there was an order that a few men from each battalion who had been continually serving in the line could be sent down to Boulogne for a three weeks' rest. The Battalion went in to hold the line at Messines Ridge and I was left out with the transport.

A Brigade doctor came over to the transport to see the men who reported sick that morning, and ordered me to hospital. He told me that I should always have trouble with my complaint, especially when marching, and that he was sending me down the line for an opera-tion. Before being evacuated to Rouen I was kept in a field-hospital about twenty miles behind the Front for two days, and whilst there I came across an old soldier of the Battalion who had left us on the retirement in August 1914. He told me that during the last three years he had been on some excellent jobs down at the Bases and had only lately been moved to this field-hospital. At this time every available man who was passed A1 was being combed out and a few old soldiers who had been on good jobs down at the Bases had lately rejoined the Battalion. When I mentioned this to him he said he was well away with the doctors and nurses, who thought the world of him as an orderly, and they would work it all right for him to remain at the field-hospital. He was quite near enough to the line, and if he could avoid it he was not going a yard rurther; he had seen enough of the poor wounded devils that had come from there since he had been at the field-hospital. He was as fat as a water-buffalo. Seven weeks later he had been combed out, rejoined the Battalion, and killed.

I arrived at Rouen and all sick men who could walk had to make their way to the hospital, which I was informed was some distance out of the town, close to the "Bull Ring". This was the place where all troops who arrived from England spent a week or two before proceeding up the line. I had left the town and was walking up a long hill when I saw a sergeant coming towards me. I stopped him and asked him the way to the hospital. As soon as he spoke I knew he had never seen the sky over a front-line trench. "Where did you land when you first arrived in France?" he asked me. "In this place," I replied civilly, "but I've not been back here lately." "Surely you have not forgot your way to the hospital? It's close to the Bull Ring where you must have spent some time before you were sent up the line. I don't suppose you have been long enough up there to have forgotten. And remember, my man, when you address me again to give me my rank."

I had my overcoat on which hid my campaigning ribbons, and he must have took me for a young soldier. I exploded and told him that when I arrived at Rouen there was not enough of tent-canvas in the place to make a patch for a sore eye, and not a hut large enough to hold a trench-louse, and that if he thought I was going to call him "Sergeant" he was very much mistaken indeed. I said I could have been a full sergeant when he was sucking milk at his mother's breast. I cursed him up hill and down, using Hindustani and French and other languages until I was blue in the nose; but he made no response and cleared off. I met many like him at the Base who were holding good jobs and were supposed to be unfit for the front line. A few weeks in a front-line trench in any bad part of the Front would have done them the world of good.

I spent the night in an hospital hut, the large hospital which consisted of marquee tents being close by. The following morning the doctor came around, who also, by the look of him, had never been no further than Rouen. Each man's complaint was on a board by the foot of his bed, and when he came to me he inquired, without picking up the board, where I had won the D.C.M. and how long I had been in France. When I told him, he picked up my board. I mentioned that I had been sent down for an operation. He then exclaimed: "Good God, man, what are you talking about? They want men like you back in the front line. But look here, I'll send you this evening for a three weeks rest to a convalescent camp which will do you the world of good." I started to explain to him what the Brigade doctor had told me, but he would not listen. He passed to the next bed where lay a nice rosy-cheeked young soldier. I had been standing by my bed fully dressed but the rosy-cheeked one was evidently more wiser than I. He was between the sheets and had a boil on his stomach. The doctor picked up his board, examined him and asked him how long he had been in France. "Three months," he answered. "Poor boy," said the doctor, "I'll send you over to the large hospital." There were twenty-eight sick men in the hut, including four old soldiers. The majority of the youngsters who had not been in France any length of time were sent over to the hospital, but the four old soldiers were sent for a three weeks rest. The doctor did not even examine me. By what I could see it was no good for an old soldier to be ill: his place was the front line where he must stay until he got killed or wounded.

The Convalescent Camp was some hours ride by train from Rouen and was known by a map reference. It was miles from anywhere and a very dismal place. There were between six and seven thousand men in it, and the majority were swinging the lead and would do anything to prevent themselves being marked A1. The morning after arriving there I appeared in front of a doctor who asked me why I had not received an operation. I explained everything and he said it was rotten, but that he could do nothing for me. All men in this camp were medically examined once a week and were marked B or C as the case might be, but as soon as a man was marked A1 he was sent back to Rouen, and from there back up the line. One young chap told me that he had been four months in France: the last three he had spent in this camp, where he now had a permanent job. He was still a C man and intended to remain one as long as he could. This young chap looked strong enough to carry an eighteen-pounder gun over his shoulder, and there were many more like him.

I received a letter and copy of Battalion Orders from

Ricco. Major Kearsley had received a bar to his D.S.O. Captain Radford and the Doctor had been awarded the D.S.O.—they had both won the Military Cross some time previous. The bank clerk and I had been awarded the Military Medal. I had did no more than the other men, and would have much preferred the young architect or Sealyham having the Military Medal instead of myself. I thought the Doctor would have been awarded the Victoria Cross. He had honestly earned it; in addition to taking charge of affairs, which of course could not be officially rewarded, he had also been under continual shell and machine-gun fire when he was wandering about attending to the wounded. I have always held that he was the coolest man under fire that ever stepped foot in France.

CHAPTER XXII

BOIS GRENIER AGAIN

I was back in Rouen in three weeks and in another week I was up the line again with the Battalion in some huts not far from Ypres. I had been away a little over five weeks and during all that time they had been out on rest and had been finding working parties up the line. I had not missed a battle with the Battalion for the last three years. I met Dr. Dunn, who asked me if I was better. I told him I was and that I was delighted with the treatment I had received down the Base. He inquired what treatment I had received and when I told him that I had received a three weeks rest, a new suit of khaki, a new pair of boots and sent back up the line, he did a good grin. He told me they would come in very handy as the Battalion was going in the line the following evening to hold the line in front of Passchendaele.

The third battle of Ypres had finished, and Passchendaele had been captured. Our Divisional General had another brainwave, and we were ordered to go in the line without puttees. It had been snowing for a few days and he thought the men would be better off without their puttees when moving about in the snow. We marched up the Frezenburg Road and then got on a duckboard track that extended a long way over the ground towards Passchendaele Ridge. What was left of the village was the other side of the ridge, and our front line was beyond it. There was a large hill this side of the ridge named Abraham Heights, and dotted here and there were pillboxes, some on high ground, others on low, and our dead were laying everywhere. When men were travelling over this area at night they could not help trampling on the dead bodies, and no doubt when it was muddy hundreds of men had received their burial in this way.

The duckboard track was constantly shelled, and in places a hundred yards of it had been blown to smithereens. It was better to keep off the track when walking back and forth, but then a man had to make his way sometimes through very heavy mud. Twenty-four hours after we were in the line the majority of the Battalion were wearing puttees. Those that did not have them in their haversacks found plenty of dead men to borrow them from. Wet snow had begun to fall, which turned into rain and some parts of the land were soon a bog of mud to get drowned in.

After four days we were relieved and went back to shell holes and dug-outs outside Ypres cemetery. Over half of the dead in the cemetery had been blown out of their graves and corpses and coffins were lying about in all directions. In the afternoon, just before we were to go back to the trenches, the regimental officers-mess cart stopped at the bottom of the road about two hundred yards from us and Sergeant Owens brought some stuff up for the officers. When he left he wished Lane and me the best of luck and had reached halfway to the

269

cart when he turned around and came back towards us. He explained that he had forgot to ask the Colonel about something. Making his way back the second time, when he had again reached about halfway to the cart a shell burst about six yards from him and he was killed instantly. The job that he had, a man could have taken an insurance policy on his life; if he had not forgot something he might have still been knocking about this ball of clay. He had did me many a good turn, and we had many a good time together, and it was rotten luck the way he had gone West.

We did another four days in Passchendaele and about a week before Christmas we were relieved and went back to Poperinghe where we billeted in a convent. The shelling around Passchendaele had been very severe and we had had heavy casualties. Although we had received drafts of officers and men after the Polygon Wood stunt we were still considerably under strength. Major Kearsley rejoined us at the convent, and everyone was glad to see him back. He told me that his wound had healed up very quickly. Either we or the Cameronians had to go up the line as a working party on Christmas day, so the two C.O.s tossed for it, and ours won.

I soon found out that the Brigade doctor was right. After a few days around Passchendaele my complaint was as bad as ever, but from now on I suffered in silence. I was doing nothing when back out of the line, and got better through resting, but when in the line if it was very muddy, and on long marches, I used to go through some agony.

Poperinghe used to get shelled now and again, but it did not prevent the cafés from doing a roaring trade,

We had a good Christmas dinner and also a good drink. The bank clerk told me that he had an invitation to spend the evening with a gunner in the Royal Garrison Artillery, whom he had met during the day. The gunner was a bank inspector in the same banking firm that he was in, and an officer in the same battery was also a bank clerk in the same firm. I thought it very funny, and wondered what the gunner's feelings would be if his officer told him to smarten himself up a bit as he was getting very slovenly in his ways.

A few days after Christmas we moved back around Ypres, the Battalion finding working parties up the line. Working parties were generally digging trenches, making roads and sometimes collecting dead within a certain distance of the front line, and were often heavily shelled. During this time I was attached to Battalion Headquarters, and one evening when on duty I received a message from Brigade which had come from England. It ran something like this: "To Major Kearsley, 2nd Royal Welch Fusiliers. Am ordered to Egypt can you do something to get me back to France. Signed, Sassoon." As I handed the message to the Major I was wishing he could do something in the matter, as it was only once in a blue moon that we had an officer like Mr. Sassoon. But he was unable. Mr. Sassoon was in Palestine for a while with a Yeomanry regiment which had been dismounted and made into the Twenty-fifth Battalion of the Royal Welch. Then they were sent to France, and he was soon back in England, wounded in the head.

The following morning Major Kearsley went out on his horse, and when riding through Ypres (it was freezing at the time) it slipped on the hard ground and

271

threw him out of the saddle, breaking his leg. I thought his luck was dead out, as he was leaving us the following day to take command of a service battalion. I heard no news of him for some years and then it was that he had been knocked over in the last month of the War, but I am glad to say that the rumour has proved false. He is alive and kicking.

In January 1918 the Division went back to St. Omer to be reorganized. While we were there a new order came into operation. Brigades, instead of having four battalions in a brigade, would now have three. Many service battalions were broken up, and we received officers and men from our Fifteenth Battalion and also officers and men from the Nineteenth (Bantam) Battalion, with some drafts from England. The drafts from home were a sorry looking lot of men, and during the next six months they got worse. The doctors that had passed some of them A1 cannot have had tender consciences. I remember one draft some months later who were very nearly all crocks. One man had a double rupture and was soon sent to hospital. Another told me that he had been a C3 man ever since the Military Service Act came into force, and had been driving a lorry in London. One evening he was warned to parade for medical inspection the following morning. There were ranks of naked men lined up in a long hut when he arrived, and he fell in, after he had stripped, in one of the ranks. A doctor passed up and down the ranks without hardly looking at one of them. He was passed A1 and, before he hardly knew where he was, he was handed a rifle and equipment and sent out to France. He was hardly strong enough to carry his rifle and equipment.

These men could not help their physical disabilities, and when I thought of the fat greasy oily men that I had seen swinging the lead at the Base I came to the conclusion that some of the doctors had gone seriously insane and were not responsible for their actions, when they passed perfectly fit men C3 and perfectly unfit men A1. I don't know what old Buffalo Bill would have done if he had had to command a company of these chaps. I expect he would have had a half dozen revolvers in his belt which he would have been pulling out, three at a time in each hand. If he had not shot the lot in a couple of days it would have been because he had dropped dead from exhaustion.

Tich and I were watching some of the Bantams drilling, and he remarked that the Battalion was coming to something when little men like that were sent to us. I laughed. Every man we were looking at was a good inch taller than what he was. He had been so long with us that he imagined he was as big as a Prussian Guard. But the Bantams turned out all right: they were good soldiers in action.

We were inspected by the Divisional General, who told us how sorry he was that we were leaving the 33rd Division and that we were being transferred to the 38th (Welsh) Division. But when the history of the Division was written we would be very prominent in it. After we were dismissed, Ricco remarked that the most prominent thing in that history should be about the way the old bun-punching wallah had docked our rum. I am told that the history did get written some years later but this important item was omitted.

I was sorry we were leaving the Brigade. There were

many in the Cameronians and 5th Scottish Rifles I was friendly with. The 38th, recruited largely by Lloyd George's influence with the chapels, had arrived in France at the end of 1915. We were posted to the 115th Brigade, the other two battalions being our Seventeenth Battalion and the 10th South Wales Borderers. We were the only regular battalion in the Division, yet with the exception of the transport we probably had more young soldiers with us than any of the others. The Division were holding the line in the Laventie Sector, which was still a quiet part of the Front. The Portuguese, whom we called the Pork and Beans, were also in this part and they looked a ragtime lot. There was a yarn going around that when they were in the front line Old Jerrie would come over whenever he liked, pinch their rations and smack their backsides before leaving, telling them that they were not worth taking back as prisoners.

The latter end of February we took over the Bois Grenier Sector. We were out of the line for a few days before going in the trenches. Paddy and I visited Bois Grenier village, our first visit for nearly three years. We went to the cemetery and I had a job to find the graves of Stevens and others I knew. The grass and nettles and poppies very nearly hid the wooden crosses. We made them a bit respectable before we left. We went down the road where the tall red-brick house and farm were. The whole of the street had been blown down and levelled to the ground, but the red-brick house with the exception of a hit by one small shell had not been touched. The ladies had left. The farm was practically untouched too and the farmer was still tilling his land. The ving blong man had vanished. He had either been killed or cleared out with a fortune. There was not much left of his house.

One night we were marching along the road on our way to the front line. I was an inside man of my section of fours and the man on my right flank had only returned from leave that evening. He was a married man and told me that he had left his home forty-eight hours before, staying only one night in the rest-camp at Boulogne. I told him that this was a quiet part of the Front and a man with ordinary luck should live for ever around here. Almost as I said these words we heard a solitary shell coming over. We checked our pace, but it burst just on our right before we had time to do more than this. He fell against me, nearly knocking me down; a piece of shell had made a big hole through his head. As soon as we were in the line one of our chaps wrote a letter to his wife, telling her of her husband's death, and a man who was going back to the transport just after with a message took it back and gave it to the Post Corporal. Some days later he received a reply saying that some terrible mistake had been made. Her husband had only left home forty-eight hours previously and he had told her before leaving that he would spend two, if not three, nights at the Rest Camp before leaving to rejoin the Battalion. Another letter arrived from her some days later saying that she had been officially notified about her husband's death, but she still believed that a mistake must have been made.

When in standing trenches at nine o'clock every morning all casualty returns were in and sent back to Battalion Headquarters, and if a man was killed at 9.15 a.m. he would not be officially reported until 9 a.m.

the following morning. When a man was killed his pal or one of his section would write a letter to his relatives which they might receive a day or two before the one from the War Office. After an attack there was a roll-call when the Battalion were relieved, and sometimes it was impossible to tell whether a man was killed, wounded, or missing.

CHAPTER XXIII

THE GERMAN MARCH OFFENSIVE

The month of March, 1918, was more like June than March. We had plenty of sun but a thick haze hung over everything early in the morning—ideal weather and conditions for either side to make an attack. Everybody seemed to have got the notion that the Germans were going to launch out with a big offensive but nobody seemed to know anything definite. Our young signalling officer asked whether I thought the enemy would break through the British Front if they did make an attack. I told him that if every man made full use of his rifle Old Jerrie would find it very difficult to break through, but that the British Army was not like it used to be and anything might happen.

Ricco decided to put in for a regular commission and being a regular soldier could do so; there were more money grants and allowances for kit than a temporary one. He tried to persuade me and Paddy to do the same, saying that we could all go to the cadet school together. But we would have nothing to do with it. He appeared in front of the Colonel and then had an interview with the Divisional General, which was the usual procedure, and a week later was informed that he could not be granted a regular commission but could have a temporary one. He told the Colonel that he would not accept a temporary one, and for the time being that finished the matter.

On March 21st the Germans launched their big offensive, down the Somme. We were in the front line near Bois Grenier. It was a misty morning but turned out a beautiful day. Nothing happened out of the ordinary for the next few days on our part of the Front, with the exception of the last day we were in the line, when the enemy shelled us very heavily and also sent a lot of gas shells over.

Early in April we left for the Somme and a few days before we left Ricco was sent for and told that he had been granted a regular commission and would proceed down to the Base that evening to go to a cadet school at home. He said he would drop a line to Paddy or me as soon as he reached England, and would be thinking of us when he was laying in his nice comfortable warm bed at home whilst we were laying in a shell hole or a wet and muddy trench. He was an extraordinary man in many ways and as tough as steel. At the battle of Loos he had been shot clean through the chest and in less than five months he was back out with us and as chirpy as a cricket. He had won the Military Medal in High Wood and it was a rotten shame he was not awarded the D.C.M.

The division that relieved us had been badly battered on the Arras Front where the enemy were also attacking and had been sent to this quiet part of the Front as a kind of rest and pick-me-up. We were lucky and they were unlucky, for less than a week after our being re-

lieved the enemy launched a big offensive on the
Laventie and Bois Grenier sectors and took the whole
line of trenches, advancing miles beyond them. I was
told that the way the Portuguese ran, the best runners
that ever lived would never have caught them. By the
time we arrived on the Somme the great German advance had more or less come to a halt, but what it had
taken us six months to gain in 1916 they had now re-
gained in three weeks, and a bit more besides.

Our transport had evidently been very busy with
their private line to Sir Douglas Haig's office during the
last week. One man told me that he had had it straight
from the horse's mouth that Old Jerrie had captured
over one hundred thousand troops and fifty million
pounds' worth of goods in the large canteens that he had
captured. I found out later that there was more truth in
what he had told me than what I gave him credit for.
The Germans were now in possession of Albert and were
dug in some distance in front of it, and we were in
trenches opposite them. The upside-down statue on the
ruined church was still hanging. Every morning our
bombing planes were going over and bombing the town
and our artillery were constantly shelling it, but the
statue seemed to be bearing a charmed existence. We
were watching the statue one morning. Our heavy
shells were bursting around the church tower, and when
the smoke cleared away after the explosion of one big
shell the statue was missing. Some of our newspapers
said that the Germans had wantonly destroyed it,
which I expect was believed by the people that read
them at the time. But I have since heard on good
authority that even if they had done so they had a good

right to it: the statue was made in Germany by a German firm and it was neither old nor valuable. The 38th Division was better for rum issues than the 33rd and we were also getting a better bread ration. The Brigadier often used to visit the troops in the front line. He was called "Merry and Bright". He was a decent old stick, and everybody seemed to like him. He must have belonged to a different kind of species than the brigadiers I had come in contact with during the last three years. There was also an excellent Divisional Concert Troupe.

The Brigade did a little attack to take a bit of rising ground and another man and I had to take some lightly-wounded prisoners back. It was very misty and we decided to make our way over some ground which would shorten our journey considerably, though if the mist rose we would be in full view of the enemy. We had not walked very far before one of the prisoners collapsed. He was only a slip of a lad and more badly wounded in the legs than what he thought. We decided to carry him between us and had covered half the journey when the mist rose. We proceeded on our way and nothing happened until we were off the ground and safe in the sunken road. Then an enemy machine-gun opened out and traversed the ground from the edge of the sunken road and along the ground we had been walking; which was as good as telling us that we had been seen and would have been riddled if we had not had prisoners with us.

Early one morning a runner was sent back to the Aid Post, which was in a cellar. This cellar was the only thing left of a farm. When he arrived there he lifted the trapdoor up and shouted down for the Aid Post Sergeant. Receiving no answer he entered the cellar and found the Sergeant unconscious and Dr. Dunn's servant and an Aid Post orderly dead. They had made a fire with a bucket of mixed charcoal and coke, and after a while had laid down for a night's sleep. The fumes had killed the two men and undoubtedly the Sergeant was saved by sleeping near the bottom of the cellar steps, where he could receive the air that was coming down through the chinks in the trapdoor and which also had a piece ripped out of one of the boards. After he was brought into the open air he was a decent time before he revived. He was evacuated to hospital. About two months later when the Battalion were in the line he was sent back up from the Base and stayed with the transport in a fair-sized town. One night the enemy shelled the place and he was killed when entering a house trying to rescue some wounded men who were inside. He was a South African veteran and Fate played a dirty trick with him. In a dug-out the fumes of coke fires were bad enough, but when mixed with charcoal were worse. Any man who went to sleep in a dug-out where there was not much air with one of those fires going, and especially if there was more charcoal than coke, would soon drop into a sleep from which there would be no awakening. I was told that a bucket of charcoal fire was a favourite method of suicide with French soldiers who were fed up with the War.

We were back in a village and the companies were paying out. Sergeant Freezer asked the young platoon officer who was paying out his company for an advance of pay, saying that he was over £40 in credit. He had been having a little drink in the morning and was slightly top-heavy. The officer refused and told him he should be satisfied with the same pay as the other sergeants were receiving. He informed the officer that he was more pounds in credit than the majority of the young sergeants were shillings: which was perfectly true. The officer said it made no difference and told him to leave the pay table, which was outside a farm-house and near the company cooker. Freezer lost his temper, seized hold of a camp dixie which had some dirty slops in it, throwed the slops over the officer and then rubbed the dirty dixie up and down the officer's coat, cursing him until he was pink. He was placed under arrest, court martialled, reduced to the ranks, and sentenced to two years' imprisonment. He was one of the few cases who were sent away to do their imprisonment. When out of action his drilling of a squad of men may have not been up to the standard of a drill sergeant but he was highly skilled in the real arts of war and in an attack the best drill sergeant in the British Army would have been a dunce alongside of him. The officers of his company were never too proud to accept his advice then and the men under him would follow him anywhere.

I remember one sergeant who was a first-class drill instructor, but when in action was no wiser than a new-born babe and as jumpy as a bag of fleas. The men whom he had been drilling when out of action soon found this out and afterwards treated him with contempt. He missed two consecutive attacks by going sick and being sent to Minimum Reserve, but the next attack he did not miss, and he was the first to pass into the next world.

Sixteen months before the War commenced I had completed my Reserve service, but had re-engaged for an additional four years on the Reserve. I had now completed seventeen years' service and was a time-expired man and was wondering if I would have the luck to get my month's leave which I was now entitled to. All leave had been cancelled for some time and no one knew when it would start again but one of the transport men wanted to bet me two to one that it would start again inside a week. He would have been an easy winner if I had accepted the bet. The transport knew everything.

The Battalion was in the line in front of Bouzicourt, which was this side of Albert, and Battalion Headquarters were in dug-outs and houses on the outskirts of the village, which was constantly being shelled. The people had stuck it in this village all through the War until the German advance, but now there was not a soul in the place. One morning the bank clerk and I took a couple of petrol-cans for water. Every well we visited had been blown in, so we made our way into the village and asked a man where was the best place to get water. He told us that there was a farm which had a long yard outside it, opposite the church, where a lot of the men were getting their water from. The enemy were shelling the village at the time and most of the shells were falling on the left and right of the church. When I said that we would find some other place to get our water, he wanted to know if I had the wind up. "Not exactly," I replied. "But I have still got some sense left." It was a small stone church with a conical tower and no good for observation purposes, but I thought it must be an excellent guide to go by when the German observation officers were observing the hits made by their batteries. About half an hour later a large shell exploded in the yard of the farm, killing or wounding twenty men who were waiting their turn to use the pump. The bank clerk and I were lucky enough to find a well which had not been blown in and got our water from it.

We had a message that leave had commenced. It was not an official one but one of the Brigade signallers had sent it us over the wire. I was warned during the night to proceed on leave. The railhead was seventeen kilometers from the front line and several villages that I passed through during the night were being shelled. I had an excellent chance of being blown to bits before ever I reached the railhead. I arrived at the railhead the following morning and just before the train left the enemy began to shell it with long-range guns. The shells were bursting about twenty yards from the train. I arrived at Abbeville, where I stayed the night. During the night enemy planes came over and bombed the town. During the course of the War I expect thousands were killed going and returning from leave. The railhead outside Poperinghe was constantly shelled and men waiting for leave trains there used to do more trembling than ever they did when in the front line.

Twenty-four hours after I arrived at my home I was surprised to receive a post card from the bank clerk, to say that he was in hospital at Cardiff which was about thirty miles from my village, and that four Battalion runners, whom I knew very well, were in the same hospital. They were all gas cases. The following day I went to Cardiff and saw him and the others. They were not so bad. Luckily they had not inhaled the gas. Their eyes looked very bad but they could see all right. The blisters on their bodies were the main things that were troubling them. The bank clerk told me that two hours after I had left the enemy bombarded them unmercifully and also sent a lot of mustard-gas shells over. They had their gas-masks on for over an hour but the gas burned through their clothes and had also penetrated some of the gas-masks. As far as he knew Paddy, Tich, Lane, Sealyham and the architect were all right when he left but he was not sure about Dr. Dunn, who had been very busy through it all. When I told him that he had met a far better fate than what he would have done if he had gone to that pump for water, he laughed and agreed with me. He also said that he was lucky to be sent to an hospital so near his home. The four of them made a quick recovery but were not sent out again to France. During the time the bank clerk had been with the Battalion he had seen much and endured much and become a pukka old soldier in action.

A lot of young miners had enlisted during the War and others had been conscripted. Some of the publicans, business men and outdoor workers, who were too old for active service but young enough for home service, now rushed to the mines and got work which exempted them from home service. Here they were doing "Work of National Importance" and they were too windy even to join their own town guard. There were a few exceptions, who wouldn't even go down the mines: they had been exempted at umpteen tribunals until the men who sat on the Tribunal Boards were ashamed to exempt them any more and at last they were forced to go. Only one of them, to my knowledge, was ever sent out on active service, and he went to France but by the time he reached the front line and got one of his boots wet, the Armistice was proclaimed. He won his medal cheap.

Everybody I met was complaining that they had to wait in queues for different articles of food, and what hardships they were enduring through lack of nourishment. I told them I didn't know what they would have said if they had to live on four army biscuits and a spoonful of jam a day. I expect they would have ordered their coffins right away. My complaint stopped me from tramping mountains this leave and I took things quietly.

A concert was given at the local theatre in honour of my D.C.M. and M.M. There was a big Pow-Wow presided over by Councillor Gathen Jenkins, who was also a schoolmaster and a man I admired very much. I made a small speech to the large audience and never felt so windy in the whole of my life before.

CHAPTER XXIV

MINIMUM RESERVE

I rejoined the Battalion, who were out of the line about two miles behind Aveuloy Wood, and the first news I received was that Dr. Dunn had left the Battalion, a gas casualty. A few days after the bank clerk had left the gas had taken its effect on the Doctor who had hung on until he could hardly see, and then had to be led away. I was sorry to hear this news and everyone that knew him said that we would never see his equal again. It is only during the last few years that I heard he was still in the land of the living and in practice at Glasgow. Here's good luck to Dr. Dunn!

Although out of the line we were sent up to do a raid. Our trenches were the other side of Aveuloy and about two hundred yards in front of our front-line trench were some old disused trenches where the Battalion holding the line had an outpost of an N.C.O. and two men who were relieved each night. The whole place was honeycombed with trenches and it was quite easy in some places for either we or the enemy to walk into one another's lines. Paddy and I and another signaller were detailed off to accompany the raiding party which was going over from the trench the post was in. An hour before we were in position the relieving post found no one to relieve. Old Jerrie had come over and captured them.

The raid was a washout and we were lucky to get off as light as we did. Paddy and I were told to assist two young soldiers to carry a wounded man back. If we went around the old disused trenches it would have taken us hours to have reached the front line, but if we travelled over the top, with ordinary luck we would be there in fifteen minutes. We decided to take the short cut and although it was breaking day we would be very unlucky if we were shot in that light. A young frail Wesleyan Minister who was now attached to the Battalion as chaplain and had come up with the raiding party volunteered to accompany us. He carried our rifles. The wounded man, whom I slightly knew, had been with the Battalion about twelve months. He was a very big man, weighing over fourteen stone, and was too heavy for two men to carry him any distance on the stretcher. So the four of us hoisted the stretcher on our shoulders. We had not walked very far before one of the young soldiers wanted a rest, but I told him to keep on. A little way beyond that they both said that they were bound to have a rest; so we put the stretcher down. Paddy and I pointed out to them that it was getting lighter and we would soon be easy targets, but they insisted on resting. We began to swear. Suddenly we heard the report of a rifle and a bullet hit up the dirt by us. That moved them. We hoisted the stretcher on our shoulders and the rate we were now walking anyone would have thought we were carrying a paperweight. Several rifles were now cracking and bullets were whizzing very close by us. When we were about fifty yards from our front-line trench an enemy machine-gun opened out on our left. They were not firing at us, but at the first burst one of the youngsters pulled his hand off the handle and ducked. The stretcher tilted and down crashed the wounded man: he had a nasty wound in his side from which he might have recovered if it had not been for this fall. The youngster said he had stumbled. "You bloody liar," said Paddy. "You ducked from underneath the stretcher, and for two pins I'd blow your bloody lights out." We arrived in the front-line trench and were lucky to get there. As soon as we arrived at the Aid Post and put the stretcher down the young soldier disappeared very quickly. The wounded man died: the fall had undoubtedly been the finish of him.

Our Colonel, Colonel Norman, had left us and our new Commanding Officer, Colonel Cockburn, who was an old regular officer of the Regiment, having the South African and, I believe, Ashantee ribbons, was a proper old war-horse and a very brave man. Forty-eight hours later we went up for another raid near Beaumont Hamel. It was a very successful raid this time and prisoners and machine-guns were brought back.

We were two miles behind the line and one morning I told a few young signallers to keep their eyes on our observation balloons, which we called "sausages", and if they had not seen an aeroplane swooping down on a sausage and setting it on fire it was quite possible they would before midday. Behind us and as far as the eye could see our sausages were up. It was a grand morning for observation but the sky overhead was covered with fleecy clouds which had formed into little pats and made an excellent cover for a plane flying above them to swoop down on the sausages. About half an hour later we saw a man jump out of a sausage and his parachute opened out. At the same time we heard the drone of a plane-engine and an enemy plane swooped down out of the clouds and opened fire with tracer bullets on the sausage, which was soon a mass of flames. The plane then disappeared back in the clouds; it had been flying so high that we never heard the engine until it swooped down. In a little over half an hour six of our sausages had been served in the same way, the airman going back above the clouds after shooting each one down; but he never fired at any of the men who were coming to earth with their parachutes. We could now see the plane quite clearly, because the clouds had cleared away. Anti-aircraft, Lewis guns, and we with our rifles, were all popping at him, but firing ceased when we saw one of our own planes had appeared on the scene and was chasing him for all he was worth and rattling away at him with his Lewis gun. We watched them until they were out of sight, but I think the German got away with it. Our planes used to bring enemy sausages down in the same way and when the sky was like it was that morning the observation officers on both sides had a rotten job. The young signallers said it had been very thrilling. I don't expect they would have said it was thrilling if they had been the occupants of the sausages.

The most interesting to watch were aeroplane fights, but the majority I saw were more over the enemy lines than ours. I witnessed a fight on the Somme in July 1916, between one of our planes and one of theirs which took place over our lines. The German was having the best of it and our airman had been wounded. He had ceased firing and was coming to earth with his machine, the German hovering above him until he had landed safe on the ground and not firing a shot at him.

We were out of the line and a few of us went for a booze to a village some miles away. An American division were billeted around the Lealvillers area and we met a lot of them in a café. They looked a fine lot of men and we found them very sociable. We spent a very pleasant evening with some of them and before we left promised to meet them again. The Royal Air Force were holding some sports and an American band was in attendance. A lot of us enjoyed the band more than the sports and when they were playing ragtime music hardly anyone was looking at the races. The bandsmen were then making some funny capers which was enough to make an owl laugh.

All officers who had done two and a half years' continuous front-line service were entitled to go home if they wished. I don't expect there were many of them left in France, although we had two of them. One of them, Captain Moodie, was one of the Artists' Rifles who had been posted to D Company when he joined us, and the old soldiers of his company at the time soon respected him. He had been commanding D Company for close on two years and was now back at Brigade as temporary Brigade-Major. (The other Artists' Rifles man, Mr. Owens, had been killed near Albert recently.) The other man to go was Captain Radford who before he left came around to Paddy and I to wish us good-bye. I was glad he was getting out of it, yet sorry he was leaving us. He said that the one thing during the War that was impossible for him to forget was the smoky dug-outs of us old signallers around the Givenchy area, which had given him more torture than anything he had been through. There was no two and a half years' rule about N.C.O.s or men, of course. A week after the Polygon Wood stunt the Battalion had been inspected by Sir Douglas Haig, who decorated Captain Radford with the French Croix de Guerre which he had been awarded some time previously. The Captain thought so highly of this decoration that he wanted to sell it for twopence. To pukka soldiers those Croix de Guerres were jokes. Even the French gendarmes in Paris were being awarded them.

About a fortnight before our last big offensive, Paddy, Sealyham, the architect, and I were sent back to Minimum Reserve. It was the first time I had been sent there, so I was not going out of my turn. We had one signaller who had been with us fifteen months and had been back there four times. He had did a few spells in standing trenches but had never taken part in any attack, always going sick just beforehand. That man swung the lead to some purpose. When he went on leave there were three columns in his local paper giving his war record and the wonderful escapes he had had. During the big offensive, when Minimum Reserve was abolished, he was killed in the first attack he had been in. We were under canvas with proper tent-lines. The Brigade carried out its drills, the Minimum Reserve of the three battalions together, under the special com mand of a major of another battalion. For the first few days signallers had to drill with the company-men, and the first morning we were doing saluting drill by numbers to improve our saluting. We then had to march up to N.C.O.s who were representing officers, and salute them. Paddy was one of the N.C.O.s, and when I marched up to him and saluted we both nearly burst out laughing. I was on other sloppy parades during the day and by the afternoon I was that fed up that I was wishing myself back in the line.

I told Paddy the following morning that I would much prefer going in the clink than doing those sloppy parades and that when he called the Roll on parade he had better report me absent. He told me not to talk rot and to stay off parade, and if any officer came along I was to tell him that I was cleaning the tents up. Orders had been given that morning that every man with the exception of the orderly corporal and cooks must be on parade. The parade moved off to the drilling ground and I was putting my coat on to move out of the camp when the Major in command came around the tents and inquired the reason why I was not on parade. I told him that I had hurt my big toe just before the parade moved off and had a job to walk. If I had told him Paddy had left me off to clean the tents up, Paddy would have been crimed for reporting the parade present when there was a man absent. I did not want to get him in a row so I made the excuse about the toe. All men that reported sick were seen early in the morning by the Doctor, so that men who received medicine-and-duty would have to do the early-morning parades. Any man who reported sick during the day would have a special sick report made out, and a man would have to be seriously ill before he had one of those. We were back so far from the line that the same system prevailed as in England. The Major roared for the orderly corporal and told him to make a special sick report for me, and after I had seen the Doctor to bring the report back to him.

I went with the orderly corporal to the Brigade Field Ambulance, which was close by, and waited in the hut where the sick were seen whilst the corporal went to look for the Doctor, whom he found in the officers' mess. He happened to be a young American doctor—there were two or three attached to the Field Ambulance—who when he looked at my sick report told me to pull my boot off. I told him there was no need for it as there was nothing wrong with my toe and would he kindly listen to what I had to say. He told me to fire away. I told him how I had been through the whole War and this was my first time in Minimum Reserve where I had to do drills which I had learnt seventeen years previously. I also gave him the true facts of the special sick report. He asked me what my medal ribbons represented and when I told him he said "Shake!" and held his hand out. He then told me to pull my boot off, as he wanted to see my toe, and when I again told him there was nothing wrong with it he said, "Who is the doctor? You or I?" After I had pulled my boot and sock off he said my toe was in a very bad state and wrote on the sick report "attending hospital and excused all duties". As I was leaving the hut he told me that as long as he was seeing the sick I was going to have an easy time while I was in Minimum Reserve. I thanked him and as

I left the hut the thought struck me that I had received more consideration from an American doctor than from any of my own countrymen.

We met the Major and when he read the sick report his jaw dropped a foot. I had denied him the pleasure of trying me the following morning on the serious crime of "going sick without a cause". He had not been in France long and he was like a good many more that I came across in Back Areas: the only thing they believed in was saluting drill and spit-and-polish parades. If the whole blasted crowd of them had been forced to do a few months in the front-line trenches in the dead of winter and where the shelling was heavy it would have made them realize that there was a war on.

I attended hospital every morning and one morning a young English doctor was seeing the sick. As soon as I went in front of him he said, "All right, Richards, carry on! I don't think your toe will get better until you leave here." Evidently the young American doctor had told him to carry on with the good work. I received a letter from the bank clerk, who was out of hospital now and soldiering at Limerick with our Third Reserve Battalion. Sealyham was sent down to the Base with a very bad knee. If ever a man earned a decoration he had, but he never got one.

CHAPTER XXV

THE FINAL ADVANCE

The big offensive had begun and we were rushed up the line to join the Battalion. On the way I passed many familiar places and picked the Battalion up on the Somme between Guillemont and Ginchy. Colonel Cockburn had been wounded in rushing a machine-gun post with the sergeant who was in charge of the runners; that was the sort of man he was. We had an American doctor in place of Dr. Dunn, who soon proved himself a brave and cool man under fire. We hung on for a few days around this spot.

I received a letter from Ricco, which, being an officer, he had censored himself. The first two pages were full of delightful language. I wouldn't have thought it possible for any man to get so many swear words on two sheets of ordinary writing paper. Ricco had been sent for, while at the Base, and had been told that owing to his long War service and magnificent record there was no need to send him home to a cadet school and that he had been granted a commission in the Field. A few days later he had been sent up country and joined a battalion of Cheshires. After the first action they were in he had been left Second-in-command of the Battalion. Shortly after this it was disbanded and he was transferred to another battalion of the Cheshires, where he was agreeably surprised to find that his new Colonel was Stanway. I was delighted to hear that my old Company-Sergeant-Major was still in the land of the living. I answered Ricco's letter and gave him all the news since he had left us, but from that day to this I have never found out whether he is alive or dead. I hope he is very much alive and enjoying all the good things on this ball of clay.

Our chaps made a small attack and took their objectives, and a few days later we were moving along and arrived at a place named Equancourt, from where we took over some trenches on the right of Havrincourt Wood, about six miles from Cambrai. Paddy and I were in Battalion Headquarters which were in a sunken road about an hundred yards behind the front line. Our telephone lines ran over the top and any breaks had to be repaired at night. We and two young signallers stayed in an upright boarded shack. One night by the aid of a candle the four of us started to play Pontoon and with our heads close together were soon deep in the game. After we had been playing some time the enemy began shelling. Some of the shells were bursting close to the shack and blowing out the candle. One of us would remark "That's a near one" as we relit it. Gas shells were also coming over and we pulled our helmets out ready to slip on as soon as we sniffed gas. There were no loud explosions with gas shells: they struck the ground with a soft thud and it was difficult to tell them from duds. We still carried on with our game and after we had relit the candle many times the shelling slackened. Paddy said, "I hope they will now give us a bit of peace." A few minutes later crash! a shell had exploded just outside the shack and we never heard even the last whine of it.

As I struck a match to light the candle one of the two young signallers shouted, "I'm hit, Dick!" "So am I", called the other. Paddy said nothing. I found him on his back with one of his wrists three parts severed and a nasty wound in the head. He was unconscious. It was not a large shell but quite large enough, and the splinters had crashed through the boards on the side of the shack. How I was not hit was a mystery. One of the young signallers had a splinter clean through the shoulder high up, and the other was hit in the muscle of his left arm. Some runners came into the dug-out and attended to the youngsters whilst I went on dressing Paddy's wrist, which I had just completed when the Aid Post Sergeant came in. He examined Paddy's head and told me he had a compound fracture of the skull, but that he had a chance. The gas was now reeking badly and we had to put our helmets on for a few minutes. Poor old Paddy must have inhaled a lot of it as the Sergeant was dressing his head. He was now talking deliriously. About an hour later he died at the Casualty Clearing Station. It was tough luck, after going through the whole War right down to September 1918 to get killed the way he did. I had lost another good pal.

There was a lot of gas hanging around that night and I felt pretty rough. Hammer Lane was wounded the following day: a small piece of shrapnel hit him high up on the back. (I am glad to say that he survived the War, returning to Birmingham, where he was well known.)

All my pals seemed to be leaving me one way or the other. During the time we were here three attacks were made to capture a strong point but each one was a failure. I overheard the colonel of our Seventeenth Battalion, who was talking with our Commanding Officer, say that he believed some of the survivors of the Boche's 1914 troops were holding the strong point. Our Colonel now was Colonel Norman, an old regular officer of the Regiment, who proved himself a very efficient man.

The first week in October the Division moved to the right and arrived on the ground where the American Division had made their attack from. About two hundred yards in front of us was a thin belt of barbed wire, three feet high and two feet in depth, which extended across the ground as far as the eye could see. I counted eleven of our tanks, a distance apart, stationary in the wire. An artillery signaller gave me an account of the attack which he had witnessed from an observation-post. The eleven tanks had gone over in advance but the belt of wire was a concealed minefield. They were all put out of action, and the Yanks had to do their attack without the aid of them. They had taken their first objective and had to wait a while before they advanced and took their final objective, which was Le Catelet, a town situated in a hollow. They rushed to take their final objective and their mopping-up party, instead of waiting behind to do their work, were so eager that they rushed forward with the attacking troops. Some of the enemy who were hidden in concealed machine-gun posts, and riflemen outside the trench in shell holes, now rose up and the Yanks were being fired on from front and rear. In spite of that some of them got to Le Catelet but were forced to retire out of it and there were not many left to tell the tale. Since then our artillery had blowed Le Catelet to bits and the enemy had retired a few miles beyond it.

The following morning we advanced slowly over this ground and halted for a few minutes by the belt of wire, which a man could easily stride over. Scores of small mines, about the size of a kitchen kettle with the spout and handle off, had been dug up inside the wire. We examined one tank: it had the bottom blown out. A hundred yards beyond the wire hundreds of dead Americans had been collected and laid out in rows, and more were still being carried to the spot. We advanced down the slope into Le Catelet. On the other side of the road leading into the town were some very high banks where a couple of machine-guns could have played havoc with any advancing troops, and when I looked at them I marvelled how any of the Yanks had got into the place. They must have had plenty of guts. We occupied some old enemy trenches on low-lying hills the other side of Le Catelet, where we stayed two days. On one of the nights our Seventeenth Battalion and a company of our own made a night attack on a village named Villers Outreaux but were held up by machine-gun and rifle-fire. Many a good man went West that night.

Early one morning just before break of day, we advanced and moved up a railway to take up a position in a sunken road about two hundred and fifty yards from Villers Outreaux. The sunken road was congested with troops of another division who had to move out for us to get in, and about an hundred of us were held up on the railway track. It was now breaking day and getting lighter every moment, and I thought if we did not soon get a move on we had an excellent chance to get riddled. I hugged the bank on the one side of the track pretty close. It was broad daylight when we finally arrived in the sunken road and from that day to this I have often wondered how we were not slaughtered like sheep. We were not in position very long before the enemy began shelling us. We had been told that the enemy were short of shells, which was the truth. Their shelling was nothing compared to what it had been, and I only witnessed one decent straffe by them from now on until the end of the War.

Our new Church of England Chaplain was in the sunken road to see what he could do for the wounded. He was a powerfully-built man and looked strong enough to carry a Lewis gun in each hand as easily as an ordinary man could carry a rifle. If he had said to one of the weaklings in the Battalion, "Here, son, give me your rifle and equipment: you are weaker than I and I will take your place in the attack," no doubt the One above would have considered it a very Christian act and would have amply rewarded him if he had gone West. But he never said anything of that order at all. The Clergy on both sides were a funny crowd: they prayed for victory and thundered from the pulpits for the enemy to be smitten hip and thigh, but did not believe in doing any of the smiting themselves. They were all non-combatants with the exception of the Catholic priests who were forced to serve in the French Army the same as anybody else.

The Brigade was going to attack the village—troops of

other divisions were also attacking on our left and right and we had two tanks to help us. Tich and I were told to act as runners. I took a message to A Company on our right flank. On their right was a main road leading into the village, where no doubt just outside the village the enemy would have a machine-gun post on each side of the road. I found the frail Wesleyan Minister I have mentioned with this company. I liked him very much, although he had chastised me several times for my language. I told him the attack would start in about five minutes and he told me that he was going over with the first wave of attacking troops, so that he could attend the wounded as soon as they were hit. I told him that he was different from all the chaplains of my experience and that I admired his pluck but not his sense. It would be far better if he waited a few minutes until after the first wave had gone over; then he would be able to go forward and attend the wounded. But if he went over with the first wave it was quite possible he would get knocked out himself and would not be able to attend anyone. He would not take my advice and went over with the first wave, dropping dead before he had run ten paces. This company lost a third of their men by machine-gun fire before they entered the village. Our tanks were there before them, but missed an enemy machine-gun which continued spitting at us infantry. At last one of our aeroplanes discovered it and swooping down very low soon put its team out of action. Once their machine-guns went West the enemy made little resistance and the village was soon taken, with many prisoners. If the German troops of 1914-1915 had been holding the positions around the village I don't believe it would have been taken in a month of Sundays.

In the afternoon the 19th Brigade staff of the 33rd Division marched along the road and I greeted several I knew. The 33rd advanced over ten miles before they were checked and took many prisoners during their advance.

CHAPTER XXVI

LE CATEAU AGAIN

From now to the finish as soon as the enemy were driven from one position, they would retire back to another prepared one. But by the look of the prisoners they seemed half starved, the majority of them being mere lads. One dark evening we entered a place named Bertry. A lot of French people were still there. They had been given the option by the enemy of either going back with them or remaining in the town. Some went back with the enemy, those that stayed being warned that they might be killed by their own shellfire. I don't believe half a dozen shells had hit the place. I was told that from now on our artillery had been ordered to shell as little as possible the towns and villages the enemy were retiring from, and only when it was absolutely necessary were these places to be heavily shelled. All the villages around this area had been occupied by the enemy since August 1914.

There had been a scrap just outside the town and the following morning some of us went on the scrounge. Two runners called Pip and Darby entered a house which was a kind of chemist shop and café combined. Darby got hold of a bottle of stuff, had a taste but immediately spit the stuff out. A few minutes later he had to be led to the Doctor with his tongue badly bleeding, who, after he examined him, said that if he had swallowed one drop of it he would have been a dead man. Darby was sent to the Base and from there to England, which was the last thing he wanted. He was the only man I ever met who enjoyed the War—of course I mean of us front-line soldiers. He had worked at different jobs in every state in America and when the War broke out he was on a ranch in Canada. He joined up and was sent to England with some remounts. He received a severe kick in the ribs and was invalided back to Canada where he was discharged with a pension as medically unfit for further service. He worked his passage to England, thereby forfeiting his pension, joined the British Army and came out to us in 1916. He had been a runner for eighteen months and wounded twice. He received a nasty wound on the last occasion and I was surprised to see him when he rejoined us three months later. He had been no further than the Base. No doubt he had asked the Doctor not to send him home. He was a well-educated man and, like the officer we called Jimmie, who was also on a Canadian ranch when the War broke out, he was always quoting Kipling. Pip had been with the Battalion about three years and was in charge of a golf course when he joined up. I am pleased to state that he is still in charge of one. In a letter I received from him twelve months after the War finished he mentioned that Darby was living not far from him, but the poison had affected his speech a little. I was sorry to hear that, and I hope he has completely recovered by now.

Tich and I went scrounging on our own and walking down the pavement in a street we saw two women approaching us who were also walking on the pavement. As soon as they saw us they got off the pavement and as we were passing them they made a deep bow to us. For the moment I was back in India and was being salaamed. I expect during the years that they had been under German rule they had to get off the pavement when German soldiers were walking on it, and it would take them some time to get out of the habit. All the villages around this area had German signs, and the names of some of the streets had been altered to German ones. Some were named after the members of the royal family of Germany and others after some of their leading generals. I expect if the United States had not entered the War there would have still been German names on them. Some of the German soldiers carried cognac in their water bottles and we were lucky enough to find two of them.

We stayed in a lovely house, the occupants having gone back with the enemy. There was some beautiful furniture in it which we soon knocked up for firewood. We got a bucket, stabbed holes in it and soon had a fine fire going in a magnificent room which had a piano. One of our chaps was a good pianist and we were soon as happy as birds. We went upstairs, pulled the beds down the cellars and slept the sleep of the just. The following morning we moved out of Bertry and just outside the town were half a dozen dead horses which had been killed by shell splinters. A lot of Frenchmen were around them with their knives, cutting the best joints away. They evidently intended to have a good feed.

During the early part of the War, on the Retirement, I had several meals of horse stew with the French, and thoroughly enjoyed them.

In one village we stayed in some of our men who were billeted in a barn attached to a little farm, accidentally found a stock of tins of condensed milk which were hidden under some straw. The people who owned the place had gone back with the Germans. They kept some and gave some to the women who were living close by, who said that the people who owned the place had been brigands. Neutral countries had been providing food and clothing for the inhabitants of the Occupied Areas and these women complained very bitterly that the people who owned the barn were too friendly with some of the distributing officials and could get anything they wanted, while they themselves were lucky to get anything at all. It was the same as everything else in the War—there were certain ways of pulling the strings. I heard the same complaint in other villages I stayed in, that some were getting a lot and others very little.

We took over a position about a mile on the left of Le Cateau, which I had not seen since August 1914, and now I could only see some of the tops of the buildings. The enemy were in a position on a ridge and railway. There was a valley between us, through which ran a little river called the Selle. One of our front-line companies was isolated and runners had to be employed. We were short of telephone wire to run out to this company, so one morning a young signaller and I went on the scrounge to see if we could get any. A thousand yards to the right of us and in a valley were some old German dug-outs and shacks. They had been occupied forty-eight hours previously by a battalion headquarters of another division, who had been shelled out of them and had many casualties. We made for this place and found some new lines which had only lately been run out and which were now lying idle. There were breaks in the wires here and there, but to us it was a godsend.

As we were coiling it up on a reel we noticed three officers coming towards us from our front. I very nearly fainted when I saw that one of them was a divisional staff officer and thought that something was bound to happen when one of his kind was so near the front line. I expect he had been visiting some battalion head-quarters and was now on his way back. They stopped by us and when the Staff Officer found we did not belong to his division he became highly indignant, saying that we were now out of our own Divisional Area and had a bally cheek to come into another division's area, salvaging wire. He ordered me to drop the reel and clear off. I began to explain to him how urgently we required this wire, which was lying idle, when he cut me short. He had just started to give me a severe dressing down for not immediately obeying his order, when Crash! Crash! a couple of shells burst not far away. Others followed. The way he and the two others sprinted back out of it, anyone would have thought they had been in strict training for months for some important track event. I shouted after him to come back and take his wire, but the three of them were soon out of sight.

The shelling was now worse, so we retired back up the slope for an hundred yards and sat in a shell hole. There was not a soul to be seen anywhere, yet for over an hour the enemy bombarded that valley, and the dug-outs and shacks which had been badly damaged before were now blown to bits. We had got the wire that we had coiled up on the reel but it was not enough, and we were waiting for the shelling to pack up to collect some more. The enemy must have used more shells that morning than what he had used for the last month on a whole divisional area. When the shelling finally ceased we had to go a little further away for our wire, but we got it, and that night ran a line out to the Company, which saved the runners some work and perhaps their lives.

We were around this spot for ten days and one morning a grand attack was made all along the Front which was a complete success. The following morning we were moving about the railway track which the enemy had occupied the day before when a German plane swooped low down over the ridge and commenced firing along the track. There were small holes dug in the bank of the track and rabbits would not have bolted into them quicker than we did. We tried to bring him down but he got away with it.

A few days later we were in a village named Englefontaine, which was a long, straggling place with woods all around and the Forest of Mormal behind it. We held one-half the village and the enemy the other. Civilians were in both parts but the civilians on our side were clearing back out of it. We Headquarters' men were in a house outside the village in an orchard. One of our companies was in a small trench. Two companies more were in houses and the other company was in the open. On the morning of November 4th a new attack was made. Our orders were to take the other half of the village and remain in it until the following morning.

Battalion Headquarters were detailed off for the mopping-up party. Our artillery put up an excellent smoke screen and the attack was made under cover of this. The company that advanced from the orchard had heavy casualties: not sixty yards from them was a solitary house which was a machine-gun post. Only thirty yards up the road from the house we were in were two machine-guns, one on each side of the road, but these did very little damage. In two hours the whole of the village was in our possession. There was some bayonet work that morning but the majority of the enemy surrendered without putting up a fight.

When bombing dug-outs or cellars it was always wise to throw bombs into them first and have a look around them after. But we had to be very careful in this village as there were civilians in some of the cellars. We shouted down them to make sure. Another man and I shouted down one cellar twice and receiving no reply were just about to pull the pins out of our bombs when we heard a woman's voice cry out and a young lady came up the cellar steps. As soon as she saw us she started to speak rapidly in French and gave the both of us a hearty kiss. She and the members of her family had their beds, stove and everything else of use in the cellar which they had not left for some days. They guessed an attack was being made and when we first shouted down had been too frightened to answer. If the young lady had not cried out when she did we would have innocently murdered them all.

A German doctor who was captured that morning and who could speak excellent English said that he was the most unlucky man in France, for if we had not made

the attack that morning he would have been proceeding
to Germany the following evening on leave. All arrangements had been made for them to retire back out of the
village that evening and through the forest behind to
some prepared positions some miles the other side of the
Sambre River. He had calculated that by the time his
leave had expired peace would have been proclaimed
and there would have been no need for him to have come
back. He honestly believed that their men could not
hold out for another fortnight. He said he did not know
how their front-line troops had stuck it so well on the
scanty rations they had been getting during the last few
months. Their men serving in Back Areas were even
worst off as regards rations and the people in his country
were more or less starving.

A German prisoner who was an excellent sketcher
drew a lightning sketch on post-cards of another man
and myself. We had not washed or shaved for days and
were in a state, and he sketched an excellent likeness of
us just as we were. We paid him with a tin of bully beef
and a cigarette. He was quite satisfied. He could speak
English and told us he had lived a couple of years in
Chelsea. Tich and I found two bottles of Black and
White Whisky which was evidently a bit of loot from the
canteens they had captured on the Somme, in their advance in March. We also found two tame rabbits, and
the thought struck me that they must have been a very
poor lot of soldiers that were holding the village, otherwise we would have never found those rabbits. The
pukka old German soldiers would have soon had them
in the stew pots. They would never have gone hungry as
long as tame rabbits were kept by civilians. There were

vegetables in the gardens and in the evening some of us had a glorious feed. The whisky livened us up and when I got down to it to snatch a few hours' sleep Tich was singing a song.

We marched through Mormal Forest, where, so the civilians had told us, British prisoners had been working for years cutting down trees. There was a railway running through it and also good roads. We crossed the Sambre River over a pontoon bridge our engineers had built. The enemy were still retiring back in a soldier-like manner. All bridges had been destroyed and all cross roads were now mine craters. We arrived at a place named Aulnoye. There was a railway junction at this place and hundreds of small mines had been dug up from underneath the metals. Not very far from the railway station had been a huge German workshop, which was now in ruins. The civilians told us that during the early part of the night three weeks previously our big bombing planes had come over and dropped their bombs on it and also on a German leave train which was getting ready to leave: train, troops and workshop had been destroyed and the explosions had been so terrific that hardly a pane of glass was left in the village.

CHAPTER XXVII

THE ARMISTICE

On the morning of November 11th, just before we left the house we were staying in, a small enemy shell crashed through the roof, but nobody was hit. We advanced about a mile out of the village and were halted behind some banks. On the right of us on the road was a cooker which had been badly knocked about, and laying alongside of it were the two dead cooks of another battalion in the Division. One of the last shells that the enemy had fired on this part of the Front had burst by them as they were moving along the road that morning.

We were ordered back to the village, where I met the architect, who was now a full corporal and attached to the Brigade Staff. He told me that all manner of yarns were flying around Brigade (where Colonel Cockburn who had recovered from his wound was now acting Brigadier) about Peace being proclaimed. He said that he knew for a fact that orders had been given to our artillery to cease fire and await orders. Shortly after, the official news came through that the Armistice had been proclaimed. Everyone was glad to hear the news though, of course, an Armistice was not the same as a

Peace and there was no booze in the village to add to our cup of happiness.

With the exception of some men of the transport there were not more than two or three of us left that had seen it through since the commencement, and ours was supposed to be a lucky battalion. I expect we had pulled off a twenty-thousand-to-one chance. Some of us celebrated the day by adjourning down the cellar of a house and playing Pontoon. We had accumulated a lot of money during the last few months and had been unable to spend it. About six hours later I rose up, stony broke. I had got the money easily and now I lost it easily. The following day I sold some German field-glasses and automatic pistols and tried my luck once more at Pontoon, with the same result as the previous day. My luck had changed with a vengeance. But I consoled myself with the thought that I had arrived in France broke and would leave it in the same way.

Since August 1914 the women living in towns and villages in the Occupied Areas had received no news of their menfolk who were serving in the French Army, and were now eagerly waiting for the French mail to arrive which would give them news of them. Some of the villages had been taken in the first German onset in 1914 without any fighting and in our advance we had retaken some of them in the same way. The people living in these places had no conception of what the War had been really like. They did not consider that even if their menfolk were now still living they might perhaps be insane, blind, or maimed for life, which was worse than being killed. There was one young woman living in Aulnoye who had a bonny little boy over four years old whom his father had never seen. When War broke out the father had been called to the Colours and the last letter he wrote was dated August 5th, 1914. Her boy had been born a few days before the Germans had occupied the village and she was now overjoyed to think that her husband would soon be back with her and how proud he would be to see the boy. The mail arrived a few days later and she was officially notified that her husband had been killed on August 12th, 1914, which was before her boy was born.

The Peer was in temporary command of the Battalion, and a few days after the Armistice was proclaimed he gave a lecture to all the non-commissioned officers in the Battalion on discipline. He told them that while the War was on it was a case of every man for himself when in action, and discipline had become a little lax. They must remember that they belonged to a Line Battalion and discipline must revert back to its pre-War standard. He said that if any N.C.O. was brought up in front of him for walking out with a private he would reduce him to the ranks. In my pre-War soldiering days an N.C.O. was not allowed to walk out with a private and even if a young lance-corporal was caught walking out with one he was brought in front of the Colonel, who would ask him to explain why he had committed so deadly a crime. All this had been altered as the War progressed and a more brotherly love had existed between N.C.O.s and men. Ninety-five per cent of the N.C.O.s that attended the lecture were men that had joined up for the duration of the War and the majority did not care a damn whether they were reduced or not. They were only waiting their time to be demobilized.

The architect, who had rejoined the Battalion, gave me full particulars of the lecture, which he considered was a lot of bally rot, and said that he was glad he had not been a soldier in pre-War days. I was doing nothing, but the Battalion was on parade all the time, doing the ordinary drills that are carried out in peace time. The Peer had another brainwave and issued out an order that every man was to parade on a certain date with his steel helmet burnished. The helmets were coated with a dark green paint and it took a man at least six hours to scrape the paint off and another two to polish it up as it should be done. There was more swearing over this order than I had heard for some time. The men who had been any length of time in the War were praying for it to break out again. The Battalion paraded in their burnished helmets. It was a beautiful day and I found it impossible to look at them with the sun shining on them. They were inspected by the Brigadier who said that the men looked very smart in their burnished helmets, but as no orders had been issued from Division regarding the burnishing of helmets they would have to be repainted. As soon as the parade was dismissed all helmets had to be taken to the pioneers' shop to be restored to their original state. The only good it had done was to improve the praying language of the men.

Miners were sent home first, so I was lucky: and after wishing my pals good-bye I paraded one day with some more of the same trade as myself and we were inspected by The Peer. He shook hands and wished me the best of luck, and I returned the wish. Just as I was getting into the motor lorry I noticed on parade with his company my old Platoon-Sergeant and Company-Sergeant-

Major, now Captain Fox, commanding B Company. I was sorry I did not have time to go over and shake hands with him, as the motor lorry was about to leave, but I hope I shall have the pleasure some day to read that he is commanding a battalion of his old Regiment of which he was so worthy an N.C.O.

We arrived in Cambrai and the following morning paraded in front of some mining officers who asked us a few simple questions about mining and seemed to be satisfied with the replies. One man admitted to me before he left the Battalion that he had never been on top of a coalpit in his life. I gave him a few particulars and he passed the mining officers all right. No doubt he had saved himself another six or twelve months' soldiering. I expect many more did the same. We stayed in a large convent for two days and then entrained for the Base.

Our train was a long one, consisting of corridor coaches and cattle trucks for the troops. There were a lot of civilian passengers in the coaches but eight of us were lucky enough to get in one of them. Before the train left we collected enough of wood, which we stacked in the coach, to last us all the way to Boulogne, and also a fire-bucket. During the whole of the journey we had the fire going and we very nearly drove the French passengers crazy with our smoke barrage. They did nothing but spit, cough and curse until they had reached their destination. We were in a coach on our own and the smoke was travelling the corridor; we were lucky we did not set the train on fire, but a fire was everything to us and it was very hard for us to drop out of habits which we had cultivated during the War.

CHAPTER XXVIII

REWARDS FOR WAR SERVICE

I was demobilized at Liverpool on December 5th and when I filed by the doctor he inquired, after looking at my medical history sheet, if I still suffered from my complaint. I replied that I did, but would see what I could do for myself. I left the Army A1 and soon got down to work. But my complaint grew worse and after spending much money and giving every known remedy a fair trial I got fed up. In two years and a half I drunk enough of medicine to float the British Navy and swallowed enough of pills which if they had been made into cannon balls would have knocked down all the concrete pillboxes on the Western Front. I was also suffering with rheumatism at the time and in August 1921 I applied for a Medical Board.

I had to go to Newport for my board and met a man from my village who was going there for the same purpose. He informed me that he had not served in the War but had been guarding a railway bridge about seven miles from his home and one night when on sentry it had rained and he had got wet. Some days later he had been admitted to hospital where he had spent a week with rheumatism. I sympathized with

318

him and said it was marvellous how he looked so well after what he had been through.

The doctors who examined me as good as told me that if I did not agree to have an operation I would not be granted a disability pension. I wanted an operation and when I asked him why I had not been operated on in the first place, they coldly informed me that they had nothing to do with the past and was dealing with the present. A few weeks later I was notified that the Medical Board had found that I was suffering with hæmorrhoids and rheumatism and that the hæmorrhoids had been aggravated by my War service: for which I had been awarded a disability pension of eight shillings a week for sixty-five weeks. Before this time expired I would be notified to appear in front of a Medical Board for a further examination. No disability pension could be awarded for my rheumatism which in their opinion had not been caused or aggravated by War service. If I wished to appeal I could do so.

I knew it was useless to appeal. I have never been in hospital with rheumatism and the War had now been over two years and nine months. I also knew that Medical Boards went by what hospital service a man had entered on his medical history sheet and not by his front-line service. If a man had only done four weeks' service in England and had been admitted to hospital for a few days he would have a better chance of being awarded a disability pension than a man who had done four years in the firing line and whose medical history sheet was clean. No matter what complaint had come on a man since the War ceased he could claim a Medical Board, but if he had never been admitted to hospital during the War with what he was now suffering from he had no more chance than a crow of being awarded a disability pension.

I met the man who had got wet guarding the bridge and he informed me he had been awarded a disability pension of twelve shillings a week for sixty-five weeks and had also been recommended for massage treatment. When I told him that I had been awarded nothing for my rheumatism he said: "I thought you wouldn't: you have never been admitted to hospital with it and that's what they go by."

Two months later I was sent to an hospital and was operated on. The Staff Nurse who was present at my operation told me that I was the worst case she ever saw with my complaint, and the most serious operation, and that also I had used the worst language she had ever heard. I apologized and said that I had probably gone back to my 1914-1915 language. I had good treatment in that hospital but was still very groggy when I left it and was granted two months convalescent treatment, which meant that I was receiving the maximum pension of two pounds a week for that period. My operation was a success in one way but not in another, and I have never been the same man as what I was before. I appeared in front of another Medical Board and was notified that I had been awarded a final weekly allowance of seven-and-sixpence for seventy weeks, and the award could not be extended beyond this period. My civilian friends were astonished that I did not receive a pension of some sort and had a job to understand me when I told them that I was quite satisfied, and thankful that I was not blind, that I had my limbs, that I was not horribly disfigured and that I was not an inmate in a mental home like tens of thousands of poor men still are who served in the War.

Yet I can well understand their astonishment. In the village where I was living the majority of men receiving disability pensions in that year, 1923, were men who had never left the British Isles or who had served at the Bases and never seen the sky over the firing line. Some of them in this year of 1932 are now drawing life pensions and larger ones than the men who were wounded or disabled in action. One man who did two months on Salisbury Plain is still drawing a pension, another who did six months somewhere else in England is still drawing a pension and doing work besides that would kill a buck nigger. Another actually went as far as Ireland and endured terrible hardships in a cook-house. He is still drawing a pension.

I could go on for a long time like this and I expect it is the same in every town and village throughout the British Isles. These men are greatly admired and are often spoken of as the men who worked their knobs during the War. Yet if the whole of the British Army had been like them during the War there would have been no pensions and not much England.

An old regular soldier had to complete twenty-one years' service with the Colours and if he was a private at the end of that period was entitled to a life service pension of one shilling a day; which I am told has now been increased to two shillings a day. During the War if an old regular soldier was invalided out of the service his Reserve service would count as Colour service, and if he had over eleven years' service was entitled to a life service pension of one halfpenny a day for every year or part of a year served. If a man was invalided out, say, with sixteen years and one months' service, he would receive eightpence-halfpenny a day.

Living not far from me is an old artilleryman who had served abroad in his pre-War days, where he had his fair share of fever. He was a reservist when the War broke out and after serving in France for three years was wounded and gassed and finally invalided out of the service with a disability pension. He was receiving this pension for some time and was then given his final award. He still suffers with his health and simply receives his service pension of roughly five shillings a week. He is what the papers call one of the Old Contemptibles, and indeed no man has been treated with greater contempt than what he has.

This is a funny world and I have come to the conclusion that lead-swingers and dodgers gets on best in it. Since 1921 I have had a pretty tough time and have had long periods of unemployment and I expect there are thousands of old soldiers like me who are worse off than I am. I was standing one day by a group of ex-Service men who had been lead-swingers and dodgers throughout the War and they were discussing the distribution of some work. One of them said that it was about time they had a say in the matter: they had done their bit during the War and it was only fair that the men who had served their Country should have a greater share of the work than the men who had never left their own homes. This particular man had contracted several dangerous complaints through shaking the Crown and Anchor dice down at the Base.

REWARDS FOR WAR SERVICE

It is Armistice day to-day and the ex-Service men are on parade wearing their War medals. The men who served at the Bases and a hundred miles behind the front line are wearing their medals more proudly than the men who served in the firing line. There is no distinction between the War medals. In former wars, for each engagement a man took part in he was awarded a bar, and a pukka old soldier would be very nearly ashamed to wear a war medal that did not have a bar attached. They were known as bare-arsed medals. The thought has often struck me during these parades how vain we all are, and how much preferable the old Red Indians were. In their belts they wore the scalps of their enemies that they had slain in action, as proof of their soldiering: but we just wear war medals, and there are some on parade to-day wearing war-medals on their breasts as if to say that they have been in action—but the only action they were ever in was with some of the charming damsels in the Red Lamps behind the Front and down at the Bases where they served. The Red Indians were vain but they were honest.

I have relied on my memory for the greater part of my story and may be out a day or two in dates, and also may have spelt the names of towns or villages wrong. But there are no fictitious characters, though I have given nicknames instead of names for safety in some cases. In 1920 the bank clerk, architect and I met and spent a very enjoyable evening together. I corresponded with them and Sealyham up to 1922 and it was my fault and not theirs that we ceased corresponding. The bank clerk was now a Second Cashier, and under him in the same branch were two clerks, one who had been a captain and the other a lieutenant during the War.

Living three miles from me is an old soldier of the Regiment who still calls me Dick. We served in the same battalion abroad and also in the War. For the first ten months of the War he was a rifle-and-bayonet man and the remainder an officer's groom. He was one of the men who used to pop over to the Native trench at Fromelles, and also the groom who gave up his billet to the Parson, and he still don't care a damn for any man. When times were good before the mines started closing down we often used to meet and adjourn to a pub for a drink and chat over old times, but if ever the conversation veered around to Native troops or parsons he would launch out with a flow of language which on two occasions was very nearly the cause of us being turned out of the pubs we were in. By stop-tap he generally had thousands of Native troops in one spittoon and thousands of parsons in another whom at times he would be fetching out again to trample them down in the sawdust with his heels. We generally wound up our evenings with the old song, set to the tune of a well-known hymn, "Old soldiers never die, they simply fade away."

893920

Printed in Great Britain by
Amazon.co.uk, Ltd.,
Marston Gate.